# Beyond Nihilism

ALSO AVAILABLE FROM BLOOMSBURY

*Heidegger and the Problem of Phenomena*, Fredrik Westerlund
*Philosophy of Finitude: Heidegger, Levinas and Nietzsche*, Rafael Winkler
*Nihilism and Philosophy: Nothingness, Truth and World*, Gideon Baker
*Mortal Thought: Hölderlin and Philosophy*, James Luchte

# Beyond Nihilism

*The Turn in Heidegger's Thought from
Nietzsche to Hölderlin*

**Dominic Kelly**

BLOOMSBURY ACADEMIC
LONDON • NEW YORK • OXFORD • NEW DELHI • SYDNEY

BLOOMSBURY ACADEMIC
Bloomsbury Publishing Plc
50 Bedford Square, London, WC1B 3DP, UK
1385 Broadway, New York, NY 10018, USA
29 Earlsfort Terrace, Dublin 2, Ireland

BLOOMSBURY, BLOOMSBURY ACADEMIC and the Diana logo are trademarks of
Bloomsbury Publishing Plc

First published in Great Britain 2022
This paperback edition published in 2024

Copyright © Dominic Kelly, 2022

Dominic Kelly has asserted his right under the Copyright, Designs and Patents Act, 1988, to be identified as Author of this work.

Cover image: Evening Glow, Grasmere, United Kingdom
(© Martin Newman / EyeEm / Getty Images)

All rights reserved. No part of this publication may be reproduced or transmitted in any form or by any means, electronic or mechanical, including photocopying, recording, or any information storage or retrieval system, without prior permission in writing from the publishers.

Bloomsbury Publishing Plc does not have any control over, or responsibility for, any third-party websites referred to or in this book. All internet addresses given in this book were correct at the time of going to press. The author and publisher regret any inconvenience caused if addresses have changed or sites have ceased to exist, but can accept no responsibility for any such changes.

A catalogue record for this book is available from the British Library.

A catalog record for this book is available from the Library of Congress.

ISBN: HB: 978-1-3501-3375-4
PB: 978-1-3503-3109-9
ePDF: 978-1-3501-3376-1
eBook: 978-1-3501-3377-8

Typeset by Integra Software Services Pvt. Ltd.

To find out more about our authors and books visit www.bloomsbury.com
and sign up for our newsletters.

*To Esther, With Love*

# Contents

*List of abbreviations* ix

Introduction 1

1   Nietzsche and the threat of nihilism 9

   Nietzsche and the problem of nihilism 11
      *Why Nietzsche?* 11
      *Nihilism as history* 13
   Nietzsche as physician 20
      *Will to power* 23
      *The overhuman* 28
   Nietzsche as metaphysician 30
   Questions concerning Heidegger's interpretation of Nietzsche 38

2   The possibility of an other beginning 43

   The end of metaphysics and the possibility of an other beginning 45
      *Ereignis* 45
      *Gelassenheit* 53
   *Physis*: Being as presencing 55
      *Original echoes of the concept of physis* 58
      *Aristotle and physis* 61
      *Physis, techne and the question of technology* 65

3   Language as the house of being 71

   Language: The house of being 72
      *The need for a reappraisal of how language works* 72
      *A traditional view of language* 73
      *Language as the advent of being* 76
      *Language as the ground of historical Dasein* 86
   The poetic word as the ground of being 96
      *The poetic as ethical* 99

**4  Hölderlin and the possibility of poetry**  105
  Why Hölderlin?  105
  How does one approach Hölderlin's poetic word?  113
  Poetic revelation as the grounding of the
  history of *Dasein*  120
  Hölderlin's word as the fate of the West  133
  The *Geviert*  140

**Conclusion**  145

*Notes*  158
*Bibliography*  178
*Index*  183

# List of abbreviations

| | |
|---|---|
| GA | *Gesamtausgabe* (Collected Works), Frankfurt: Klosterman, 1975–. |
| BQP | *Basic Questions of Philosophy: Selected 'Problems' of 'Logic'*, trans. R Rojcewicz & A Schuwer. Indianapolis: Indiana University Press, 2004. |
| BT | *Being and Time*, trans. Macquarrie and Robinson. Oxford: Blackwell Publishing Ltd, 1962. |
| BW | *Basic Writings*, trans. and ed. David Farrell Krell. London: Routledge, 1993. |
| CP | *Contributions to Philosophy (From Enowning)*, trans. Parvis Emad and Kenneth Maly. Indianapolis: Indiana University Press, 1999. |
| DT | *Discourse on Thinking*, trans. John M Anderson and E Hans Freund. New York: Harper Perennial, 1966. |
| EHP | *Elucidations of Hölderlin's Poetry*, trans. Keith Hoeller. New York: Humanity Books, 2000. |
| EP | *The End of Philosophy*, trans. Joan Stambaugh. Chicago: Chicago University Press, 2003. |
| FS | *Four Seminars*, trans. A Mitchell and F Raffoul. Indianapolis: Indiana University Press, 2003. |
| HC | *The Heidegger Controversy*, ed. Richard Wolin. Cambridge: MIT Press, 1993. |
| HCT | *History of the Concept of Time: Prolegomena*, trans. Theodore Kisiel. Indianapolis: Indiana UP, 1985. |
| IDS | *Identity and Difference*, trans. Joan Stambaugh. Chicago: Chicago University Press, 2002. |

| | |
|---|---|
| IM | *Introduction to Metaphysics*, trans. Gregory Fried and Richard Polt. New Haven: Yale University Press, 2000. |
| KPM | *Kant and the Problem of Metaphysics*, trans. Richard Taft. Indianapolis: Indiana University Press, 1990. |
| M | *Mindfulness*, trans. P. Emad and T. Kalary. London: Continuum, 2006. |
| N1 | *Nietzsche*, Vol. I: *The Will to Power as Art*, trans. D. F. Krell. New York: Harper and Row, 1979. |
| N3 | *Nietzsche*, Vol. III: *Will to Power as Knowledge and Metaphysics*, trans. D. F. Krell. New York: Harper and Row, 1987. |
| N4 | *Nietzsche*, Vol. IV: *Nihilism*, trans. Frank A. Capuzzi. New York: Harper and Row, 1982. |
| OBT | *Off the Beaten Track*, trans. Julian Young and Kenneth Haynes. Cambridge: Cambridge University Press, 2002. |
| OWL | *On the Way to Language*, trans. Peter D Hertz. San Francisco: Harper and Row, 1971. |
| P | *Pathmarks*, trans. Frank A Capuzzi *et al.*, ed. William McNeill. Cambridge: Cambridge University Press, 1998. |
| PLT | *Poetry, Language, Thought*, trans. Alfred Hofstadter. New York: Harper and Row, 1971. |
| TB | *On Time and Being*, trans. Joan Stambaugh. Chicago: Chicago University Press, 2002. |
| WCT | *What Is Called Thinking*, trans. J Glenn Gray. New York: HarperCollins, 1968. |
| ZS | *Zollikon Seminars*, trans. Franz Mayr and Richard Askay. New Haven: Northwestern University Press, 2001. |

# *Introduction*

This investigation seeks to unify two themes in the interpretation of the thought of Martin Heidegger, both of which justify – despite the vast amount of secondary literature on his work – further consideration. The first theme concerns further clarification of Heidegger's turn from a purely philosophical discourse to an examination of thought that is other than metaphysical. This turn can be traced in the movement of Heidegger's thought from his engagement with the philosopher Friedrich Nietzsche to his investigation of the work of the poet Friedrich Hölderlin. The second theme concerns the Nietzschean heritage in this move, that is, the explication of a properly historical dimension of thought as outlined in his work on Hölderlin and given direct expression in his texts of the late 1930s and early 1940s – namely, *Contributions to Philosophy*, *Mindfulness* and *The History of Being*.

It is for this reason that this book is entitled *Beyond Nihilism: The Turn in Heidegger's Thought from Nietzsche to Hölderlin* as it sets out to discover in the movement of Heidegger's thinking a change in how history is to be thought at the end of the metaphysical tradition. In tracing this movement, I intend to show that for Heidegger the history of the West thus far – from its inception in the thought of the ancient Greek philosophers to its culmination in Nietzsche's determination of being as *Will to Power* – is to be understood as the history of the forgetting of being (*Seinsvergessenheit*). However, that this is the case only comes to light as this history draws to a close, and in so doing the possibility of a new relation to being and thus a new beginning also comes into view. This is what Heidegger refers to as the 'turning' that occurs within being, the moment when history thus far is revealed out of its origins as determining being in such a way that it fails to do justice to being's essential nature (if we can speak of such a thing). It is also the moment when thought is called to think being more authentically.

Further, Western history, as the forgetting of being, is also referred to by Heidegger as the history of metaphysics, a history that ends in modernity and is revealed in the incapacity of philosophy to any longer *think* about the nature of being. This incapacity is best exemplified for Heidegger in the thought of Friedrich Nietzsche, a thinker whose work Heidegger regards as both compelling and bringing metaphysics to its conclusion insofar as Nietzsche constructs a metaphysics of pure subjectivity. What Heidegger means by this is that Nietzsche's thought is the ultimate expression of what philosophy has attempted to articulate since its inception in ancient Greek thought, i.e. the beingness (*Seiendheit*) of beings (*Seiendes*). That the metaphysical tradition thinks being (*Sein*) in these terms means it reduces the truth of what *is* to the way an entity presents itself, as a result of which the meaning of being as such goes increasingly unthought. This thoughtlessness reaches its climax in Nietzsche's notion of *Will to Power*, which thinks being in terms of beings understood as pure loci of power, a determination that reduces life to the purely present by removing anything beyond life towards which it can be directed. Thus the history of metaphysics ends in nihilism, a point in the history of Western thought when 'there is nothing going on with being' [OBT 197]. Hence, it will be revealed that for Heidegger nihilism is the culmination of Western thought's historical failure to properly attend to being.

However, what will also be revealed is that the reason that thought is unable to do justice to being lies within the origins of metaphysical thinking as it arises in Greek philosophy. To this end Jennifer Gosetti-Ferencei notes that for Heidegger the history of the West hitherto 'has wandered into a crisis of withdrawal'.[1] What this means for thought is that what *is* appears to be self-given and immediate and the sheer wonder at the presence of things that belongs to the ancient Greeks (and gives rise to the Western tradition) has disappeared. Why this should be the case is that today we no longer experience beings as the Greeks did, that is, aletheically. To say that the Greeks experienced beings aletheically is to say that for the Greeks beings in their beingness are experienced as *emerging* into presence (from out of hiddenness). However, Heidegger argues, in bringing this experience to thought the Greeks fail to account for the hiddenness from which beings emerge and think the beingness of beings solely in terms of presencing. This determination gives rise to and shapes the Western tradition, whereby beings are thought in terms of presence and that from which they emerge into presence, namely being, is forgotten. In modernity, this view of beings is apparent in scientific thought, which approaches beings as objects insofar as they are strewn of any temporal relations and as simply lying present before the knowing subject.[2] The truth of beings on this count is a-historical and being *as such* is missing from the picture.

As we shall see, the implicit danger here is that not only does thought not attend to being, but that the human being as such runs the risk of being reduced to an object that has no meaning beyond its scientific calculability. Consequently, Heidegger thinks, not only do we need to establish a new relation to being but a properly historical sense of ourselves in order to open up ourselves to something beyond the immanence of our own existence. Heidegger thinks that to do this requires that we establish an open relation to being whereby the hiddenness that is essential to the emergence of beings into presence comes to light in itself. For Heidegger, it is this hiddenness or withdrawal of being that provides 'food for thought', that is, that opens up a path within being along which thought can travel and thereby humanity can have a destiny towards which it can comport itself. It is for this reason that Heidegger turns to poetry and to the poetic word of Friedrich Hölderlin in particular, as in the latter Heidegger discovers the possibility of opening up a properly historical dimension for thought and thereby a new relation to being as such.

This is because Heidegger regards the poetic word (*Dichtung*) as essentially having the potential to originate a new history, and Hölderlin's poetry in particular as being decisive in this respect:

> Hölderlin puts into poetry the very essence of poetry, but not in the sense of a timelessly valid concept. This essence of poetry belongs to a definite time. But not in such a way that it merely conforms to that time as some time already existing. Rather, by providing anew the essence of poetry, Hölderlin first determines a new time. It is the time of the gods who have fled *and* of the god who is coming.
>
> [EHP 64]

Hölderlin's poetic word is one of absence, of loss. Consequently, for Heidegger, it is a poetry that opens up for modern sensibilities the possibility of experiencing a feeling or sense of loss in the face of the departure of the old gods. In other words, Hölderlin's poetry makes possible an experience of modernity as a time of spiritual crisis. What this means for Heidegger is that Hölderlin, in his poetry, discloses the current age as one that lacks a meaning, a direction, a historical (*geschichtlich*) sense of itself. Thus, in the face of the forgottenness of being Hölderlin's poetry provides a way of remembering what has been lost to modernity, that we are no longer 'at home' within being, that we are no longer able to heed its call. Viewed in this light, it has been said of Hölderlin's poetry that it is a way out of the forgottenness of being insofar as it is a 'courageous venture into that darkness – an investigation of that withdrawal (of being) – in order to uncover poetically a new beginning'.[3]

Moreover, if Hölderlin's poetry is a remembrance of what has been lost, it also points to the future as it opens up the space for the preparation of the arrival of the new god. This is because, as we shall see, Heidegger thinks Hölderlin's poetry is transformative – it reveals both the truth of the West (German people)[4] as it stands in relation to being and being, as that in which Western people dwell, as having an element of mystery attached to it. Hölderlin's poetry does this by revealing beings (and thus the world in which they appear) not as something on-hand, but as something that is essentially strange. This is because beings and the world in which they appear are defamiliarized as they occur in the poem, they come forth not as they seem to be (in everyday experience) but as they actually *are*. And the ground on which a historical people stand, on which its world is based, is revealed for the first time in the poem as abyssal, that is, it comes forth as indeterminate. It is for this reason that Heidegger thinks Hölderlin's poetry holds out the promise of a new beginning, of originating a new time. As we shall discover, Heidegger thinks that the defamiliarizing of the world in the poem calls a people into its truth. Hence, in Hölderlin's poetry the truth of Western people is revealed in the flight of the gods which simultaneously hints at the mystery that lies beyond what is present – this, for the West, is its historical situation. Consequently, Hölderlin's poetry is seen to open up Western people to a decision, to what kind of relation it shall sustain within being.

However, this decision does not reside with Western people, nor is it a decision about the happening of the truth in the poem. Rather, it is a decision about what the truth of being shall be in the future. As Felix Ó Murchadha notes, Heidegger is here directly addressing GWF Hegel's proclamation that art, as originating the truth of a people, is a thing of the past.[5] This proclamation is metaphysical in nature, Hegel regarding art in modernity as aesthetically determined. In other words, the artwork is no longer experienced as originating the truth of a people and is instead understood purely in terms of how it affects, in one way or another, human sensibilities. Consequently, for truth to be seen to happen in the artwork, for it to transform a people, means that a people must be receptive to the happening of truth as it occurs there, which means it must have a properly historical relation to being, one that lies beyond the history of metaphysics. However, in order to fully clarify what is at stake here I need to situate this thesis in the general sweep of Heidegger's work.

In his *What Is Called Thinking?* Heidegger tells us that '*Most thought-provoking is that we are still not thinking* – not even yet, although the state of the world is becoming constantly more thought-provoking' [WCT 4]. As strange as this may sound it encapsulates the single thought that preoccupies Heidegger throughout his philosophical life – namely, how are we to think being so that we can do justice to it and to ourselves? The question of being arose early in Heidegger's life. Indeed, it can be located at that point when he was still a high school student and received from his teacher a copy of Franz Brentano's book *The Several Senses of Being in Aristotle*.[6] It is this book that convinced Heidegger that the question of being must be revived, due to the fact that Brentano's book points out that Aristotle distinguishes many different meanings of being (which he categorized in terms of different types of entities) but that consequently a unified meaning of being could not be arrived at. Heidegger found this state of affairs 'untidy', as it rendered the concept of being as essentially empty.

Heidegger's dissatisfaction with the notion of being intensified with his immersion in medieval and modern philosophy which understood being solely in terms of the beingness of beings until in his magnum opus from 1927, *Being and Time*, we are met with the following:

On the basis of the Greek's initial contributions towards an interpretation of being,[7] a dogma has been developed which not only declares the question of the meaning of being to be superfluous, but sanctions its complete neglect.

[BT 21]

Indeed, Heidegger here not only has his sights set on philosophical thinking but scientific thinking also, both of which can be summed up in the term 'theoretical attitude', a viewpoint from which beings are thought as objects that stand over and against the knowing subject, as a consequence of which being as such is occluded from thought. However, in making the above declaration, Heidegger does so from the position of having made a breakthrough in his own researches into the nature of what we mean by being. This breakthrough has two aspects to it. In the first instance, Heidegger adopts a phenomenological approach to the question of being. Briefly, what this means for Heidegger is that thought, rather than merely categorizing and conceptualizing what is to be thought about, instead lets itself be guided by the matter (*Sache*) of thinking, that is, by being. The other aspect is the point from which Heidegger begins his examination of being, as it is to the human being in its average 'everydayness' to which he turns.

This approach has a couple of important advantages to it. In the first instance, as both the sciences and philosophy tend to understand beings solely in terms of objects that stand over and against the human subject, it allows Heidegger to look beneath this ontic understanding of beings by revealing the ontological foundations that give rise to it. Further, this approach also reveals the historical distortions that undermine any notion that we can question beings from a neutral perspective, thus undermining the claims of the sciences that they establish universal truths. The importance of this insight – given Heidegger views truth and being as inextricably linked, our understanding of one necessarily affecting how we view the other – which will be brought out in the course of this thesis, is that it can no longer be claimed that truth is essentially a-historical. As we shall see, Heidegger's approach here is hermeneutical – he attempts to interpret being from the perspective of the historically situated human being. What this leads Heidegger to discover in *Being and Time* is that in modernity, being is essentially understood in terms of the utility of beings.

The dangers inherent here I have already alluded to above in terms of nihilism, but what is of equal significance is that metaphysical thought is unable to grasp this danger. This comes to light through Heidegger's critical disengagement (*Auseinandersetzung*) with the thought of Nietzsche.[8] If Heidegger seeks an overcoming of nihilism in Nietzsche's work as the thinker whose thought is the culmination of metaphysics, what he is confronted with instead is the realization of the absolute occlusion of being. However, Nietzsche's work not only reveals the limitations of philosophical thought, of how it is inadequate to the task of overcoming nihilism, but so thoroughly does Nietzsche's thought occlude being, it points in the direction from which being might be actually thought (historically).

Thus it is to art that Heidegger turns and in particular poetry which, as the essence of language, allows humanity to dwell within being. The importance of the poetic word for Heidegger is that it originates truth – it initiates the struggle between hiddenness and unhiddenness that is the essence of being. Most importantly, poetry (and we are here talking about great poetry) opens up being to thought, that is, opens up truth for the thinker. Indeed, Heidegger refers to thinking as almost a 'co-poetising', as the poet and the thinker are both involved in questioning into the nature of existence.[9] However, the poem itself brings being to the word in such a way that being retains its mystery, in which it essentially goes unspoken. And as that which is to be thought about, being comes forth in the poem as that which withdraws from thinking, opening up a path that allows humanity to exist historically. It is within this context that Heidegger turns to Hölderlin as that poet who points beyond metaphysical thought to a properly historical thinking of being. That is, as that poet who opens up a people to decision Hölderlin's poetry holds out the possibility of opening up a new beginning for the West.

Consequently, the first and second chapters of this text concern Heidegger's engagement with the question of the dangers of nihilism as the final convulsion of the history of metaphysics. The first chapter analyses Heidegger's confrontation with Nietzsche, who he regards as the last great thinker of metaphysics. This confrontation allows Heidegger to reveal nihilism in its absolute form, a form that is then taken up and dealt with in Chapter 2 in terms of the technological determination of the world as it stands today.

Both chapters allow me to show why Heidegger not only begins to distance his own thinking from a strictly philosophical approach to things but also why his turn to art (specifically in the form of poetry) – thought poietically – offers a possibility of opening up a history beyond metaphysics.

Therefore, in the third and fourth chapters I turn to language as the most fundamental way that the human being dwells within being and thus where the battle to move beyond nihilism is to be fought. For Heidegger, as we shall see, language is essentially poietic, which means that it brings forth beings into their being through the word. In the case of the human being, it is the poet who is called forth into the word, whereby she grounds being as the truth of a people and thereby offers up the hope of establishing a new history for that people. It is for this reason that we look to Heidegger's engagement with Hölderlin in the final chapter, as it is in this poet's poetic word that Heidegger sees the possibility of establishing a new time.

Finally, in the conclusion I sketch out how the movement of Heidegger's thought away from that of Nietzsche's towards a properly historical thinking of being owes a debt to Nietzsche's attempt to move away from metaphysical thought towards a historical thinking grounded in the temporality of life. And I will further show how this movement happens in relation to Heidegger's positive engagement with Hölderlin's poetry as that which opens up the possibility of a new history.

# 1

# *Nietzsche and the threat of nihilism*

Heidegger views modernity as standing precariously on the precipice of meaninglessness, that is, of losing its historical sense of itself. To this end he says:

> Beings *are*, but the being of beings and the truth of being and consequently the being of truth are denied to beings. Beings *are*, and yet they remain abandoned by being and left to themselves so as to be mere objects of our contrivance. All goals beyond men and peoples are gone, and, above all, what is lacking is the creative power to create something beyond oneself. The epoch of the highest abandonment of beings by being is the age of the total questionlessness of being.
>
> [BQP 159]

That we have arrived in this situation is due to a decline in Western humanity's relation to being – disclosed as the history of the West – a relation that is opened up with the ancient Greek thinkers and reaches its final stage in the modern world. This decline has been fittingly described as an 'ossifying amnesia',[1] the process by which a primordial impetus to question into the nature of being is forgotten in favour of an understanding of being that rigidly focuses on the presence of beings. It is a decline that heralds the modern age as one in which humanity is immersed in a stultifying darkness, a darkness that, in Heidegger's terms, bears the mark of (and is grounded in) the 'abandonment of being'.[2] But in what exactly does this darkness consist? And wherein lies its danger?

Nominally, at least, the response to both questions can be straightforwardly summed up in the word nihilism. At the heart of this word lies, quite literally, nothing – i.e., the *nihil*, the Latin term for nothing or nil. Accordingly nihilism, as the insidious danger that lies at the heart of modernity, sees modernity as that era which is, so to speak, dominated by nothingness. It is the era in which nothingness – the inability to find anything meaningful beyond the sheer presence of things – emerges as 'a psychologically necessary affect of the decline of belief in God'[3] in the face of which there are no longer any illuminated paths along which humanity is free to traverse and in which anything meaningful in existence is reduced to one's experience of it, and nothing beyond this.

We must, however, be guarded against mistaking the symptoms of the disease for the disease itself. Gianni Vattimo, for example, suggests that as nihilism is still developing as a historical event, then it is not possible to properly define its exact nature.[4] And yet whilst true, this lack of clarity does not mean that we cannot at least try to venture forth a preliminary diagnosis, at least try to understand at what stage it stands with the disease so that a decision can be made with regard to its remedy, or if indeed a remedy can be found. Heidegger's analysis is a little bleaker than Vattimo's, questioning the very possibility of ever attaining a proper perspective on nihilism when he opens his essay of 1943, 'Nietzsche's Word: "God is Dead"', with the statement: 'The following commentary is an attempt to point in the direction where, perhaps, the question about the essence of nihilism can one day be posed' [OBT 157].[5]

What Heidegger is intimating here is that not only are we unable to grasp nihilism in its essential nature, but that the reason for this is that its essential nature is tied to Western humanity's destiny as it stands in relation to being. In other words, and as will become clearer in the next chapter, Heidegger thinks that the task of confronting the problem of nihilism is one that can only be entered into if we attend to the historical movement of *Dasein*[6] in relation to being, both with an eye to how this movement unfolds in the past and an eye to what this might portend for the future. This will prove to be not so much a call to action on Heidegger's part but a call to reflection on the part of *Dasein* in its relation to being.

Hence, in approaching the problem of nihilism, there are two related difficulties which need to be addressed. To begin with, there is the problem of how nihilism manifests itself so that it is recognized as such and thereby speaks out beyond our immediate experience of it. Further – and in direct relation to how we resolve this problem – there is the difficulty of how we respond to the challenge of nihilism or even if a response is possible. What follows shall be an examination of these difficulties, initially through an analysis of what nihilism means in the thought of Friedrich Nietzsche, both in terms of how he views its challenge to humanity and how he responds to this challenge. This will then be followed by an attempt to clarify Heidegger's response to Nietzsche's analysis before drawing out of the tension that exists between these two thinkers a deeper understanding of Heidegger's confrontation with the problem of nihilism itself.

## Nietzsche and the problem of nihilism

### Why Nietzsche?

Why turn to Nietzsche as the starting point of an investigation into nihilism? Of course, one does not have to read too much of the tonnage of secondary literature regarding Nietzsche's philosophy to find him proclaimed the philosopher of nihilism, or even more crudely to see him described simply as a nihilist.[7] Both designations, however, are predicated on the assumption that nihilism is some form of philosophical movement or doctrine that takes its place in the pantheon of philosophical thought alongside German Idealism and Existentialism, for example. Understood as such, Nietzsche's thinking on nihilism can be simply discarded as mistaken by those who disagree with it, or assimilated as correct by those who do not, which amounts to the same thing: nothing changes on engaging with Nietzsche's work. Such an approach neither does justice to Nietzsche's thought nor does it sufficiently take seriously the threat of nihilism as it is elaborated in his work, an elaboration that lays bare the fundamental implications of our nihilistic age.

However, if we do engage thoughtfully with Nietzsche's work, then we are confronted with the stark reality of the matter to be thought: it is 'the history of the next two centuries […] (of what) can no longer come differently: *the advent of nihilism*' [WTP Preface]. What Nietzsche is here directing his reader to meditate on is the ineluctable, historical movement that *is* nihilism as something that must be *endured*. In other words, nihilism can only be understood in terms of the sweep of history itself, and this history as something that modernity must undergo. The importance of this insight is not lost on Heidegger:

> Nietzsche uses *nihilism* as the name for the historical movement that he was the first to recognise and that already governed the previous century while defining the century to come, the movement whose essential interpretation he concentrates in the terse sentence: 'God is dead'.
>
> [N4 4]

This is a crucial statement. To begin with, it opens up a critical dialogue between Heidegger and Nietzsche which sees the former engage seriously with the latter as *the* thinker of nihilism and sees him as perhaps the first philosopher to do so.[8] As will be shown, Heidegger takes Nietzsche's thinking to be the ultimate expression of nihilism whilst simultaneously appropriating, to a certain extent, Nietzsche's own analysis of the condition of nihilism in order to be able to do so. This means that in turning to Nietzsche we are able to garner an understanding of what Heidegger regards as the essence of nihilism and so give a philosophical context to Heidegger's own thinking on the subject.

Further, this contextualization necessarily situates the problem of nihilism historically. This is significant insofar as Heidegger takes Nietzsche seriously when the latter claims that his thought is the culmination of the whole tradition of Western thought. This, from Heidegger's viewpoint, means that Nietzsche's work can be considered as the final convulsion of this tradition, not only signalling the advent of nihilism but also indicating the point at which the history of metaphysics comes to an end. As such, Nietzsche's philosophy can be viewed as a transitional path from metaphysical thinking to a thinking that is other than metaphysical, even if we cannot be certain what form this thought might take. Thus, it is on the basis of a thoroughgoing engagement with Nietzsche's work that Heidegger thinks it is possible to take a stand on nihilism, to be able to recognize it in its essence and thereby to try to distance our own thinking from it.

## Nihilism as history

Given Nietzsche's claim that nihilism is a historical phenomenon, we should not be too surprised to learn that its manifestation is alluded to by thinkers prior to – and in distinction from – Nietzsche and his own particular understanding of it. Philosophically speaking, it is Friedrich Jacobi who first uses the concept in a letter to Johann Fichte dated from 1799, in which he imputes to the latter's idealism a nihilistic ego-centrism.[9] The word is then taken up and transformed in nineteenth-century Russian thought in which its earlier, German conception as applying to either epistemological or metaphysical concerns is now thought in terms of its socio-political ramifications, whereby it is seen to play a significant part in devaluing existence. This is best exemplified in the works of Ivan Turgeniev where nihilism is synonymous with positivism, insofar as only that which is given to the senses can be regarded as real, rendering superfluous such notions as tradition, authority and value.[10] Finally, nihilism attains its Nietzschean determination in his work *The Will to Power*, where in response to the rhetorical question: 'What does nihilism mean?' Nietzsche replies that it is when '*the highest values devaluate themselves*' [WTP §1]. What is to be made of this statement?

The first thing to note is that Nietzsche associates a historical decline in the 'highest' values with the onset of nihilism. But what does Nietzsche mean by highest values, and how is he able to recognize their loss of potency? Could it be, for example, that he is alluding to the decline in belief in the Christian God in nineteenth-century Europe? It could certainly be argued that a decline in religious belief may well signal an increasing disregard for moral standards as well as an abandonment of shared values. Yet is it not also the case that the old order gives way to the new, by which the decline in Christian values is mirrored in the turn to a more measured, rational approach to morality, such as is witnessed, for example, in the rise of Utilitarianism in the same century?[11] Certainly, it could be argued that Utilitarian morality, which bases the value of an act on its consequences rather than the authority of God, forms a much broader basis from which to judge an action than is afforded by religious doctrine (i.e. it is founded on the rationally verifiable rather than the merely interpretative). Consequently, in exchanging the Christian standard of moral values for that of the Utilitarian, cannot the case be made (at least from a rational standpoint) that this decline is rather its opposite – namely, progress?

And yet, although it is true to say that this decline in values can be located historically – in the movement from one set of values to another – it is not at the level of values themselves that nihilism is to be located, according to Nietzsche. If this were the case, then it would mean that nihilism itself was some kind of value, i.e. that a particular value is somehow placed on nothing or that nothing itself would be in some way a consciously given value. However, what Nietzsche does think is that this decline can be located in the underlying value of values as such. This is not to say that if we attempt to locate a decline in values by looking to the basis of a particular value system – whether it is God or human reason – we shall discover it. As far as Nietzsche is concerned, in moving from God to rationality as the basis for the evaluation of human existence one simply swaps one interpretation of life for another, and in doing so, one fails to pay heed to the essentially detached, ideal viewpoint from which value is placed on life as such. This is the key to understanding Nietzsche's thinking on nihilism. To this end we only need to look to his criticism of Utilitarianism, which he sees as condemning the origin of moral evaluations (that is, the Christian belief in absolute values), whilst in fact 'it believes them just as much as the Christian does' [WTP §253]. Hence, it is the foundations of moral evaluations themselves, insofar as they are based on the application of absolute values to life, on which Nietzsche has his sights set in his attempt to uncover the dangers of nihilism.

If we are to get to the crux of Nietzsche's understanding of nihilism, however, then we will have to make one further observation: for Nietzsche, nihilism is the process by which the highest values *devaluate themselves*. This begs the question not only of what devaluation means in this context, but also of the reflexive nature of a process by which values are able to undermine themselves. A clue to what Nietzsche has in mind here is given by him when he says of devaluation that 'the aim is lacking; "why" finds no answer' [WTP §1]. Although this response is a little enigmatic, it is crucial to understanding the historical inevitability of modernity as the era in which humanity in general lacks a purpose, and the individual is increasingly alienated from her world.

That the 'why' finds no answer further signifies for Nietzsche that not only is human existence directionless in the West, but that the origins which direct this existence, which lie within the ancient Greek philosophical tradition, give this existence an impetus that proves to be both illusory and unsustainable. Or to put it another way, the values that give rise to and sustain the path of Occidental history necessarily lead Western humanity to the brink of meaninglessness. Further, in failing to recognize the truth of this historical event, Western thought issues in nihilism in its most virulent form. Hence, for Nietzsche, nihilism is the historical phenomenon of the foundations of Western values giving rise to a devaluation of Western existence.

Now the concern must be to investigate how Nietzsche is able to both recognize and describe the current age as nihilistic, especially in the face of the modern sciences' claims that through their researches humanity is making 'progress'. To this end Nietzsche's famous proclamation in *The Gay Science* serves as a good starting point. In a section illuminatingly entitled 'The Madman', which has been described as an attack upon adherents of a secular version of old Christian ideals,[12] Nietzsche says:

> The madman jumped into their midst and pierced them with his eyes. 'Whither is God?' he cried; 'I will tell you. *We have killed him* – you and I. All of us are his murderers. But how did we do this? How could we drink up the sea? Who gave us the sponge to wipe away the entire horizon? What were we doing when we unchained this earth from its sun? Whither is it moving now? Whither are we moving? Away from all suns? Are we not plunging continually? Backward, sideward, forward, in all directions? Is there still any up or down? Are we not straying as through an infinite nothing?'
>
> Here the madman fell silent and looked again at his listeners; and they, too, were silent and stared at him in astonishment. At last he threw his lantern on the ground, and it broke into pieces and went out. 'I have come too early', he said then; 'my time is not yet. This tremendous event is still on its way, still wandering; it has not yet reached the ears of men. '[13]

The first of these passages gives us a clear indication of Nietzsche's thoughts regarding nihilism as concluding the movement of Western history and is encapsulated in the phrase 'What were we doing when we unchained this earth from its sun?' Nietzsche here conjures up the powerful image of nihilism as the setting of the sun on the history of the West: the hour of darkness is upon us. Indeed, the notion of light is a much used motif in Western history, redolent as it is of certain significant crossroads that mark its progress. For example, at the origins of Western thought stands Plato and his determination of the philosopher as the person who 'sees the light' (and thereby philosophical thought as illuminating life) as outlined in Book VII of his *Republic*.[14] Here Plato, in his famous 'Allegory of the Cave', depicts the philosopher as the person who ascends from the darkness of the cave (life) to the realm of eternal truth, to the light of the Ideas. But the philosopher does not escape the darkness in this way; rather, she returns to the darkness in order to try to reveal life in its true light. Thus philosophy is a way in which the philosopher tries to stimulate the human being to direct her life towards discovering truth, to see the light for herself.

There are also relatively modern equivalents, such as can be seen in the Copernican Revolution, which in turn leads to the ideas of rational progress that spring from what we term, aptly enough, the Enlightenment. It should not surprise us to discover, then, that the Christian God is categorized in this way by Nietzsche. Indeed, Nietzsche equates the Platonic and the Christian interpretation of life to the extent that he claims, 'Christianity is Platonism for the "common people."'[15] Thus, a look to Nietzsche's above pronouncement of the death of the Christian God, as the unchaining of the earth from its sun, should give us some insight into the historical happening of nihilism, even as it relates to Platonic thought.

To this end, one only has to look to the Christian Bible for confirmation of the significance of Nietzsche's insight. There, in the New Testament, the Christian God's representative on earth, Jesus, declares: 'I am the light of the world; he who follows me will not walk in darkness, but will have the light of life.'[16] This call to follow the Christian path is also the call to walk in the light of God and find one's truth in the salvation to which this path leads. This signifies that in imitating the life of Jesus, one redeems oneself from sin and finds salvation in being united with God. But given that Jesus *represents* the way to the ultimate truth that lies in salvation, the question is, on what authority does his proclamation rest? It transpires this authority resides in that which transcends life – namely, God. To this end Jesus says: 'I bear witness to myself and the Father who sent me and bears witness to me.' Thus the path to salvation is lit from without and is that towards which the Christian directs her life.

We are now in a position to say that the truth that lights the Christian path is founded upon that which does not come into the light, which is to say that life is understood in terms of that which does not partake of life but marks life with its stamp. In Nietzschean terms, this means that Christianity, through the incarnation of God in Jesus, is a way in which becoming bears the stamp of being, untruth is marked by truth and the Christian life, understood in terms of one's salvation in God, means that life is interpreted in terms of that which lies beyond life – i.e. in terms of death.[17] To speak of death here is to speak of the ideal. The ideal or true world is the world in which truth resides as eternal and unchanging, and in relation to which the world of everyday life is reduced to one of semblance and error. From Nietzsche's viewpoint, the Christian interpretation of existence sees life as an illness whose only cure is death; the truth of life is that the human being needs saving from it – the ideal is more real than life itself: Christianity diminishes humanity.

One would think that Nietzsche's declaration of the death of God in the above citation would be something to be welcomed, given his views as I have just outlined them. However, and as Walter Kaufmann draws to our attention, it is not modernity's loss of faith in God that Nietzsche bemoans so much as what this loss of faith signals, i.e. a fundamental loss of meaning and value in the world *per se*.[18] The question arises, how does the death of God affect a complete loss of meaning in the world, especially as the world is open to interpretations other than the religious?

From Nietzsche's viewpoint, the danger implicit in the loss of faith in the Christian basis of truth is concealed in its supersession by the determination of the world as rationally knowable. Historically speaking, this danger stems from the debt owed by Enlightenment thinking to its Christian forebear, at least insofar as in the former we witness a continuation of the ideal notion of truth that belongs to the latter. Enlightenment thought simply replaces the absolute truth as it is found in the word of God with the universal truth of human reason. In other words, rational judgement becomes the sole arbiter and guarantor of what it is for something to be true. Philosophically speaking, the origins of this movement in thought can be traced to Descartes' separation of the human subject from its world, as contained in his famous pronouncement *cogito sum* (I think, I am), whereby it is the transcendent subject that guarantees knowledge of the material world, thanks to its privileged position as one of God's created beings.[19] There is a further movement in thought to be seen in the work of Immanuel Kant, whereby human reason becomes transcendent and *autonomous*, and truth becomes what can be known only insofar as it can be knowledge for the human subject (and insofar as this knowledge can be termed objective). It is just a short step from here to nineteenth-century positivism and the idea that the world is essentially mechanical in nature, whereby truths are presented as cold, hard facts.

However, the danger that Nietzsche sees here goes beyond the historical movement of truth as grounded in the Christian God to one grounded in human reason. Truth, for the Christian, is a way of existing – it gives meaning and purpose to life. Insofar as she interprets her life as the pursuit of truth, and truth insofar as it is found in God by following the path of Jesus, then Christian truth is redemptive. However, for Nietzsche, when truth is determined in terms of positivism, then both the historical and interpretive dimensions of truth are masked. To this end Nietzsche says, 'Against positivism, which halts at phenomena – "There are only *facts*" – I would say: No, facts is precisely what there is not, only interpretations. We cannot establish any fact "in itself": perhaps it is folly to do such a thing' [WTP §481]. In other words, thought positively, truth loses any bearing on life and becomes purely a-historical.

The resultant danger that positivism brings is what Nietzsche refers to as nihilism. From Plato's Allegory of the Cave, which urges us to spend our lives in pursuing knowledge of the unchanging truth of ideas, to Christianity and its requirement that we lead a life in pursuit of unity with God as the one true meaning of life, truth has been understood in terms of that which is worth pursuing insofar as it gives value to life – indeed, the highest value. And yet this pursuit of truth has led to positivism, where truth means nothing more than the bald facts of a universe understood as matter in motion. This mechanistic understanding of life is wholly indifferent to human existence, viewing it as nothing more than an abstract, a-historical phenomenon – another thing amongst a universe of things. Thus this absolute value, this pursuit of truth for the richness and meaning it gives to human existence, eventually devalues itself as it empties all meaning out of human life. Painted in this light, nihilism is the belief in the value of truth when its pursuit no longer has any impact on how we direct our lives.

We have now gained an insight into what Nietzsche means when he refers to nihilism as 'the highest values devaluating themselves'. The history of the West can be viewed as a path lit by the light of truth which from its very beginnings is fated to estrange the human being from its world. The pursuit of truth in modernity no longer gives an impetus to human existence: the human being no longer *becomes* something in its pursuit of truth (i.e. it is no longer historical in nature); rather, the human being *is* something (i.e. an abstraction from life, a thing). What must now be asked is where do we stand in relation to nihilism after Nietzsche traces its outline? This is not simply in the sense of whether or not we have a better understanding of nihilism, but instead in the sense of whether we are moved enough by Nietzsche's thinking so that we take a stand in relation to nihilism's pressing danger.

In Nietzsche's terms, it is a question to which our response will reveal just how deeply entrenched nihilism is in modernity. If we take the above citation, it is the case that the madman's proclamation of the death of God is met with silence, leaving him little option but to throw his lantern to the ground and thereby extinguish its light. The response of the madman's listeners leads him to bemoan the fact that the event of nihilism 'is still on its way', and that he is unable to make himself understood as his 'time is not yet'. And yet, the fact that his listeners cannot heed the madman is not a sign of nihilism, but its very embodiment. This is because Western humanity remains tied to the language of metaphysics, to the language of representation, in which words stand in for the things they name. Nietzsche is alive to this problem: 'Like a form, a concept is produced by overlooking what is individual and real, whereas nature knows neither forms nor concepts and hence no species, but only an 'X' which is inaccessible to us and indefinable by us.'[20] In other words, the language of metaphysics gives us a detached perspective on life; it speaks in metaphors that give us the illusion of truth. However, the madman speaks from the perspective of life: from out of the concrete historical truth of nihilism. For the madman to be heeded, then his listeners will have to be free from the shackles of rational thought which restrict them to a dispassionate, neutral view of the world. This is what prompts Nietzsche to say that 'faith in the categories of reason is the cause of nihilism' [WTP §12]. Until we are able hearken to the madman's word that God is dead, that is, until we are able to recognize that which we value most has devalued itself, then we are to remain in the dark about ourselves and hence passive in relation to our lives.

We are now in a position to say that, for Nietzsche, nihilism is the historical movement of Western history thought in terms of the devaluation of its highest values. It is the means by which Western life, which above all places its highest value on the pursuit of truth, loses all sense of purpose. Nihilism, in short, is the fate of the West. As the 'perfect nihilist' who 'relate(s) the history of the next two centuries', how does Nietzsche suggest we respond to the challenge of nihilism?

## Nietzsche as physician

For Nietzsche, the philosopher is not simply someone who pursues truth just for the sake of being able to able to say what is true. Rather, the philosopher is also a physician. A physician is someone who is tasked with bringing back to health an unhealthy body. If we regard modernity as suffering from an illness, and that illness is diagnosed by Nietzsche as nihilism, then the philosopher is the person who has the specific job of helping the human being move from passivity to activity in the face of nihilism.[21] And yet, as we have already noted, when the madman diagnoses modernity as the era of nihilism, he is met with silence: the patient does not recognize that she is ill – let alone that she is in need of a cure – and so the process of recovery cannot even begin. Thus the philosopher is confronted with the problem of how she is to re-invigorate the health of a patient when the patient is not responsive to her entreaties. This situation calls for further clarity as to the role of the philosopher-physician. To this end Nietzsche says:

> I am still waiting for a philosophical *physician* in the exceptional sense of that word – one who has to pursue the problem of the total health of a people, time, race or of humanity – to muster the courage to push my

suspicion to its limits and to risk the proposition: what was at stake in all philosophising hitherto was not at all 'truth' but something else – let us say, health, future, growth, power, life.²²

When the shadow of nihilism is cast upon us, the duty of the philosopher-physician is not to proffer one truth in place of another, but to enquire into and lay bare the value of truth as such, with particular regard to the affect it has on the health of a people or an era. Thus, nihilism can be brought into relief by the philosopher-physician if she is able to reveal that truth is not something that both transcends and superintends human life, but is rather historically predicated on the exigencies of this very life. As Ullrich Haase rightly puts it, for Nietzsche nihilism is a historical malady, we suffer from having lost our essential relation to history.²³ Our pursuit of truth has led us to view ourselves as beings that are abstracted from life and the only remedy for this is to answer to how we have become what we are, to reveal the human being as essentially historical in nature. Accordingly, Nietzsche thinks that if this task can be achieved, then the constrictions placed on modern existence by the tightening bonds of nihilism can be loosened, at least to the extent that modernity becomes aware that it is suffering from the malady of nihilism and so can actively respond to its threat.

In uncovering the historical origins of nihilism Nietzsche turns to ancient Greek philosophical thinking, particularly as it is found in the work of Plato, rather than to Christian thought which merely makes what originates in Plato's thought 'more cunning, more insidious, more incomprehensible'.²⁴ In imputing to Platonic thought the initial stirrings of nihilism Nietzsche means to reveal it as giving rise to the history of metaphysics. This is because, according to Nietzsche, Plato is the philosopher who first stamps being onto becoming – who first posits an ideal or true world over and against the world of the senses and error, although this claim does not go uncontested.²⁵ At its most basic this means that any finite being that can be met in sensible experience is only understood in terms of that which is infinite, i.e. in terms of what Plato calls its Form or Idea. Thus the world of sensible experience, the physical world, a region 'mingled with darkness, the world of becoming and passing away', is apprehended in terms of the metaphysical realm, the world of the idea, a 'domain where truth and reality shine resplendent'.²⁶ Thus a rose, a being that becomes what it is (that comes into bloom and dies away), is understood in terms of its ideal form, in terms of that in which it participates but which in itself is unchanging. Yet, on first blush, what seems an interesting epistemological insight on Plato's part has far more destructive ramifications for Nietzsche, who says:

> Plato measured the degrees of reality by the degrees of value and said: The more "Idea", the more being. He reversed the "concept" reality and said: "What you take for real is an error, and the nearer we approach the 'Idea,' the nearer we approach truth.
>
> [WTP 527]

In other words, Plato is positing a stable world of ideas as having more reality and a greater degree of being than the unstable world of the senses. This is what leads Plato to have Socrates say in his *Phaedo* that anyone who is properly philosophical will welcome death, and indeed it is this thought that allows Socrates to willingly take his own life.[27] This is because, Plato argues, if we wish to live a good life then we should give ourselves over to gaining knowledge of that which is most real. And as that which is most real is also that which stands to the greatest degree in the light of truth, and as the light of truth shines brightest in the ideal realm, then the human being should direct her life towards death as a way of leading the soul away from the errors to which it is prone in the sensory realm and towards the truth as that which is most ideal.

Hence, the path to truth leads away from the world of appearance, away from life and towards the ideal as that which has *greater value* for humanity, as that which enables us to live better lives. We thereby measure the world of appearances against that of the ideal only to find that the former comes up short, whilst the latter holds out the promise, upon death, of coming into the full light of truth. This judgement that Plato passes on life (by which life is diminished in Nietzsche's eyes) is transformed under Christianity in favour of transcendence towards the absolute truth in God. In modernity, as Nietzsche highlights, upon the death of God this grounding and possibility of ideal truth, along with its value to the transcendent human subject, disappears as the subject no longer has anywhere towards which she is able to transcend – she is trapped within the immanence of her experience, although she is not aware of this.

## Will to power

Such critical analysis on Nietzsche's part, however, is not to be viewed in purely negative terms, as it also opens the way to a more positive outlook. If the transcendent subject lacks an ideal world towards which she can direct her life, she is nonetheless still left with this life itself, towards which she can no longer feel indifferent and upon which she is free to take a stand. If we bear this in mind then we can understand why Nietzsche is able to frame a more positive view of Plato the philosopher. In positing the ideal world as the locus of truth Plato, from Nietzsche's viewpoint, is able to stamp an image of being onto becoming. That is, Plato stamps upon the temporal flux of life the eternal, unchanging world of the ideal. In doing so, Nietzsche argues that Plato gives the creative impetus to the illusion of stability within the midst of instability. Nietzsche sums up this state of affairs in a terse statement from his 'How the "Real World" Finally Became a Fable' which reads: 'I, Plato, *am* the truth.'

This statement is revelatory of something essential to Nietzsche's thinking on nihilism. Plato, in stamping being onto becoming, is the embodiment of the kind of person who – rather than merely passively standing by on the lookout for truth – is actively involved in *creating* it, in bestowing it as a value upon the world by positing it as the meaning of human existence. Thus Plato is a prime example of what could be argued is the central thought (alongside *The Eternal Return of the Same*) of Nietzsche's work, namely, (the) *Will to Power*,[28] a prime example of what Nietzsche means when he says that 'to impose upon becoming the character of being – that is the supreme Will to Power' [WTP §617]. But what exactly is *Will to Power*? It is both a much misunderstood and difficult concept to come to terms with and the thought, it could be argued, that underpins the whole of Nietzsche's work. Consequently, I shall refrain here from analysing the minutiae of these difficulties with the exception of mentioning that difficulty which greets every serious reader on their first encounter with this thought, and that is, as a response to nihilism, it reveals the profundity of what Nietzsche views as the plight of modernity. *Will to Power* is nothing less than a re-thinking of the notions of truth, world and life that gives to all three a unity that re-vitalizes the human being by demanding of her a return to a creatively active existence. To this end Nietzsche says in

Section 1067 of his *The Will to Power*: 'This world is the Will to Power – and *nothing besides!* And you yourselves are also this Will to Power – and nothing besides.'

As a response to the loss of the supra-sensuous world and its concomitant devaluating of human existence, Nietzsche offers the thought of *Will to Power*, a 'yes-saying' return of humanity to the flux of life. Here the individual is thought in terms of functioning as an active element within a world of creative activity, a willing participant in a process of fluctuating power relations. This is not to say, however, that the individual is an agent consciously willing this or that action. Nor is it to say that the individual is bent on an accrual of power in the sense of being able to dominate others, a criticism that has often been levelled at Nietzsche's thought. Instead, the individual here is thought of as given over to the flux life itself, as given over to creative activity. To understand fully what Nietzsche means by life as 'creatively active', we need to take a brief excursus and look at how he views life in one of his earliest works, *The Birth of Tragedy*.

In *The Birth of Tragedy*, Nietzsche argues that Greek tragedy – as the apotheosis of Greek civilization – arises out of the conflicting forces that are embodied in the Greek gods Apollo and Dionysos, 'artistic powers which erupt from nature itself'.[29] The Dionysiac side of the conflict stands for all that is dark in life, an 'intoxicated reality' that seeks the abandonment of the individual to the point of 'self-forgetting'. The Apolline side is the drive for measure, to clarity and to sobriety in the midst of intoxication. Brought directly into conflict through the creative will of the Greek tragedians, these powers collide on the Greek stage and make manifest for the Greek people a genuine sense of human life as torn between two conflicting perspectives: the individual as the dispassionate onlooker of life; life as a turbulent flux to which the individual is necessarily given over. For Nietzsche, Greek tragedy hits on what is most meaningful to life in its attempt to reconcile the unstable relation of these two creative powers. On the one hand we see the human being as a vulnerable individual at prey to the vicissitudes of life, on the other we see the human being as at one with a greater reality.

Thus, in the form of the gods Apollo and Dionysos, Nietzsche thinks the Greeks are able to bring into relief a manifestation of the creative struggle between being and becoming that reveals truth as conflictive prior to the advent of Platonic thought and the decisive step taken along the path of truth that sees the supersession of becoming in the stamp of being. Nonetheless, this struggle serves as a paradigm for Nietzsche's notion of *Will to Power* as it collapses the supra-sensuous and sensible worlds into a process of conflicting drives in which the one responds to the other and through which either one can only be understood in terms of the other. Truth here is the struggle to bring measure to the 'confusing multiplicity' of life and sees the human being as the locus of this struggle.

It is also important to note that Nietzsche's conception[30] of life thought as *Will to Power* is not simply limited to the confines of human existence. For Nietzsche, all life demonstrates *Will to Power* insofar as all beings belong to the struggle *to be*. This leads Nietzsche to say that 'being – we have no idea of it apart from the idea of "living"' [WTP §582]. From a Heideggerian viewpoint, Nietzsche's argument is that being is in fact becoming, that all beings are essentially understood in terms of becoming. From Nietzsche's viewpoint, he is arguing that all beings belong to life understood as *Will to Power*, which means that all beings are loci of conflicting powers striving amidst a continuous flux of power-relations. Understood in this sense, as a being amongst other beings, the individual is not someone who possesses *Will to Power* – rather, she is *Will to Power*. Consequently, the individual is not to be understood essentially as a subject or an isolated being that stands by passively making judgements about the world. Instead, she is regarded as an active *being* that is given over to becoming the being that she is. The more the human being actively engages with life (the more she is open to other willing beings), the freer she will be to *become* who she *is*. Thus, the human being here is not thought of as a subject that transcends life but as given over to life which in itself is transcendent. In a very real sense the individual is challenged by Nietzsche to be a being that overcomes itself, that wills to become what it is not as much as willing not to be what it is. It is a challenge to return the human being to its essence as a being-historical. Or it can be thought of in the sense that Heidegger draws to our attention in his Nietzsche lectures, in which he says that Nietzsche thinks that 'art is the basic occurrence of all beings' [N1 12], and so the individual is a locus of creative forces that discovers itself as existing amidst a confluence of creative forces.

We can see that what Nietzsche has in mind with *Will to Power* is an understanding of the world from the perspective of life. However, as Ullrich Haase notes, this idea opens up Nietzsche's philosophy to much of the misunderstanding it has subsequently received.[31] This is due to the fact that Nietzsche's notion of the will tends to be understood in the sense of the conscious will of the human subject. In other words, it is thought in the sense that it is a possession of the human being who uses it to overpower others. But for Nietzsche, life understood as *Will to Power* breaks down this notion of human subjectivity in favour of viewing the individual as an actively creative being given over to life as a confluence of pure activity. What does this mean exactly? Willing, according to Nietzsche, never implies the willing of a state of affairs that already obtain, as that would essentially make willing a passive activity. Instead, willing always implies the willing of something beyond what already *is*, of willing towards a future state of affairs. Thus willing, and so *Will to Power*, can be regarded as the creative impulse to give rise to something unfamiliar, to create something new out of that which *is*, to go beyond the immediacy of one's own being. In the case of the human being, insofar as she is given over life, she has the freedom to strive to go beyond herself, to become who she is.[32] This is life viewed from the perspective of art, and so it retains the vestiges of the Dionysian, thought as a creative process of self-overcoming, which in turn points away from metaphysical history towards a truth that lies beyond. What Nietzsche is attempting to do here is to open up the possibility of what he terms a *Revaluation of all Values*, of which he says in his preface to *The Will to Power*:

> For one should make no mistake about the meaning of the title that this gospel of the future wants to bear. "*The Will to Power*: Attempt at a Revaluation of All Values" – in this formulation a countermovement finds expression, regarding both principle and task; a movement that in some future will take the place of this perfect nihilism – but presupposes it, logically and psychologically, and certainly can come only after and out of it. For why has the advent of nihilism become *necessary*? Because the values we have had hitherto thus draw their final consequence; because nihilism represents the ultimate logical conclusion of our great values and

ideals – because we must experience nihilism before we can find out what value these "values" really had. - We require, sometime, *new values*. [WTP Preface]

This is to say that at some point during the history of metaphysics there comes a moment when our highest values become impotent and need to be revoked, at least in terms of their transcendental nature. It is in this context that Nietzsche talks about 'revaluation', but what exactly does he mean? What Nietzsche does not mean, according to Walter Kaufmann, is that we come to a time when we replace the old values with new ones.[33] Instead, Kaufmann argues, revaluation is the simple becoming conscious of prevailing values as bearing the mark of a mendacious morality and accepting that we are living in the shadow of a dead God. In other words, revaluation is the acceptance that what we hold to be most virtuous is without foundation. However, we should also bear in mind that this is also a positive moment in Western history. To this end Nietzsche says in *Ecce Homo*: '*Revaluation of all values*: that is my formula for an act of humanity's highest self-examination, an act that has become flesh and genius in me. My lot would have it that I am the first *decent* human being, that I know myself to be opposing the hypocrisy of millennia.'[34] As hyperbolic as this sounds, it is no mere exercise in self-aggrandisement by Nietzsche but a declaration that has historical significance.

As I have already noted, Nietzsche views himself as the 'perfect nihilist'. Having taken on the burden of nihilism it did not crush him: he lived through the experience, accepted it and came out the other side. Hence, Nietzsche saw himself as best placed to pronounce a verdict ON the state of modernity. This is because Nietzsche sees himself as looking at the world from the perspective of one who has accepted the death of God. Having done so, Nietzsche looks to the creative possibilities of life thought as *Will to Power* as offering a way beyond nihilism. And, as Kaufmann argues, what Nietzsche affectively does here is to reverse the prevailing valuations that originally reversed the ancient Greek valuations that were manifest in Greek tragedy prior to Platonic thought.[35] In other words, Nietzsche 'reverses' Platonism by calling for a return to life understood in terms of becoming rather than being. Whilst Plato stamps becoming with the image of being in the form of the 'empty fictions' of unity, substance and duration, Nietzsche instead tries to give us the truth of life by revealing it as essentially fleeting and protean. Thus any overcoming of nihilism can only be based on *Will to Power*, on the confluence of creative forces that give humanity a new perspective on life.

## The overhuman

It is in this light that Nietzsche, in his *Thus Spoke Zarathustra*, has Zarathustra say: 'God has died: now *we* desire – that the overhuman shall live (trans. mod.).'[36] Further, he has *Zarathustra* say: 'I love him who lives for knowledge and who wants knowledge that one day the overhuman may live. And thus he wills his own downfall.'[37] The thought that needs thinking at the time of nihilism is that of the 'overhuman'. The person who has the courage to think this thought is the active nihilist. The active nihilist is the person who in the spirit of self-overcoming, by giving in to the creative impulse to go beyond herself as she *is*, wills the overhuman in place of the transcendent realm as the locus of truth. Consequently, truth is to be thought in terms of life itself. But what does Nietzsche mean by the overhuman that it can fill the void where once stood our highest values? Rather enigmatically, he says that the overhuman is the meaning of the earth, but says little more of any substance.[38] This is because, as a genuinely historical thought, the notion of the overhuman must be approached obliquely. One cannot use the language of representation to think that which is genuinely historical, as to re-present means to bring what is fully present before thought and what is genuinely historical can only be understood in terms of its historical *movement*.

This is why *Zarathustra* speaks in riddles.[39] The overhuman cannot be present for modern thought as it belongs to another history, that is, to a history that is yet to come. This new history is necessary as Western history has come to an end as directionless. In the face of this lack of direction, all that is left for the active nihilist is to create something that goes beyond herself, by which she negates her current standing in life and thereby hands herself over to becoming – that is, she must become properly historical. This overcoming is directed towards the idea of the overhuman, the 'type that has the highest constitutional excellence, in contrast to "modern" people'.[40]

However, we would be mistaken if we thought that Nietzsche means that the active nihilist wills herself to become the overhuman. This would simply suggest that the active nihilist in some sense views herself as she currently is but at some point in the future, with perhaps some enhanced sense of her own superiority. However, creative self-overcoming towards the notion of the overhuman is a way for modern humanity to cut its links with its past and give itself over to a new history. It is in this way that Nietzsche views the current plight of humanity: 'Man is a rope, fastened between animal and overhuman – a rope over an abyss.'[41] That is, humanity is no longer the goal of life but a bridge across it. This is Nietzsche's way of saying that when we no longer have meaningful values to apply to life, life itself becomes our meaning. But as life itself is sheer becoming – that is, *Will to Power* – then what is left for the active nihilist is to become properly historical, to will her own overcoming in the hope that one day something beyond the modern human will arise. Thus life is ultimately a creative act: to will one's own overcoming by making the overhuman the meaning of the earth. But this is both to say and not say that humanity finds its goals in the overhuman; as the idea of the overhuman is not determined in any way, it is a path along which thought can travel but which has no designated stop. It is, in fact, truth thought historically:

> 'Truth' is therefore not something there, that might be found or discovered – but something that must be created and that gives a name to a process, or rather to a will to overcome that has in itself no end – introducing truth, as a *processus in infinitum*, an active determining – not a becoming conscious of something that is in itself firm and determined. It is a word for the 'will to power'.
>
> [WTP §552]

I wish to conclude this section with a recapitulation of the general points I have outlined on Nietzsche's thinking regarding nihilism. For Nietzsche, nihilism is that historical event by which the highest values devaluate themselves, insofar as that which we find most virtuous finally reveals itself as having no firm basis. Nietzsche argues that the origins of this event are to be found in the thought of Plato, whereby the drive to ideal truth leads away from the tragic manifestation of life at its most meaningful and towards the history of metaphysics. Thus the meaning of human existence is no longer thought in terms of becoming, but in terms of being as that which transcends life. Over the millennia, this ideal truth becomes Christianized and eventually ends in positivism and the alienation of the Western individual from her world which we call nihilism.

In response to this, Nietzsche posits the notion of the overhuman as the meaning of life, a notion towards which those of a strong disposition (active nihilists) are to orient their lives. For Nietzsche, this is a way of getting beyond the metaphysical history of the West by creating a new history based on life thought as *Will to Power*. Truth thus becomes properly historical as the self-overcoming of humanity. We have now arrived at a point at which to examine the influence Nietzsche's thought on nihilism has on Heidegger, and how Heidegger responds.

## Nietzsche as metaphysician

Before we come to what distinguishes Heidegger's thought on nihilism from that of Nietzsche's (and Heidegger's view of Nietzsche as the last great metaphysician of Western thinking), it is briefly worth noting the former's debt to the latter, particularly with regard to Nietzsche's influence on Heidegger's own thought on nihilism and his ability even to critique Nietzsche. To do so at this juncture means that we can deal immediately with a difficulty that often arises in the secondary literature with regard to Heidegger's interpretation of Nietzsche's thought – namely, that it does violence to it.[42] To say that Heidegger does violence to Nietzsche's thought would seem to impute to him the wilful misinterpretation of Nietzsche's work in furtherance of his own philosophical project. This is exemplified by the eminent Nietzschean scholar Walter Kaufmann, who refers to Heidegger's thought as 'deeply authoritarian'.[43] What Kaufmann means by this is that Heidegger's method leads him to read his own ideas into texts and consequently to regard his own interpretations of those texts as authoritative. The claim is that this leads Heidegger to tread such a narrow path through a given text that much of philosophical merit, as well as alternative viewpoints, get passed over as inconsequential. In other words, in doing violence to a text, Heidegger does not do it justice. Yet doing justice to a text is exactly what Heidegger's thinking is about, as we shall see.

I have already noted in this chapter that doing justice to Nietzsche's thought involves more than merely assimilating what he says as either correct or incorrect and thereby allowing the world itself to remain untouched. Nietzsche's thought confronts his reader with the problem of nihilism, with the problem of what to do in the face of a world that lacks direction. As such, Nietzsche's thought throws down a challenge to his readers: do we have the courage to face up to the historical crisis that is nihilism? Heidegger accepts the challenge, he agrees that Western humanity lives at a time that requires of it 'great decisions', but he accepts it on his own terms. For example, whilst Nietzsche thinks that we should will the overhuman as the meaning of the earth as a way of getting beyond nihilism, Heidegger's approach (eventually) leads him to think that we should adopt a stance of 'active non-willing', as a way of *letting being be*.[44] This might make it appear that the division between the two thinkers lies in Nietzsche's call to action and a more 'passive' approach from Heidegger. Yet this would be a mistaken assumption. Both philosophers share a similar appreciation of the threat that nihilism poses, and both maintain that a decision about nihilism must necessarily involve a decision about the role played by language in determining truth. What separates the two thinkers, however, is how they interpret Western history. Heidegger sums up the historical situation that both men face as follows:

> There is a danger that the thought of man today will fall short of the decisions that are coming, decisions of whose specific historical shape we can know nothing – that the man of today will look for these decisions where they can never be made.
>
> [WCT 66]

What I am suggesting here is that both men agree that Western thought. i.e. metaphysical thought, occasions the advent of nihilism as well as hindering any move beyond it, given that our destiny is to view the world through metaphysical concepts. Against this background, Nietzsche's positing of the notion of the overhuman along with willing its arrival (returning thought to the temporal experience of life), and Heidegger's refraining from willing through a thoughtful comportment to being, can both be seen as similar responses to the problem of a creeping indifference to and alienation from the world. In other words, both thinkers look to a thinking that is other than metaphysical as a way of responding to nihilism. However, what underscores the similarity of these responses is a fundamental divergence as to what the history of metaphysics means, as to what it reveals in its unfolding, a divergence which is due to the differences in the way that both men *think* this history. As we shall see, Heidegger discovers in Nietzsche's notion of the overhuman the apotheosis of metaphysical thought as well as its concluding form.

And yet, in so thoughtfully engaging with Nietzsche's work, in seeking to discover the problems of modernity in the light that Nietzsche sheds upon them, Heidegger makes Nietzsche's problems his own.[45] In doing so, Heidegger not only does justice to Nietzsche's thought by taking up Nietzsche's challenge to seek out 'all that which is foreign and question-worthy in existence' but he also opens up a discourse with Nietzsche's thought in which his own philosophical thinking undergoes a transformation. Thus the question of nihilism is approached from a purely ontological viewpoint as mediated through the prism of Nietzsche's own thoughts on nihilism. Consequently, if the criticism is that Heidegger does violence to Nietzsche's thought, it can be seen that he does so whilst simultaneously doing justice to it. So much so, in fact, that Gianni Vattimo suggests not only does Heidegger open the door to Nietzsche as a thinker, but that an understanding of Nietzsche opens the door to Heidegger's own philosophy.[46]

Equally significant as far as the importance of Nietzsche's work for his own thinking is concerned is that Heidegger engages with Nietzsche's thought more than with any other thinker's. As far as Heidegger's published works are concerned, we can see this from as early as *Being and Time*. Here, Heidegger's engagement with Nietzsche – despite only mentioning him by name on three occasions – is clear to see. It is revealed in *Being and Time*'s destruction of the Western metaphysical tradition, understood as a history of decay that originates in the fertile ground of ancient Greek thought which ends in the sterility of positivism. Almost thirty years later Heidegger publishes *What Is Called Thinking?* in which he points to language as a possible way to move beyond metaphysical thinking, and to Nietzsche as that thinker whose thought must be overcome if we wish to do this. Thus Heidegger's concern with Nietzsche as a thinker can be seen to sustain much of Heidegger's own work for much of his life.

However, as it becomes increasingly clear that Heidegger views Nietzsche's thought as an impediment to overcoming metaphysics we should not be surprised that he describes Nietzsche's thought in his 1943 essay 'Nietzsche's Word: God Is Dead' (important as it contains the distillation of a series of lecture he gave on Nietzsche between 1936 and 1940) as a 'countermovement against metaphysics (that) remains embroiled in it and has no way out; in fact it is embroiled in it to such a degree that it is sealed off from its essence and as metaphysics is unable to think its own essence' [OBT 162]. Briefly, what Heidegger is driving at here is that in heralding the death of God, Nietzsche sees himself as bringing to an end the idea of a supra-sensuous world by replacing it with idea of a world of pure becoming, thereby reversing a tradition that begins with the thought of Plato. However, as Heidegger points out, as a countermovement to metaphysics Nietzsche's thought is still metaphysical as it essentially understands being in terms of *Will to Power*, which is being thought as the being of beings, whilst being as such disappears from sight. Yet we should not read this as a criticism of Nietzsche as just another thinker in a long line of metaphysical thinkers stretching back to the ancient Greeks. For Heidegger, Nietzsche's thought signals the culmination of the metaphysical tradition as he is the thinker that undermines this tradition from within. As such, Nietzsche's thought is of critical importance as it contains within it the essence of the whole metaphysical tradition as attaining its fate in nihilism. This is why Heidegger says of Nietzsche's proclamation 'God is dead' that he is here giving expression to 'the word that has always been implicitly spoken within the metaphysically determined history of the West' [Ibid 160].

Nietzsche's thought does not merely contain the thought of a single thinker, then, but the essence of the whole history of metaphysics from its origins, that is, its motivating, nihilistic force. This is why Heidegger regards Nietzsche as the thinker that is both closest to us *and* the one from whom we need most to distance ourselves. In other words, Nietzsche's thought is transitional (*ein Übergang*) and as such it is a 'pointing before and beyond' in which 'all the themes of Western thought ... gather together' [WCT 51]. Thus, as the self-proclaimed 'first perfect nihilist of Europe' who heralds the end of the metaphysical tradition, Nietzsche struggles to rid himself of its influence upon his thought. To this end Heidegger says:

> Nietzsche sees clearly that in the history of Western man something is coming to an end: what until now and long since has remained uncompleted. Nietzsche sees the necessity to carry it to a completion. But completion does not mean here that a part is added which was missing before; this completion does not make whole by patching; it makes whole by achieving at last *the wholeness* of the whole, by thus transforming what has been so far, in virtue of the whole.
>
> [WCT 55]

Hence, the thought of the thinker that is Nietzsche is not open to simple refutation as his thought bears the historical weight of the whole of the metaphysical tradition. As such, Nietzsche thought brings thought itself into question as the vehicle that harbours the fate of the West as nihilism hidden within. This is why Heidegger insists on a critical disengagement with Nietzsche's thought as a way of locating the danger which lies within. Similarly, the words of the madman in the market square who pronounces the death of God may be mocked – nonetheless, his words demand a serious hearing (as this is an historical thought, one which opens up a path for thought to travel along). Anyone attentive enough to heed the call will be awakened to the fate of the modern individual: cast astray in a barren landscape, out of which there are no paths signposted and whose formerly familiar landmarks have suddenly receded into their own shadows. The question arises, what does Heidegger discover about the nature of nihilism in Nietzsche's thought?

As has been noted already, for Nietzsche this situation speaks directly of values – the death of God signalling the end of the ideal world and its absolute values, ushering in the end of metaphysics in the form of nihilism along with the loss of the *telos* of Western humanity heretofore. Yet this is not, according to Heidegger, an observation about the decadence of Western history, but speaks instead of what Nietzsche calls its 'inner logic' (*innere Logik*), a logic that does not leave us world-less but with a world devoid of its former meaning. Moreover, this situation also impels us 'toward a new dispensation of value', or better, a revaluation of the basis of values. Consequently, we discover that nihilism is thought by Nietzsche as Janus-headed: it is a nay-saying look to the past and its ideal values and a yes-saying look to a future in which a new dispensation of values is to be founded on life.[47] In both cases values are understood as arising out of *Will to Power*; what changes in the transition from the one to the other is our stance on nihilism itself. We are to say no to the 'weak', pessimistic stance that says life has no meaning and is thereby rendered worthless, and instead say yes to an acceptance of life understood as *Will to Power*. Herein, according to Heidegger, lies the danger hidden in Nietzsche's thought. What reason does Heidegger have for thinking this?

It is because, Heidegger says: 'Will to Power, becoming, life, and being in the broadest sense have the same meaning in Nietzsche's language' [OBT 172]. In other words, all reality is understood in terms of fluctuating power-relations in which each being wills a preservation and increase in its own power. Thus, all beings are understood in terms of *Will to Power*, which in turn means – given that *Will to Power* is to form the basis of the revaluation of all values – that the ultimate value of beings as a whole is *Will to Power*. It is here that Heidegger locates the implicit danger of Nietzsche's thought insofar as it is the ultimate manifestation of metaphysics. Why? Because reality is given its value in terms of *Will to Power*, which is to say that what is real are beings determined insofar as they are the embodiment of *Will to Power*. Thus, *Will to Power* is the value that determines beings in their being, and being as such disappears from view:

> For it is precisely in the positing of new values from the Will to Power, by which and through which Nietzsche believes he will overcome nihilism that nihilism proper first proclaims that there is nothing to being itself, which has now become a value. [...] Value thinking is now elevated into a principle. Being itself, as a matter of principle, is not admitted as being. According to its own principle, in this metaphysics there is *nothing* to being.
> [N4 203]

Thus *Will to Power* is the fulfilment of metaphysics as far as Heidegger is concerned, and is best exemplified in Nietzsche's notion of the overhuman. As has already been noted, 'God has died: now *we* desire that the overhuman shall live'[48] is a desideratum that cannot, as such, be determined. All one can say of it is that it is an idea that is intended to lead humanity beyond nihilism by making itself properly historical, that is, by willing its own self-overcoming.

Consequently – and because it understands itself as essentially *Will to Power* – the notion of the overhuman determines human *being* in terms of an unremitting will to its own self-overcoming which forms the basis of all its value-positing and thus the basis of all becoming. Hence, from Heidegger's viewpoint, the notion of the overhuman places a value on being *as such* and so being is completely hidden from view.

If this is indeed the case, if Nietzsche's thought is indeed essentially metaphysical, then it must retain some sense of the subjective about it that can be brought forth in evidence against it. Of course, it could be countered immediately that for Nietzsche there is no such thing as truth and that Nietzsche said as much himself, describing truth as an illusion.[49] This being the case, then surely there is nothing to be gained from a discussion of truth as it stands in Nietzsche's thought. And yet, Nietzsche's notion that truth is an illusion – far from making an irrelevance of the notion of truth as such – proves to be the very basis on which Nietzsche views truth as having any meaning whatsoever for the human being. To this end he says: 'Truth is the kind of error without which a certain species of life could not live. The value for *life* is ultimately decisive' [WTP §493]. Thus truth is a value for Nietzsche, and as such needs to be understood in terms of whether or not it is beneficial to life, and not as existing disinterestedly in some transcendental, ideal realm.

However, given that the human being is normative in the sense that it prescribes the value 'truth' to life – even if that truth is understood as overcoming oneself in order to will the overhuman – the problem of the subjectivity of value-giving necessarily arises. To this end Heidegger says in his 'Nietzsche's Word: God is Dead':

> But within modern metaphysics the being of beings is determined as will and thereby as self-willing; however, self-willing is intrinsically already self-knowing-itself; Beings (*subiectum*) present (*präsentiert*) themselves, in fact they present themselves to themselves, in the mode of the *ego cogito*. This self-presenting, the re-presenting … is the being of beings qua *subiectum*. Self-knowing itself becomes the quintessential subject … Modern metaphysics, as the metaphysics of subjectivity, thinks the being of beings in the sense of the will.
>
> [OBT 182]

Values for Nietzsche are not something that in themselves are grasped from out of the metaphysical realm but can only be understood from the perspective of life. However, this means there must be a perspective, a viewpoint from which values are posited. For Nietzsche, this viewpoint is understood in terms of the self-overcoming of the individual in willing the overhuman as the meaning of the earth. Thus truth is understood from the perspective of the individual's will to overcome herself. But this does not mean that truth becomes subjective insofar as everyone has their own perspective on truth, and thereby truth is reduced to the level of opinion. Rather, truth, as *Will to Power*, as that which determines beings in their being, becomes the viewpoint from which all of life is determined. As such, Heidegger suggests, *Will to Power*, which as the being of beings determines all beings insofar as they present themselves as both loci and enhancers of power, means that the truth of the world resides in *absolute* subjectivity. In other words, truth is reduced to the enhancement of power from the perspective of the human subject, and the human subject makes all other beings conform to its will. Thus human subjectivity is nothing other than the absolute power to dominate the earth as the embodiment of *Will to Power*. Hence truth is the accrual of power, the being of beings. It is for this reason that Heidegger seeks to distance his thought from that of Nietzsche, as Nietzsche not only does not think being as such, his thought occludes it.

We shall return to this point presently when I seek to clarify – by looking at some critical voices regarding Heidegger's interpretation of Nietzsche's thought – just what is at stake in this confrontation between Nietzsche and Heidegger with regard to nihilism. However, it should prove helpful here to draw together briefly the various strands of Heidegger's argument that consigns to Nietzsche his status as the last metaphysician. Firstly, this status is not accorded to Nietzsche on account of his singularity as a thinker but because in reversing Platonism, in thinking truth in terms of *Will to Power* rather than as residing in the realm of the supra-sensuous, Nietzsche simply encapsulates it. Consequently, Nietzsche's thought is to be understood in terms of the whole metaphysical tradition reaching its destiny. As such, Nietzsche's thought can be considered transitional, heralding the end of metaphysical thinking in this reversal and indicating the necessity for a thinking that is other than metaphysical. This can be seen in Nietzsche's understanding of Western history as the devaluation of our ideal values, a devaluation that empties life of all meaning and leaves humanity in need of a new basis for the revaluation of values as such. For Nietzsche, the basis for this revaluation is life understood as *Will to Power*. However, this does not in itself get us beyond metaphysics as it is dependent on the perspective of absolute subjectivity as thought in the notion of the overhuman as the dispenser of values. The overhuman is the dispenser of values as that being who will 'determine all beings in their being' [OBT 193] based on *Will to Power*. Hereby the path to being itself is blocked insofar as it is reduced to a value, and what can be said to lie at the heart of nihilism as the end of metaphysics is 'that there is nothing going on with being' [OBT 197].

## Questions concerning Heidegger's Interpretation of Nietzsche

At the beginning of his lecture courses on Nietzsche, which began in 1936, Heidegger says the following:

> The confrontation with Nietzsche has not yet begun, nor have the prerequisites for it been established. For a long time Nietzsche has been either celebrated and imitated or reviled and exploited. Nietzsche's thought and speech are still too contemporary for us. He and we have not yet been sufficiently separated in history; we lack the distance necessary for a sound appreciation of the thinker's strength.
>
> [N1 4]

The confrontation begins, of course, with Heidegger, but the question remains as to what can be can be said about this confrontation in the time that has since elapsed. The first thing that can be said is that it is not a simple question of who is right and who is wrong, or who has the stronger argument. It is, rather, a matter of how we come to terms with nihilism as it is thought by these two thinkers, both in the sense of how we grasp its shadowy and shifting form and how we can try to find our way beyond its ever-increasing influence. It also remains (unsurprisingly, given what I have just said) a matter of grave philosophical concern, with Gianni Vattimo asserting that in the latter part of the twentieth century, much European philosophical thought is concerned with the connections that obtain between the thought of both Nietzsche and Heidegger, and which particularly revolve around the question of Nietzsche as the last metaphysician.[50]

I shall turn first to what has been said with regard to the question of truth that Heidegger discovers in Nietzsche, a notion that is essentially representational, in which the viewpoint of absolute subjectivity allows for something to be valued as true insofar as it is beneficial to life. It has been argued that whilst Heidegger is not being unfair to Nietzsche insofar as he views Nietzsche as thinking truth as *Will to Power*, he is too quick to judge Nietzsche insofar as he does not pay heed sufficiently to the fact that Nietzsche's fundamental concepts should be understood as transitional concepts – with an eye to the future as well as the past.[51] This is to say that Heidegger understands Nietzsche's concepts as the fulfilment of a general impetus found within metaphysics from truth thought as the manifestation of being to the complete occlusion of being in the evaluative dominance of the overhuman. However, it could be equally argued that Nietzsche's concepts can be understood in terms of *setting thought on its way* into an openness towards the future. Indeed, as Nietzsche's notion of truth springs from life itself, it must be thought as essentially temporal, i.e. as finite in nature. This means that his notion of truth does not determine wholly or absolutely; rather, it brings truth into the sweep of history, by which it can only be understood in its essence as finite.

Whether this reading of Nietzsche's concepts would be possible without an understanding of Heidegger's own philosophical insights is a moot point, as it would be equally difficult to understand much of Heidegger's philosophy without the influence of Nietzsche thought upon it. What it does show is the closeness of the two thinkers in philosophical outlook, particularly when we recognize that thought in this way, Nietzsche's conceptual understanding reminds us of the notion of preparatory thinking (*das anfängliche Denken*) in Heidegger's work, a thinking that does not ground thought, but opens it up to possibilities 'whose coming remains uncertain' [BW 436]. Indeed, it could even be argued that through his engagement with Nietzsche's work Heidegger's own thinking had been opened up to future possibilities.

Eugen Fink (as an early and important contributor to this debate) also sees an openness to being in Nietzsche's thought that he thinks Heidegger overlooks. In his *Nietzsche's Philosophy* – where much of his own thought bears the mark of Heidegger's influence – he counters Heidegger's assertion that Nietzsche is the last metaphysician by suggesting that greater attention should be paid to Nietzsche's notion of *play* [*Spiel*] as a central concept of his thought. Fink argues that through the notion of *play* the human being stands in 'an ecstatic openness' to the world rather than as one being amongst others. This is significant insofar as Nietzsche's overhuman, understood in this sense, would no longer be regarded as standing over life as a value-dispensing locus of power but as given over – in a Dionysian sense – to the play of being and becoming and so an active participant in the fate of the cosmos.[52]

This is an interesting insight on Fink's part, seeing the possibility in Nietzsche's notion of *play* of locating the human being within an open relation to being (in the Heideggerian sense) by handing her over to the historical vicissitudes of becoming, and thereby slewing off the last vestiges of metaphysical dependency in Nietzsche's thought. However, Fink fails to make the case as to why, despite the fact that Heidegger pays little heed to the notion of *play* in Nietzsche's thought, Heidegger goes wrong in not putting this notion at the centre of Nietzsche's thought in place of *Will to Power*. Thus in failing to make the case – whilst bringing to light an interesting insight into Nietzsche's thought – Fink's claim does not prove critical for Heidegger's general interpretation.

Ernst Behler brings out an important methodological point in his *Nietzsche in the Twentieth Century*. Having examined two important texts on Nietzsche by Karl Jaspers he concludes that Jasper's main insight is that Nietzsche's work is so fragmentary and contradictory – not to say, finally, aberrational – that one should abandon a mere reading of his work in favour of a perusal of his 'intellectual experience'.[53] In view of this Behler contrasts Heidegger's approach to Nietzsche's aphoristic and openly structured texts as one which Heidegger thinks he can read in the style of traditional metaphysics. This begs the question of Heidegger's approach to a given text, particularly if we also recall Kaufmann's assertion that Heidegger's philosophy is deeply authoritarian.

We can understand Heidegger's approach to Nietzsche's texts, and any other texts of the tradition for that matter, if we bear in mind that he understands the tradition as a process by which being is approached in terms of the being of beings and that any text of the tradition will manifest this in its own particular way. More fundamentally, however, this process increasingly manifests this understanding of being as grounding beings in a *being present* that simultaneously coincides with an increasing disregard for that which remains hidden in this presencing. Therefore this grounding can be traced in modern philosophical thought from, for example, Descartes' *Cogito Sum* on to Kant's transcendental subject, Hegel's movement of absolute spirit and finally Nietzsche's *Will to Power*.[54] That Heidegger can assert this of Nietzsche's thought is because Nietzsche's concept of *Will to Power*, as a way of revealing beings as loci of power and nothing besides, is thus the fundamental concept of Nietzsche's thought. Thereby Nietzsche's thought, however fragmented, can still be shown to belong to the metaphysical tradition given its underpinning by the notion of *Will to Power*.

On the basis of these observations it can be seen that there are certain pressing and problematical concerns regarding nihilism that need further explication, and which will only be furnished by a deeper understanding of Heidegger's approach to the problem as a way of distancing his thought from that of Nietzsche. This is most pertinently summed up by Will McNeill when he says that as far as Nietzsche's engagement with nihilism is concerned, at least from Heidegger's perspective, the question of the 'is' does not arise.[55] That is, being as such is no longer brought into question. This is the starting point for Heidegger's engagement with nihilism, and the point from which it is possible to begin to distance our thinking from that of Nietzsche, and thus the tradition of metaphysical thought, as we shall see in the next chapter.

# 2

# *The possibility of an other beginning*

In his *Contributions to Philosophy*, which Heidegger worked on contemporaneously with his Nietzsche lectures, he remarks:

> Nihilism in Nietzsche's sense means that all *goals* are gone. Nietzsche has those goals in mind that grow of themselves and transform humans (whereunto?). [...] Directed toward the other beginning, nihilism must be grasped more fundamentally as the essential consequence of the abandonment of being.
>
> [C 96]

This sounds decisive – fatal even, and written as it was between 1936 and 1938, with a world war looming on the horizon, such a statement reveals more a sense of urgency than one of melancholy. It would, then, be timely to ask: where to from here for Heidegger? In the face of the seemingly ineluctable will of Western humanity to annihilate itself – measured by Heidegger in the thorough-going occlusion of being from *Dasein* – what use is the thinking of the philosopher if her thoughts go unheeded? And what is more, if nihilism is a *fait accompli*, what is to be gained from its further analysis, even if valuable insights are to be gained and were to be heeded? Would *Dasein* not be better served by the philosopher if philosophical enquiry was put aside in favour of a harkening to the claims of reason or art as ways of obscuring the fact of nihilism and therefore alleviating its affects? Or specifically in Heidegger's case, perhaps a claim could be made for the conservation of a more 'natural' mode of existence, with the ancient Greeks serving as a model. Michael Gillespie notes in response to such claims that Heidegger, whilst sympathetic, would regard any of these suggestions merely as ways of rejecting modernity and that the issue for Heidegger is to overcome both it and antiquity as a means of overcoming metaphysics itself.[1]

In following Gillespie's analysis it would seem that for Heidegger a confrontation with the history of metaphysics is required as both a precursory and necessary step in its overcoming. But what is meant here by the overcoming of metaphysics? Certainly, given what I have just said about nihilism, Heidegger will have to show that despite metaphysics attaining its historical completion as nihilism, the possibility of a new relation between *Dasein* and being can be opened up in some way, that is, if *Dasein* is not to remain in the dark about being. If Heidegger can make the case, then he should also be able to demonstrate what else is necessary to such an overcoming. For example, how does this new relation reveal a new understanding of truth, and in what sense will this truth be borne out in *Dasein* appropriating a properly historical sense of itself? Further, and allied to these observations, is the seemingly insurmountable necessity for *Dasein* to unshackle itself from the language of metaphysics and the restraints it places on *Dasein*'s view of being.

Briefly, and as an immediate response to these demands, we can say that the overcoming that Heidegger has in mind here lies simply in the recognition of the fact that the history of Western thought, understood philosophically (and for Heidegger this means understood in its essence and out of its essence as metaphysics), comes to an end in nihilism. As such, it is also the recognition that this end – in and of itself – signals the approach of another beginning: a beginning as yet un-thought and, for the philosopher, perhaps properly speaking unthinkable. Nonetheless, Heidegger insists, it is a beginning for which we must prepare ourselves, a beginning that requires us to try to step back from metaphysical thinking and into a new way of thinking that is able to open up a new history. Therefore in the remainder of this chapter I shall examine the historical event of nihilism – as Heidegger interprets it – in order not only to situate the Western individual in her current historical relation to being but also to see how this helps us come to terms with the problem of nihilism itself, and thereby to look beyond metaphysics.

# The end of metaphysics and the possibility of an other beginning

## Ereignis

What, then, does the philosopher do in the face of nihilism? I agree with Gillespie's analysis that Heidegger passes over the rejection of modernity in favour of an overcoming of metaphysics, and that therefore the philosopher must in some way indicate a way beyond or outside of nihilism from within nihilism itself. Yet such a stance still retains the implicit danger that Heidegger sees in Nietzsche's philosophy – that it does not attain the necessary standpoint to be able to determine metaphysics in a non-metaphysical manner. This is said in light of the fact that it is the philosopher (i.e. the metaphysical thinker) who diagnoses nihilism as the fate of the history of metaphysics, and who then makes a decision as to how it is to be remedied, or even if a remedy, as such, is possible. How, then, is Heidegger's thought able to avoid the same fate as Nietzsche's and instead wrestle itself free from the constraints of metaphysics?

It is certainly not possible, Heidegger tells us, if we view the end of metaphysics as an event that occurs due to 'a very cheap "anthropological" anchoring of the discipline of metaphysics in humans' [C 121]. That is, metaphysics is not something that *Dasein* 'does' and then is at some point free to decide not to do. Still, the fact cannot be escaped that *Dasein* is the site whereby 'that ground is obtained where the truth of be-ing[2] is grounded' [Ibid]. That Heidegger can make such a distinction – that truth as metaphysics is grounded by *Dasein* and yet it is not determined by *Dasein* – should not strike us as strange. In *Being and Time Dasein* is described by Heidegger as being both in truth and in untruth (*Unwahrheit*) and that such a notion need not be regarded as subjective.[3] Indeed, for Heidegger truth is *Dasein*'s mode of being, and so its way of *having* a world rather than being subjected to one. What this distinction does signal, however, is that the unfolding of the history of metaphysics – as revealed in the movement from the understanding of truth experienced aletheically to truth understood as the correspondence between subject and object – is something that can be viewed as happening *through Dasein*. Hence, Heidegger can make the claim that the end of metaphysics is made manifest, not by *Dasein*, but by *being* itself, as revealed in its gradual occlusion from *Dasein* in what might be termed its 'question-worthiness'. But what form ultimately does this occlusion take, in the sense that it signals both the ending of metaphysics and the approach of another beginning in terms of the promise of an opening up of a new relation of *Dasein* to being? To this end Heidegger says:

> The first beginning's coming originally into its own (and that means into its history) means gaining a foothold in the other beginning. This is accomplished in crossing from the *guiding-question* (what is a being? the question of beingness, being) to the *grounding-question*: What is the truth of be-ing? (Being and be-ing is the same and yet fundamentally different.)
>
> Historically grasped, this crossing is the overcoming – and indeed the first and first possible overcoming – of *all* 'metaphysics'. 'Metaphysics' now first becomes recognisable in what is its ownmost; and, in thinking in the crossing, all talk of "metaphysics" becomes ambiguous. Put into the domain of the crossing to the other beginning, the *question*: What is metaphysics … already inquires into what is ownmost to 'metaphysics' in the sense of gaining an initial footing in the crossing to the other beginning. In other words, the question already asks from within this [other beginning]. What it makes manifest as determination of "metaphysics" is already no longer metaphysics but rather its overcoming.
>
> [C 120]

The key to understanding what Heidegger has in mind here is given above parenthetically in the phrase 'Being and be-ing is the same and yet fundamentally different'. Put simply, at the end of the history of metaphysics being should no longer be thought in terms of the being (*Sein*, *ousia*, substance) of a being (*Seiende*). Rather, be-ing (*Seyn*) should be viewed as an event (*Ereignis*)[4] in which the meaning of beings in their being unfolds historically. *Ereignis* is not, however, an event that occurs within history – more fundamentally, it is an event that *gives rise* to and unfolds *as* history. This leads Heidegger to write: 'Be-ing needs man in order to hold sway; and man belongs to be-ing so that he can accomplish his utmost destiny as Dasein' [C 177]. Thus history is understood fundamentally as the constant interplay between *Dasein* and be-ing in which the former belongs to the latter and the latter is dependent on the former as its way of coming to light. Thereby history marks the 'essential sway' (*Wesen*)[5] of being; it is *how being happens* in an ongoing process of concealment and unconcealment.

The notion of *Ereignis* is therefore significant for Heidegger as it enables him to think the truth of being from out of a more authentic experience of being. This experience, though not something to which *Dasein* can wilfully give over itself, is opened up in the crossing from metaphysical history to the beginning of another history, a point to which I shall return presently. As far as Heidegger's thought is concerned, however, the notion of *Ereignis* signals a decisive break from any metaphysical determination of being, including that which resides in his own thinking. As already mentioned, Heidegger thinks of *Dasein* in *Being and Time* as essentially aletheic – *Dasein is* insofar as it uncovers and conceals. However – and as Heidegger acknowledges – this determination of *Dasein* means that it is still possible to understand truth as belonging to metaphysical thinking.[6] This is because *Dasein* provides the temporal horizon for the possibility of truth by transcending its own particular being. This in turn can be interpreted in such a way that *Dasein* is thought of as the entity that gives a fixed, temporal structure to being, providing the possibility for the presencing of beings in their being. It is only a small step from here to representing this horizon in a quasi-objectifying way, i.e. as a ground. The notion of *Ereignis* allows Heidegger to overcome this difficulty as it enables him to think of being from out of a fundamental experience of being in which *Dasein* stands in an open relation to being. Hence, the truth of being is no longer to be thought of in the sense of a horizon towards which *Dasein* transcends itself, but as an openness (within being) in which *Dasein* is given over to the event or happening of being. The question now arises as to what extent viewing the truth of being as an event helps Heidegger to loosen the constraints of metaphysical thought.

If the truth of being happens as an historical event, then metaphysics can be said to be finite. Indeed, the possibility of another beginning rests on the recognition of this finitude. But what also comes to light is that metaphysics, as the grounding of the truth of being for the West, has an origin.

Moreover, Heidegger locates this origin in the primordial Greek experience of being (which Heidegger, following Plato and Aristotle, calls wonderment (*thaumazein*)) out of which the being of beings is first thought aletheically as unhiddenness. Consequently, truth thought as the unhiddenness of beings both originates Western thought and simultaneously spells its decline – as outlined in the movement from Plato's notion of the Idea to Nietzsche's *Will to Power* – to the correspondence of the thought and the thing, with a concomitant forgottenness of the mysteriousness of being as that which stimulated Western thought at its inception. It is this decline as the history of Western thinking that delimits metaphysics for Heidegger. With this in mind, Richard Polt is able to say that the history of metaphysics, understood as an event of being, 'brings out the limited validity of the tradition'.[7] In other words, at the origins of Western thinking, in the primordial experiences of being that give rise to it, there is more to being than is captured in *Dasein*'s initial determination of it as the unhiddenness of beings.

Crucially for Heidegger, it is only at a time when the shadow of nihilism is cast over *Dasein* that *Dasein*'s fundamental abandonment by being, as its historical fate, comes to light. This is because the origins that give rise to the history of metaphysics are not, so to speak, abandoned to the past to become ossified, historical facts. Instead, these origins shape the course of this history as the history of being (*Seinsgeschichte*) in such a way that they accomplish their fate in its completion as nihilism.[8] In other words, metaphysics occurs as the unfolding event of being in which being is thought originally as the unhiddenness of beings and ends when this interpretation is revealed historically in its limitations. As we might by now imagine, it is a revelation that does not occur from within the restricted purview of metaphysical thought. Instead, this revelation is something that modern *Dasein* experiences as the abandonment of being. As such, it is an experience that *Dasein* undergoes in which *Dasein* is revealed as uprooted from any relation to being, in which *Dasein* shows itself in its utter groundlessness, and which signals that the history of metaphysics has come to an end *in essence*. The question arises: what form does this experience take?

Essentially, the end of metaphysics is given its impetus through *Dasein*'s fundamental attunement (*Grundstimmung*) to being. Significantly, fundamental attunement has no object, but is rather a basic mood experienced by *Dasein* in which *Dasein* is given over to being to the extent that that which is familiar becomes strange. These basic moods are revealed in Heidegger's work as experienced either on the personal level – as with the case of anxiety as it is outlined in *Being and Time* – or on an epochal level, as in the case of wonderment for the ancient Greeks.⁹ On the epochal level, fundamental attunement is what allows *Dasein* to have an insight into its historical situation in relation to being and so 'fundamental attunement *attunes Dasein* and thus attunes *thinking* as projecting-open the truth of be-ing in word and concept' [C 16, trans. mod.]. The fundamental attunement of modernity is characterized by Heidegger as, amongst other things, startled dismay (*Erschrecken*). Heidegger writes:

> Startled dismay means returning from the ease of comportment in what is familiar to the openness of the rush of the self-sheltering. In this opening what has been familiar for so long proves to be estranging and confining. What is most familiar and therefore the most unknown is the abandonment of being. Startled dismay lets man return to face *that* a being *is*, whereas before a being was for him just a being. Startled dismay lets man return to face that beings *are* and that this – be-ing – has abandoned all beings and all that appeared to be beings and has withdrawn from them.
>
> [C 11]

Startled dismay allows *Dasein* to experience its historical situation as its abandonment by being. And it is true to say that this abandonment signifies for Heidegger the West's rootless relation to its past, and this in two significant ways.¹⁰ In the first instance, it is revealed as the gradual withering of an original impetus to thinking that is rooted in being and which concludes with modernity's falling prey to free-floating worldviews (*Weltanschauungen*), views such as communism or conservatism that are ways of seeing the world in a meaningful way. On the other hand, it is revealed in the forgottenness of the fecundity of *Dasein*'s native soil to provide a primordial relation to being, a situation Heidegger refers to as *Seinsvergessenheit* ('the forgetting of being'). But what is most significant in this revelation is that in the face of startled dismay, being once again becomes question-worthy (*fragwürdig*) for *Dasein*.

Hence, the experience of the fundamental attunement of startled dismay – which re-attunes *Dasein* to the question-worthiness of being – holds out the possibility for *Dasein* of a future beyond the history of metaphysics. As such, this possibility is given in the transition *from* the *Leitfrage* that lies at the heart of metaphysics and *to* the *Grundfrage* that lies at its end, a movement Heidegger refers to above as 'the crossing' (*der Übergang*). For Heidegger these two questions give shape to the history of metaphysics. The *Leitfrage* is concerned with questioning into the truth of beings at the outset of philosophical thinking in ancient Greece whilst the *Grundfrage* is the question for our times which addresses itself to the meaning of being.[11] Further, it should be noted that from its sketchy beginnings in *Being and Time*, the distinction between the two approaches to the question of being becomes clearer in Heidegger's thought throughout the 1930s, due to his thought's shifting focus from *Dasein* as a being to the historical being of *Dasein*. However, towards the end of the 1930s, in his *Contributions to Philosophy*, this distinction becomes, if anything, a little more problematic.

This is because, thought historically, in the crossing from the *Leitfrage* to the *Grundfrage*, we move from what Heidegger calls the first beginning (*der erste Anfang*) to the other beginning (*der anderen Anfang*).[12] For Heidegger, this is significant as these beginnings are self-referential and encapsulate the history of metaphysics. In the first beginning the history of the West is set on its way by the ancient Greeks in questioning into the beingness of beings. Consequently, and viewing being as an event, both *Dasein* and being come to presence historically – and into mutual relation – as grounded in the unhiddenness of beings in their being. As Heidegger emphasizes, 'there is in that occurrence a definite opening up of beings as such, so that man thereby receives his essential determination, which stems from this opening' [C 123]. Importantly, what is missed in this opening up is a questioning into the nature of unhiddenness itself. However, what the Greeks fail to account for in the first beginning is a necessary step on the way to the question concerning the meaning of being as such:

> When the question of beings as such, the inquiry into beingness, occurs, there is in that occurrence a definite opening up of beings as such, so that man thereby receives his essential determination, which stems from this opening (*homo animal rationale*). But what opens up this opening of beings

to beingness and thus to be-ing? There is a need for a history and that means for a beginning and its derivations and advancements, in order to allow for the experience (for the beginners who question) that refusal belongs to the essential sway of be-ing. Because this knowing awareness thinks nihilism still more originally into the abandonment of being, this knowing is the actual overcoming of nihilism; and history of the first beginning thus completely loses the appearance of futility and mere errancy. Only now the great light shines on all the heretofore [accomplished] work of thinking.

[C 123]

The first beginning brings to light what essentially belongs to being in such a way that it escapes expression in how being is thought in this first beginning. This is because the ancient Greeks, in looking to being in the disclosure of beings, fail to account for the fact that being itself withdraws as part of the process of disclosure. This is the destiny (*Geschick*) of Western humanity that Heidegger calls the history of metaphysics. But destiny for Heidegger is not understood here in the sense of an ineluctable fate. Rather, it is a process by means of which being and *Dasein* adapt to each other in such a way that the absencing that is essential to being's coming to presence itself comes to light *as* this absencing. And it becomes the destiny of the West only to the extent that *Dasein* recognizes nihilism as *its* destiny and engages with it as such. This is what Felix Ó Murchadha refers to as the moment when *Dasein* comes to the decision *to be* historical, to accept its fate as its own and so to choose the possibility of change.[13] It is this moment that Heidegger thinks heralds in the other beginning.

The other beginning, then, is the destiny of the first beginning insofar as *Dasein*, in its thinking, first comes to recognize that untruth or errancy (*die Irre*) attaches itself to the unhiddenness of beings from out of its very origins. But errancy is not thought here in the sense that *Dasein* goes astray in its pursuit of being – which indeed it does according to Heidegger – but more fundamentally in the sense that being itself leads *Dasein* into error in its refusal to fully come to presence in the presencing of beings. Thus, the question of the truth of being is not only not yet decided, it is revealed ultimately as always open to question for the simple reason that being never gives completely of itself, but always withholds itself in coming to be. Therefore, to be able to ask about the truth of being is only possible for *Dasein* insofar as an initial questioning into the being of beings accomplishes its fate by opening out into the questioning about the meaning of being as such. In other words, the question about the truth of being becomes a question about the being of truth.

Viewed from this perspective, metaphysics can be seen to come to an end when truth is no longer seen to be grounded in *Dasein* (as that being to which all other beings reveal themselves) and instead *Dasein* is itself revealed as grounded in truth as the historical unfolding of being. Consequently, the question of being once more becomes a concern for the thought of *Dasein*, whilst revealing *Dasein*'s metaphysical mode of thinking to be ultimately insufficient for the task. This allows Heidegger to say that metaphysics has been overcome – not in the sense we saw in Nietzsche by reversing it, nor in the more general sense of a counter-movement – but in such a way that metaphysics is undermined from within. This leads Heidegger to venture emphatically: 'Now everything is and becomes different. Metaphysics is no longer possible' [C 128]. It is no longer possible because *Dasein*'s relation to being, through the movement of thinking from truth thought metaphysically to truth thought out of *Ereignis*, means that *Dasein*'s view of its own being changes. In accepting its fate, *Dasein* chooses to belong to the historical unfolding of truth and rejects the notion that in its being it transcends this unfolding.

Heidegger's thought here is significant in two ways. Firstly, his thought is distanced from Nietzsche's insofar as it points to a markedly different future than does the latter's. It is not possible on this account of the end of metaphysics to posit the idea of an overhuman as the meaning of the world because, put simply, the meaning of any possible world cannot be willed by *Dasein*. Further and directly related to this point, Heidegger makes the case that at the end of metaphysics *Dasein* is no longer to be tasked with thinking being as the unhiddenness of beings, but instead comes into its own by *allowing being to happen as truth*. *Dasein*'s role as such is later described by Heidegger in his 'Letter on Humanism' in the following manner:

> The advent of beings lies in the destiny of being. But for man it is ever a question of finding what is fitting in his essence that corresponds to such

destiny; for in accord with this destiny man as ek-sisting has to guard the truth of being. Man is the shepherd of being. [BW 234]

The other beginning holds out the possibility of a new destining of being in which being holds sway over *Dasein* so that *Dasein* no longer grasps hold of being in thought but allows thought to attend to being. But the form that this destining might take, or even if such a possibility can be realized, is unknowable for *Dasein* as it lies strictly within the historically unfolding hiddenness and unhiddenness of being thought as *Ereignis*. Now, it may well be the case that what partly motivates Heidegger's thinking here (at least initially) are the political contingencies of 1930s Germany, and the need for some form of political autochthony for the German people in the face of the uncertainties that existed in Europe at this time.[14] But of more long-term (philosophical) significance is the fact that at the outset of the other beginning, *Dasein* faces its future armed only with the *Grundfrage*.

I say armed only with the *Grundfrage*, but this does not necessarily have to be thought of in a negative sense. At the end of metaphysics the question into the meaning of being leaves behind any notion of foundational thinking. Unlike in the first beginning, when being is grounded in the beingness of beings, the other beginning leaves open any decision about being. Being now can only be grasped insofar as it is an event in which it simultaneously both reveals and hides itself – it is an abyss (*Abgrund*), to use a favourite word of Heidegger's, a groundless ground. Thus the essence of truth, thought from out of the essence of being, is devoid of any firm footing in the crossing to the other beginning. This is why man is described above as the 'shepherd of being'. *Dasein* must attend to the unfolding of being – waiting on what being sends and bearing witness to it – as *Dasein* is no longer able to lay hold of being with any certainty.

## Gelassenheit

The need for *Dasein* to adopt such an attitude towards the question of being becomes an increasing concern for Heidegger in his later philosophy. It is revealed in a move from the earlier perceived voluntarism of *Being and Time* (and other works of this period) to the increasingly significant role played in

Heidegger's thinking by the notion of *Gelassenheit*. *Gelassenheit* is commonly translated as 'releasement' and is understood in terms of the fundamental attunement to being that allows *Dasein* to twist itself free from its willing-relation (to being) in favour of a non-willing letting-be. *Gelassenheit* is contrasted in Heidegger's thought in particular with the notion of the will in Nietzsche's thought, a notion which Heidegger describes in his *Nietzsche* lectures as 'the fundamental mood of one's being superior' [N3 152], not only insofar as one excels others but also insofar as one excels oneself.[15]

We have already met this idea in Nietzsche's overhuman, of course, as that which is the meaning of the world to the extent that it is the highest embodiment of *Will to Power*. But in contrasting *Gelassenheit* with this notion of will Heidegger is not suggesting a merely passive response on the part of *Dasein* to being, understood in terms of a strict non-willing. This would only be to repeat Nietzsche's error of reversing that which one opposes and so of assimilating it essentially into this opposition. Instead, *Gelassenheit* is to be thought of as an openness to being, a form of thinking that is a 'relinquishing of the willing of a horizon' [DT 79] and simultaneously as a waiting (*Warten*), an allowing things to be, an allowing beings to come into the open as the beings that they are. As Babette Babich notes interestingly, Heidegger is here following Nietzsche (but necessarily in a different direction) in the sense that he makes the case for letting thought do something with *Dasein*, rather than *Dasein* doing something with thought.[16] What this means for Heidegger, in effect, is that rather than positing (in an oblique, enigmatic way) the notion of the overhuman as a way of willingly overcoming nihilism (as we have seen with Nietzsche), *Dasein* is to remain thoughtfully open to being and so to participate fully within its unfolding. Thus, far from being a passive response to being, the notion of *Gelassenheit* gives back to *Dasein* the responsibility of once again engaging with being and to what being brings to *Dasein*. This points to what Heidegger would term a more authentic (*eigentlich*) mode of being for *Dasein*.

We have seen that Heidegger views nihilism as the final convulsion of the history of metaphysics, and that metaphysics itself is undermined in the recognition that this is the case, at least insofar as *Dasein* accepts nihilism as its fate. Hereby, metaphysics is circumscribed as the history of the West, one that begins with the ancient Greek determination of being as the beingness of beings, and one that ends in the revelation that being is an unfolding event of hiddenness and unhiddenness. Thus, the first beginning comes into its own, fulfils its destiny, in the other beginning in the movement from the *Leitfrage* to the *Grundfrage*. It is in this movement that metaphysics is not so much overcome as undermined, if unpredictably. The question again arises: whereto from here for Heidegger? Certainly, in the crossing to the other beginning the oblivion of being is now no longer covered over for *Dasein* but has become a genuine historical problem for it. It is a problem that brings in its wake the question of the meaning of truth which, as *Dasein's* way of being in the world, no longer has a firm grounding. All that *Dasein* can do in such circumstances is to prepare for the possibility of a new beginning, a new destiny (*Geschick*), in which *Dasein* re-attunes itself to being. In such circumstances Heidegger calls on *Dasein* to properly re-engage with being, to become the 'shepherd of being' – to await on what being sends. But to await on what exactly?

It is true to say that no matter what Heidegger's analysis of the West's historical situation reveals, it does not point beyond the fact that the West is chained to metaphysical thinking, and to the question of how *Dasein* re-attunes itself to being if it still thinks in the same limited way. However, the idea of the other beginning also speaks significantly to the first beginning. If it is possible to throw light on the distinctiveness of metaphysics from out of its historical beginnings it is possible, to borrow a phrase from George Pattison, to look *behind* metaphysics.[17] That is, we can try to ascertain what makes metaphysical thinking distinct in relation to what went before by entering into a dialogue with the original thinkers who preceded metaphysics and thereby, through them, gain an understanding of what non-metaphysical thinking might look like. It is with this in mind that we now turn to the Greek notion of *physis*.

## *Physis*: Being as presencing

In his 'Letter on Humanism', written in 1947, Heidegger states that 'language is the house of being. In its home human beings dwell' [BW 217]. In doing so, Heidegger makes the point that it is in language that being becomes manifest in such a way that human beings come to dwell historically.[18] With regard to the history of metaphysics, this is significant as its fundamental concepts (*Grundbegriffe*), concepts that delineate and predominate over the main content of this history, attain their original determinations through the primordial experience of being as given in the thought of the ancient Greeks. Consequently, the fundamental concepts of Western thought provide a path for questioning into the very basis of metaphysics as well as holding out the promise of a view of what lies beyond.

It is for this reason that we shall turn to Heidegger's examination of the concept *physis* as it stands in ancient Greek thought. To this end I shall concentrate on Heidegger's essay *On the Essence and Concept of Φύσις in Aristotle's Physics B, I* (henceforth *Aristotle's Physics*), written in 1939, as Heidegger claims it is in this work of Aristotle that there is to be found 'the first coherent and thoughtful discussion ... of the essence of φύσις' [PM 185].[19] The reason we turn to this particular concept from amongst all other possible fundamental concepts is twofold. In the first instance, Heidegger argues that *physis* is for the Greeks the word that determines their primordial experience of being. As such, it is the concept in which are harboured 'decisions about the truth of beings' [Ibid]. Of course, these decisions (*Entscheidungen*) do not give us a notion of being *as such*; rather, they point to the beingness of beings, to the truth of beings as a whole. But what Heidegger attempts to do in this essay is to distinguish between the essence of the concept of *physis* and the essence of *physis* itself, as a way of drawing out what is presumed of the latter but which goes unspoken in the former. This leads Heidegger to say:

> If we recall that today the truth about beings as a whole has become entirely questionable; moreover, if we suspect that the essence of truth therefore remains thoroughly in dispute; and finally if we know that all this is grounded in the history of the interpretations of the essence of φύσις, then we stand outside the merely historical interests that philosophy might have in the 'history of a concept.' Then we experience, although from afar, the nearness of future decisions.
>
> [PM 185]

Thus Heidegger involves himself in an attempt to think more originally what the Greeks thought themselves (that is, to get to what goes un-thought and unexpressed in Greek thinking and yet forms the essential basis of this thinking) in order to restore to the Greek concept of *physis* its unthematized basis. That Heidegger does this should not surprise us as we have already seen how he de-structures or dismantles (*Destruktion*) the notion of truth by revealing it as arising out of the Greek experience of being thought aletheically. In the case of the concept of *physis*, a concept that determines the meaning of being in a way that helps give rise to the history of the West, Heidegger is seeking to retrieve the temporal experience of being that lies behind this determination.[20] In doing so, he attempts to uncover the traces of a non-metaphysical understanding of being that are retained in Aristotle's text.

The other reason for turning to the concept of *physis* is because, as that which names the fundamental determination of being for the Greeks, it is a word that literally lies at the heart of Western history as the history of metaphysics. As Heidegger says, 'In a quite essential sense, meta-physics is "physics," i.e., knowledge of φύσις' [PM 185]. Thus, an understanding of what the Greeks determine by the term *physis* will throw light on the essence of metaphysics. And yet, we must ask, does such a claim on Heidegger's part amount to anything more than a simple form of word-play? Are we to understand him quite literally here? Indeed, the notion of metaphysics would have sounded alien to Aristotle's ears. Rather, the subject-matter or science of the work we call *Metaphysics* was instead referred to by Aristotle as 'first philosophy' or the study of 'being qua being'. The word metaphysics itself is only a later attribution that is taken from a title given to the work by an early editor of Aristotle's texts. As such, metaphysics translates the Greek τά μετά τά φυσικά, meaning 'those writings coming after the Physics' which is commonly, though not invariably, held to indicate chronologically the place where this work stands in the Aristotelian canon.[21]

Heidegger dismisses such claims as unimportant, however, as 'metaphysics is just as much "physics" as physics is "metaphysics"' [PM 185]. He says this because whilst Aristotle's *Physics* is a study of particular beings (i.e., natural beings), knowledge of beings in this sense provides the cornerstone of Aristotle's work that we now call *Metaphysics*, which is the attempt to ground knowledge of (natural) beings as a whole. Heidegger's argument is that to ground knowledge of beings as a whole – which depends upon an understanding of beings as physical entities – is to presuppose knowledge of what is named in the word *physis* (ἐπιστήμη φυσική). Subsequently, whether or not one work takes precedence chronologically is superfluous as far as Heidegger's main assertion stands, that knowledge of *physis* lies at the heart of the origins of metaphysics. What, then, does Heidegger find that is decisive in Aristotle's determination of *physis* in his *Physics*?

## Original echoes of the concept of physis

Perhaps surprisingly, and yet crucially, Heidegger finds in Aristotle's text a derivative (*Abkömmling*) interpretation of *physis*, one that is indebted to a more original understanding that is found in the thought of the pre-Socratic thinker Heraclitus. This derivative interpretation, however, marks a decisive point in the history of metaphysics, a point at which a transition in the notion of *physis* takes place the consequences of which the West is still living with today. It is a point at which can be located a shift in the conception of being in Greek thought that not only signals the distant arrival of nihilism but can also be viewed as the culmination of Greek thinking on the subject hitherto. Seen in this light, Aristotle's conceptualization of *physis* in his *Physics* still bears the traces of a more original notion. It is a notion that is found in the extant fragments of Heraclitus, a notion that lies at the origins of philosophical thought and so perdures in and predates Aristotle's text.

The first question to ask is: what can be said of the original determination of *physis* that means a transition from it can be located in Aristotle's thinking? This, according to Heidegger, can be gleaned from Heraclitus' fragment 123 in which he says: *physis kruptesthai philei*, commonly translated as 'nature loves to hide itself' but which Heidegger renders as 'being loves to hide itself'.[22] The difference in translation here will prove fruitful when we come to examine the decline in the original naming power of *physis* alongside the unfolding of metaphysics, but currently we need to see what Heidegger is able to retrieve from Heraclitus' words. Heidegger writes:

> Being is the self-concealing revealing, φύσις in the original sense. Self-revealing is a coming-forth into unhiddenness, and this means: first preserving unhiddenness as such by taking it back into its essence.

> Unhiddenness is called ἀ-λήθεια. Truth, as we translate this word, is of the origin, i.e., it is essentially not a characteristic of human knowing and asserting, and still less is it a mere value or an 'idea' that human beings (although they really do not know why) are supposed to strive to realise. Rather, truth as self-revealing belongs to being itself. Φύσις is ἀλήθεια, unconcealing, and therefore χρύπτεσθαί φιλεῖ.
>
> [PM 230]

Thus being is equated with *physis* and *physis*, on this reading, is what emerges in and of itself – it is the origin and ordering of unhiddenness, i.e. truth. Understood as such, being is originally viewed by the Greeks as that which in its essence emerges in such a way that in becoming unhidden it has a predilection (*Vorliebe*) for hiding itself. Yet we must not make the mistake of trying to understand what Heraclitus is saying here in a metaphysical sense. If being 'loves to hide itself', then this self-limitation of being is not something that will come to light if only it is approached in the right way, if only it is thought 'correctly'. Rather, this refusal on being's part, this darkness that lies at its heart, is not to be penetrated by thought – it belongs to the very essence of being to withhold itself in this manner. To be truthful to being on this account means that what one should do is attend to it in such a way that allows it this predilection to hide itself as it emerges into presence, that is, if one wishes to avoid subjecting it to the will of *Dasein*.

If *physis* is that which *is*, is that which comes to presence whilst simultaneously withdrawing itself, then truth is an inseparable part of this process as the self-revelation of being that Heidegger discovers in the Greek word *aletheia*. This is why Heidegger argues that *Dasein* exists within both truth and un-truth and that truth, subsequently, is properly thought as *a-letheia* (un-hiddenness). That is, truth is of a privative nature, i.e. it is essentially the play of disclosure and withdrawal.[23] And yet being only comes to light through that which emerges into being – namely, beings, and beings can be true only insofar as they participate in the essential sway of being. This is to say that beings can be true only to the extent that they are grounded in the play of truth as the revealing and concealing of *physis*. Consequently, Heidegger argues, Heraclitus phrase 'being loves to hide itself' not only gives us the original conception of *physis* as being, but also points to that experience of being out of which this conception arises.

Heidegger argues that in this retrieval (*Wiederholung*) of the primordial conception of *physis*, we hear an echo of something which lies beyond the original naming power of metaphysical thought – we get the sense of an experience of being which promises other possible conceptions of being, possibilities in which the truth of being holds open alternative historical vistas. What Heidegger is not saying here is that the Greeks somehow 'went wrong' at this particular point in their history. Nor is he trying to retrieve a more authentic (*eigentlich*) truth that lies at the origins of metaphysics but was somehow overlooked by the Greeks. What he is attempting to do is to retrieve those possibilities that lie at the first beginning of Western thought, but in a *more original* way than was open to the Greeks. By being more original, Heidegger means to make these possibilities *more problematical.* Heidegger does this by engaging in what he calls a dialogue (*zwiegespräch*) with the thinkers of ancient Greece, bringing to the fore what these thinkers give voice to in their texts but to which nonetheless they remain in the dark – namely, that the withdrawal of being lies at the heart of the coming to presence of beings. It is in light of the retrieval of the darkness that lies at the heart of being that Heidegger seeks to make more problematical our understanding of being, and so open up modern humanity to the possibilities that are to be found at the inception of the first beginning – possibilities that only emerge as such in the crossing to the other beginning.

However, in making what goes unsaid (and unthought) in the Greek thinker's texts more explicitly our own is to involve ourselves in something beyond the mere matter of simply interpreting what the Greeks said. Retrieval is for Heidegger – as Felix Ó Murchadha points out in referring to how one should approach Heidegger's own texts – the 're-vitalizing' (*wieder-holen*) of an event which takes place in one's actual engagement with the text.[24] Thus, it is not a matter of reiterating the problems that the Greek thinkers face but of re-developing these problems through a confrontation with these thinkers and making their problems our own. Heidegger addresses this point in his 1929 text *Kant and the Problem of Metaphysics*:

> By the retrieval of a basic problem, we understand the opening-up of its original, long-concealed possibilities, through the working out of which it is transformed. In this way it first comes to be preserved in its capacity as a problem. To preserve a problem, however, means to free and keep watch

over those inner forces which make it possible, on the basis of its essence, as a problem.

[KPM 143]

It is with this in mind that Heidegger engages with Aristotle as a means of getting to the primordial difficulty that lies at the heart of the Western conception of *physis*. This is because not only does Aristotle's thought contain within it the echo of the primordial experiences that give rise to the Greek conception of being, but because a decision is made about being in Aristotle's thought that opens up a path along which tread all future metaphysical interpretations of the essence of *physis*. So it is with this in mind that we turn to Aristotle's interpretation of *physis*.

## Aristotle and physis

In Aristotle's *Physics* the term *physis* is not thought in a uniform manner, particularly with regard to the domain which it names, as on the one hand it names beings in their beingness in general, and on the other it names one particular domain of beings in their being – namely, natural beings.[25] Nonetheless, both conceptions retain an element of Heraclitus' original naming force with the latter notion in particular carrying a sense of *physis* as a presencing that simultaneously conceals, and it is this latter conception that is the main focus of Heidegger's concern in his text.

Heidegger argues that Aristotle's conception of *physis* has two fundamental aspects. On the one hand it is *arche*: that which originates and sustains in emergence that to which it gives rise. This is not to say, however, that we should think *arche* in a causal sense (as one external force acting upon another). Rather, *arche* should be thought in the sense that emergence both restrains and dominates that which emerges. In other words, *physis* thought in terms of *arche* is the movement that allows beings to emerge, although not in the sense of relocation (of movement from one place to another), but in the sense of change, of movement taking place *within* a particular being. On the other hand, *physis* is *kinesis*, movedness (*Bewegtheit*) in the sense of that through which any form of movement as such is possible. Both aspects taken together signify, Heidegger argues, that Aristotle thinks *physis* as the movement of that which originates itself and orders that which is originated as change. As such, *physis* is the fundamental mode of the movedness of natural beings (*phusei onta*), through which they emerge and sustain themselves, which is to say, *physis* is the beingness (*Seiendheit*) of natural beings.

Nonetheless, it is not just movement alone that is attached to movedness for the Greeks. Heidegger thinks that what is most definitive of the Greek notion of movedness is 'rest', not in the sense of cessation of movement, but where movedness 'is gathered up into *standing still*, and where this ingathering, far from excluding movedness, includes and for the first time discloses it' [PM 217]. This sounds counter-intuitive, to say the least. However, Heidegger makes his case by singling out a passage in Aristotle's *Metaphysics* in which the Stagirite says that 'someone sees, and in seeing he or she has also at the same time (precisely) already seen' [Ibid].[26] Heidegger's point is that for the Greeks movedness comes to be what it is, attains its end (*telos*), by coming to rest as that which it is. Therefore, in the process of seeing, in the repose of the seen, seeing firsts comes to be what it is in the gathering to itself of that which it is (*entelecheia*), i.e. seeing.

To truly come into its own, however, a being must, in attaining its end, come into presence. And for a being to come into presence ultimately means for the Greeks that it comes into its *eidos*, which means nothing less than 'the manner and mode in which something stands "finally and finitely" in its appearance' [PM 217]. This notion of *eidos*, of course, reminds us of Plato's conception of truth, and there is certainly an element of the Platonic Idea here in the sense that beings *appear* in their beingness as movedness.[27] And yet, for Plato the movedness in which beings appear is somewhat shadowy and tends to lead us astray when it comes to the truth of beings. Instead, Plato thinks that the appearing of beings can only ever be of a secondary reality, in which beings partake of – that is, come into presence as a semblance of – their primary reality as 'forms'. The truth of beings as such only comes to light in the realm of the forms, which in turn is dependent on the transcendence of the human being. Aristotle, on the other hand, thinks the truth of a (natural) being specifically in terms of how it comes into presence, in terms of how it reveals itself in the movedness of its being. If Platonic thought determines the shadowy nature of *physis* as hiding the real truth of beings from us, then

Aristotle's insight is that this shadowy nature lies at the heart of the truth of any given being. It is also an insight that brings to the fore an important aspect of Greek thinking on *physis*, namely, that at the heart of *physis* lies *steresis* or, as Heidegger puts it: 'in στέρησις is hidden the essence of φύσις' [PM 227].

Heidegger says that *steresis* means privation (*Beraubung*) for the Greeks, but in a special sense.[28] It is an 'absencing', and as such lies at the heart of the movement of a being as it comes to presence and sustains itself in its *eidos*. It is, so to speak, the internal workings of this process. But it is not an absencing in the sense of a simple negation (a denial or no-saying). Rather, it is an absencing that comes to presence in this absencing. This is best understood in terms of Greek notion of *genesis*, which we today understand as generation, and which Heidegger describes as 'the self-placing into the appearance' [PM 223]. Heidegger defines the Greek sense of *genesis* thus:

> Specifically it is production of itself, from out of itself, unto itself. Nonetheless, it is essentially "being on the way", each being that is produced or put forth (excluding artefacts) is also put *away*, as the blossom is put away by the fruit. But in this putting *away*, the self-placing into the appearance – φύσις – does not cease to be. On the contrary, the plant in the form of fruit goes back into its seed, which, according to its essence, is nothing else but a going-forth into the appearance.
>
> [PM 227]

The *genesis* of the plant is thus a 'being on the way', and this being on the way is the movement or change that the plant undergoes in its appearance as it comes into presence. We thereby see the plant come into blossom, and in the process, we note the leaves that prepared the way for this blossom fall-off. In turn, the blossom disappears as the plant comes to bear fruit, and the fruit gives way in favour of the seed it contains. This is a continual (though not circular)[29] process to which belongs essentially the 'no more' or the 'not yet' – e.g. the plant that is no more in blossom but is not yet gone to seed. We can see then that there is an absencing to *physis* that comes to presence in its absencing, and as such belongs to the *eidos* of the being that comes forth in this process. Which is to say that for Heidegger, both withdrawal and withholding belong to the essence of being understood by the Greeks in terms of *physis* and can be *seen* do so in the unfolding appearance of natural beings as they come into unconcealment from out of concealment.

It is Heidegger's contention that this sense of concealment, at least, is what Aristotle's thought retains of the original understanding of *physis* that is found in the thought of Heraclitus. However, we can also see that what is most immediate in the unfolding of *physis* is that it is understood in terms of beings as they come into their beingness, as they come-forth into presence. On the one hand, this makes plain why Heidegger persists in his analysis of Greek truth as based on the notion of *a-letheia*, and why he says at the conclusion of his essay that 'truth as self-revealing belongs to being itself.Φύσις is ἀλήθεια, unconcealing, and therefore χρύπτεσθαί φιλεῖ' [PM 230]. On the other hand, Heidegger says:

> In the *Physics* Aristotle conceives of φύσις as the beingness (οὐσία) of a particular (and in itself limited) region of beings, things that grow as distinguished from things that are made.
>
> [PM 228]

In other words, *physis* is limited to the beingness of one type of being, the natural being, and in the process shifts from its primordial sense (as it stands in Heraclitus) as accounting for the being of beings as such, that is, for all beings. Thus, *physis* in Aristotle's conception takes on the aspect of the presencing of natural beings, which historically speaking – and thanks to its Latinate translation as *natura* – comes to account for natural beings in terms of a regional ontology – namely, as belonging to nature. This opens the way for the question concerning the essence of *physis* to become a question into the nature of natural beings. Any questioning into the essence of beings *per se* thus goes beyond natural beings as such, and for the Greeks to go beyond natural beings is rendered as *meta ta phusika*, which we today translate as metaphysics.[30] Hence at the heart of metaphysics lies *physis* and *physis*, thought as the beingness of beings, as the presencing of beings from out of concealment, is reduced to the being of a particular region of beings – namely, natural beings. The question now arises as to how this analysis of *physis* throws light on the nature of metaphysics, so that perhaps a way beyond nihilism can be envisioned. The answer lies in the relation that obtains between *physis* and what the Greeks called *techne*, a word from which we derive our modern notion of technology.

## Physis, techne and the question of technology

Walter A Brogan observes that in 'Aristotle's Physics' Heidegger draws out the distinction between natural beings and things that are made, a distinction thought in terms of the Greek conceptions of *physis* and *techne*.[31] It is Brogan's contention that in doing so Heidegger is trying to draw to our attention the complicity that exists between these two ways of disclosing beings. According to Brogan, Heidegger thinks that *techne*, as a form of producing or making things, is understood by the Greeks as a way of knowing and revealing, a way of bringing-forth [*Hervorbringen*] beings from out of concealment into unconcealment. In the case of natural beings, whose being is *physis* (which means they come forth from out of themselves), the truth of their being, i.e. that they are open to change, that they can 'not-be' what they are, only comes to light insofar as this hidden possibility is brought forth through the power of *techne*.

Consequently, Brogan argues, modernity (thought in terms of nihilism) can be viewed as the predominance of *techne* over *physis*, by which *physis* is subsumed under the modern reign of technology. But technology is here not thought of as something technological – rather, it is 'a way of revealing … it is the realm of revealing, i.e., of truth' [BW 318]. To fully understand what Heidegger is driving at here we will have to uncover the complicity that exists between *techne* and *physis* as it is determined originally in Greek thought. However, Brogan's point is that this complicity exists in the modern era, and it is in the abandonment of *physis* in favour of *techne* that is the mark of nihilism for Heidegger. Consequently, what Heidegger tries to do in his thinking on *physis* is to call for a return back to the mutual relation between *physis* and *techne* as a way of getting beyond nihilism. It is with this in mind that we now look to Heidegger's retrieval of the essence of the interrelationship that obtains in ancient Greek thought between *physis* and *techne*.

*Techne*, translated into the Latin as *ars*, is commonly thought to mean either art or technique and forms the root of what we today refer to as technology. But, Heidegger warns, we need to be careful how we use this term as:

> Τέχνη does not mean "technique" in the sense of methods and acts of production, nor does it mean "art" in the wider sense of an ability to produce something. Rather, *techné* is a form of knowledge; it means know-how in, i.e., familiarity with, what grounds every act of making or producing.
>
> [PM 192]

To this end, Heidegger translates the Greek determination of *techne* into the German as *Sichauskennen*, which he defines as 'to be entirely at home in something, to understand and be expert in it' [BW 318]. Yet this is not strictly, as might be expected, a being at home in the sense of being comfortable at producing or creating something. More significantly, it is a being at home amidst beings as they come to presence and therefore a knowing how to allow beings to come forth into appearance. *Techne* as such is a mode of *aletheia*, a way of bringing-forth into the world that allows *Dasein* to participate in truth. As a way that truth happens, however, *techne* both differs and shares certain similarities with *physis*, as Heidegger notes in his essay 'The Question Concerning Technology', published in 1954:

> It is of the utmost importance that we think bringing-forth in its full scope and at the same time in the sense in which the Greeks thought it. Not only handicraft manufacture, not only artistic and poetical bringing into appearance and concrete imagery, is a bringing-forth, *poiēsis*. *Physis*, also, the arising of something from out of itself, is a bringing-forth, a *poiēsis*. *Physis* is indeed *poiēsis* in the highest sense. For what presences by means of *physis* has the irruption belonging to bringing-forth, e.g., the bursting of a blossom into bloom, in itself (*en heautōi*). In contrast, what is brought forth by the artisan or the artist, e.g., the silver chalice, has the irruption belonging to bringing-forth, not in itself, but in another (*en allōi*), in the craftsman or the artist.
>
> [BW 317]

On this account it can be said that both *techne* and *physis* are ways of bringing-forth beings into appearance from out of concealment and therefore both can be regarded as modes of *poiesis*, of bringing out of concealment into unconcealment. They can, consequently, also be regarded as modes of *aletheia*, as ways in which beings are brought-forth into appearance and therefore into the truth of their being. *Techne* and *physis* are therefore ways in which beings are brought forth into truth. In this respect they differ insofar as the *arché* or movedness of beings that are brought-forth through *physis* is self-generating and sustaining, whereas that of beings brought-forth through *techne* lies within the knowledge of the craftsman (*technites*). However, distinct as these modes of *poiesis* maybe, they do not exist independently of each other. Instead, the two should be thought together.

We can see this in an example that Heidegger uses of an artefact (in this case a table) to describe *poiesis* as a bringing forth into truth in the sense of *techne*. The movedness of a table in its being brought-forth into unconcealment is dependent on the knowledge of the craftsman of the *eidos* or appearance of the table. Here the *eidos* serves as a paradigm or guide (*paradeigma*) that allows the craftsman to produce (*Hergestellen*) what we might term an 'actual' table – that is, to bring this *eidos* into the stable appearance of a table as 'having-itself-in-its-end' (*Sich-im-Ende-Haben*) [PM 218], as Heidegger says following Aristotle.[32] The craftsman does this by taking wood suitable to the making of a table and bringing-forth the table from out of the wood so that this change from the suitable to the actual appears within the wood itself. Thus the table attains its *telos*, comes to be that which it is and as is revealed through the change that takes place in the wood, due as it is to the foresight (*prohairesis*) of the craftsman.

Yet this foresight is not limited solely to a pre-view of the *eidos* or appearance of the table. We have already noted that *techne* is not merely knowledge of how to do things but a being at home amidst the presencing of beings. For the craftsman to bring forth the table he must also have knowledge of beings as they come to be, of natural beings, of beings not only as they are presently but in the ways that they unfold into coming into presence. This is because if the craftsman intends to bring forth into presence any artefact whatsoever he is dependent on the appropriateness (*dynamis*) of naturally occurring beings to do so. Appropriateness, as a way in which natural beings come to presence, is 'that manner of emergence which, while still holding itself back and within itself, comes forth into the appearance wherein such appropriateness is fulfilled' [PM 219]. In other words, natural beings emerge into appearance in ways that they both *are and are not* by way of this emerging. This means that the craftsman can approach the wood and see in it something that is not there but can still come to be there – namely, the table.

We can see that the coming to presence (*Anwesenheit*) of the table as a coming into its truth (*aletheia*) through *techne* is possible only insofar as it is dependent on the presencing into truth of natural beings (i.e. the wood) through *physis*. However, *techne*, as a mode of *poiesis*, sees *Dasein directly involved* in the bringing forth into truth, of revealing beings in their being. That is, *Dasein*, as craftsman, brings forth beings from out of the darkness (absence) that is attached to the being of *physis* and into the light of its world. This collusion between the two modes of *poiesis* as a way of presencing beings into the truth of being provides the circumstances through which a critical point is reached in Greek thinking on being, one that has repercussions for the whole of Western history subsequently. For Heidegger, this notion of *techne*, as a mode of *poiesis*, as a way of bringing something new into the world is superseded by an understanding of *techne* as a way of making or producing things. This is due in large part to the direct implication of *Dasein* in the bringing forth of beings into the presence of being, allied to an increasing neglect in accounting for the openness of beings that allows for this bringing-forth to begin with. The craftsman produces the table; thus, the being of the table is *to be* produced. Subsequently, *techne*, as a knowing way of bringing beings into the truth of their being, eventually becomes a way of understanding beings as being produced.[33] Here is born the productive horizon of the truth of being that Heidegger calls metaphysics, in which *techne* is the mode of revealing the truth of beings that in modernity we now call technology, and through which *physis* is relegated to naming that region of beings we call nature. Thus the question arises: how is technology a threat to humanity, particular if we think of it in terms of the application of science for the betterment of life?

The short answer is that the essence of technology, as Heidegger famously states, is not in itself something technological.[34] Rather, the essence of technology is the way that the modern world gets determined as an object that stands over and against the human subject to be exploited and disposed of in a calculating manner. The essence of technology is thus a way of revealing beings, of bringing them into truth. How, then, are we to recognize this form of revealing? Heidegger names the modern technological mode of revealing *Gestell*, which he says comes to the fore in the age of the modern natural sciences – not as a result of these sciences – but rather in the form of these sciences. In 'The Question Concerning Technology' Heidegger refers to *Gestell* in the following terms: 'The revealing that rules in modern technology is a challenging (*Herausfordern*) which puts to nature the unreasonable demand that it supply energy which can be extracted and stored as such' [BW 320]. Hans Ruin notes that as Heidegger's thinking on this subject develops, then *Gestell*, which names the essence of nihilism, is used by Heidegger to encircle a constellation of phenomena that includes the human being.[35] As such, *Gestell* names the propensity for all beings to present themselves as resources to be exploited. But exploited to what end, and by whom? In a very real sense, *Gestell* names the destiny of the West thought in terms of (productionist) metaphysics, in which the truth of beings is no longer to reveal them in their being but to make a demand upon them to present themselves as resources to be exploited (either as raw material or as human resource). Thus the essence of technology is to reveal beings in terms of a static presence or standing-reserve (*Bestand*), a way of revealing beings that not only hides their nature in the sense that they belong essentially to *physis*, but also disguises the fact that it does this. The danger of technology, then, is that not only is it a way of revealing beings that blocks off other ways of revealing beings but it prevents them from being revealed as anything other than resources.

As far as we are currently concerned, however, it is enough to say that the technological age, as signalled in the domination of *physis* by *techne*, is marked by the fact that beings are challenged forth in a way that prevents *poiesis* – that stops revealing as such. That is, and as George Pattison puts it succinctly, 'technology does not let what is to be made show itself, but places a demand upon its product that it answers to a predetermined purpose'.[36] Thus the bringing forth of the craftsman out of *physis* is replaced by the challenging forth of modernity in which that which naturally gives rise to itself disappears.

This is nihilism for Heidegger. Thus the question concerning technology, as Jennifer Gosetti-Ferencei observes, is not one of whether we should accept or reject technology but one of whether the questioning of technology itself is still possible.[37] In order to address this danger what is needed is a re-balancing in the relation between *techne* and *physis* in which a new relation is opened up to that which *is* insofar as it is disclosed in *Gestell*, in which thought is able to lay claim to *physis*. To this end, in 'The Question Concerning Technology' Heidegger cites the German poet Friedrich Hölderlin's lines from his poem *Patmos* in which he says, 'But where the danger is, grows the saving power also' [BW 340]. *Techne* is for the Greeks a mode of *poiesis*, a way 'that brings forth truth into the splendour of radiant appearance' [BW 339]. As such, *techne* also named the *poiesis* of the fine arts for the Greeks. Thus art and technology originally share a common ground in *poiesis*. It is in light of this that Heidegger asks whether art 'may expressly foster the growth of the saving power, may awaken and found anew our vision of, and trust in, that which grants' [BW 340]?

Heidegger's point is that art and *techne* share a common ground – they are both ways of revealing the world, both ways that *poiesis* happens. However, unlike *techne*, art does not challenge forth beings but essentially attempts to show beings in their true light. Hence, if we wish to overcome nihilism in its technological form, Heidegger thinks that we should turn to art as a way of confronting technology, of revealing the truth of the world, and thereby perhaps discover in the poietic something redemptive for humanity, that is, of revealing *techne* in itself as a mode of revealing and thereby making being once again question-worthy. What is needed is a redirection of thought towards that which eludes the grasp of metaphysics – that is, towards *physis*. It is with this in mind that the next two chapters examine Heidegger's thinking on the redemptive power of art thought specifically in terms of the poetical.

# 3
# *Language as the house of being*

I have just said that Heidegger, in 'The Question Concerning Technology', quotes the following from Hölderlin's poem Patmos: 'But where the danger is, grows the saving power also.' Heidegger's claim here is that the possibility of moving beyond the history of metaphysics and of opening up a new history is a possibility that resides within the dynamics of art. However, we should be minded that for Heidegger 'all art is in essence poetry' [BW 198]. This is not to say, however, that architecture, music and sculpture can be traced back to the poetic word, but that they all share Heidegger's broader conception of poetry as the setting-to-work of truth. On the other hand, Heidegger suggests, poetry thought in the narrow sense, that is, as a linguistic work (poesy), 'has a privileged position in the domain of the arts' [Ibid]. This privileged position can be summed up as follows: poetry brings truth to the word by letting beings appear as the beings that they are. In fact Heidegger, thinking language as essentially poetic, goes so far as to say that where there is no language then there is no world, no openness to being. Thus Heidegger is making the case that language, thought poetically, is the most profound revelation of what is, and thereby offers the greatest possibility for *Dasein* to dwell once again in the openness of being. However, if we wish to understand the privileged place that poetry holds within the domain of the arts, then 'the right concept of language is needed'. Thus, to see how poetry holds out the possibility of originating a new history beyond metaphysics we turn first to how Heidegger views language in its essential nature.

# Language: The house of being

## The need for a reappraisal of how language works

On more than one occasion Heidegger refers to language as 'the house of being', the place in which the human being dwells amidst the unfolding truth of being – a truth to which the human being not only belongs, but for which she must also take on full responsibility.[1] The strangeness of such a 'definition' of language can be seen in the ontological implications of what Heidegger is saying here – that language is not fundamentally something the human being possesses (in the sense of *having* or *using* language), but is rather something that the human being *undergoes* and through which it endures. In other words, the human being exists within language and so experiences both being (including its own being) and beings in terms of how they are brought to light in and through the *word*. That Heidegger thinks this should not surprise us too much, given that this thesis has examined his thinking with regard to some of the key concepts of Occidental history (e.g. *physis* and *poiesis*) and how these concepts reveal the unfolding of this history in relation to being.

Yet the full import of what Heidegger has in mind here goes beyond any notion of language in the sense that things are simply discovered in the world, named and thereby come to be represented categorically *in* language. Instead, and as will be seen, Heidegger argues that language brings beings (essentially) into the open – it is the site where truth is founded in being and where being is grounded as truth. Consequently, that there are beings, that there is a world in which beings come to be and that the human being is able to negotiate her way around the latter in relation to the former is granted by the naming power of language itself, as a way of bringing beings into the truth of their being. Hence, Heidegger is making the case that language be viewed as the way in which truth unfolds primordially, as the 'clearing-concealing advent of being itself' [BW 230].

Such a description is redolent of the way Heidegger talks about how art functions in 1936's 'The Origin of the Work of Art' (henceforth 'The Origin'). In this text Heidegger tells us that as a mode of *poiesis*, what we call art is the way in which truth happens in the artwork (as the struggle between earth and world). This is *poiesis* thought in its broadest sense 'as the letting happen of the advent of the truth of beings' [BW 197]. However, poetry in the narrower sense (i.e. as a linguistic work) has, as already noted, 'a privileged position in the domain of arts'. This privileged position is given in poetry's fundamental naming power, in poetry's unique mode of preserving truth in language by grounding truth in the word (*das Wort*). As such, 'what is spoken purely is the poem' [PLT 192], it makes present in the word what was formerly absent – that is, poetry originates, it 'brings beings as beings into the open for the first time' [BW 198]. Hence, Heidegger argues, language is not only the path along which *Dasein* makes its way in the openness of being, as poetry, it affords us the strongest possibility of finding a way beyond the language of metaphysics and so beyond nihilism, given its power to bring truth to the word. As Heidegger says, 'art as poetry is founding [...] founding as beginning', that is, in poetry proper, 'a thrust enters history, history either begins or starts over again [BW 74]. But to understand how language (thought poetically) is able to do this we will first need to examine Heidegger's re-thinking of how language works.

## A traditional view of language

It has been long held that it is language that distinguishes the human being from all other types of being. Heidegger discovers this way of thinking in the ancient Greek formulation *zoon logon echon* which, whilst it traditionally renders the human being as a 'rational animal', Heidegger – by pointing out that in the ancient Greek lexicon *logon* shares a root with the verb *legein*, meaning to talk or to discourse – interprets it instead in broader terms as 'that living thing whose being is essentially determined by the potentiality for discourse' [BT 47]. This 'potentiality' points to a difficulty within language to which we shall return.[2] But the essential point to be gleaned here is that the human being is distinguished in its being insofar as it is given over (potentially) to speech: the human being is that being that has the capacity to speak.

It is not a giant leap to move from this interpretation to what can be termed the 'commonly' held belief about language, that it is fundamentally a form of communication between people, a way of informing ourselves about the things of the world. A prime example of this view of language can be seen in the thought of prominent linguist and cognitive scientist Steven Pinker. Pinker (along with a reductionist flourish all of his own) expresses his thoughts on the essence of language in the following manner:

> In nature's talent show we are simply a species of primate with our own act, a knack for communicating information about who did what to whom by modulating the sounds we make when we exhale.
>
> Once you begin to look at language not as the ineffable essence of human uniqueness but as a biological adaptation to communicate information, it is no longer as tempting to see language as an insidious shaper of thought, and, as we shall see, it is not.[3]

Language here is a kind of unique instinct through which human beings talk about the world as a way of coping with it. More importantly for this study, it seeks to lend a certain legitimacy to the idea that language can be understood in terms other than itself. That is, language can be regarded as being incorporated into a larger picture of how the human being functions, and the human being can be regarded in terms of how she relates to a world in distinction to who she is.

Further, it is this distinction (by which language is seen as a mode of communicating meaning *between* individuals *about* the world, and the word is seen as the embodiment of this meaning) that has come to obscure our understanding of what discourse *is* fundamentally. According to Heidegger in his *Zollikon Seminars*, we can see this in the representational view of language, a view that exists amongst English-speaking philosophers from Hobbes to Hume, and a view which begins with Descartes and finally includes both Husserl and Frege, to varying degrees.[4] Here, the spoken word is the communication of the inner thoughts and ideas of the human mind. These ideas represent nominally (and a-historically) things that are found in the external world. Contrarily, as with German Romanticism and on through to the thought of Nietzsche, words have a historical significance insofar as they are the expression of a historically unfolding 'worldview' (*Weltanschauung*), in which hermeneutical context the human being plays out its existence. Yet both views fail to get to the fundamental, ontological significance of language as far as Heidegger sees it, coming up short by viewing language solely in terms of it being rooted in the human subject, and so by definition viewing language through the prism of a dualism that sees the human being standing aloof in some sense to what is named in the word.

Heidegger levels this criticism of language thought dualistically both early and late in his thinking, although his stated views as to why it falls short of an adequate interpretation of language alter along with his change of focus after *Being and Time*. In *Being and Time*, Heidegger says that 'to significations, words accrue. But word-Things do not get supplied with significations' [BT 204], thereby pointing out that language, as discourse, is a way of articulating a pre-given meaning that is to be found in *Dasein*'s being-in-the-world, in the way that *Dasein* is concerned (*Besorgen*) for its existence amidst beings. However, even given Heidegger's primary interest in *Being and Time* as a way of undermining metaphysical thinking in 'the attempt to lead this metaphysical thinking in itself only to its own "presuppositions"' [M 187], his stated view of language there stills involves a dualism between the pre-thematic significance of a word and the actual word itself.

Heidegger's later philosophy, particularly, though not exclusively, from the mid-1940s on, seeks to undermine all forms of dualism in language through a re-examination of its ontological significance in relation to the advent of being as such. Language comes to be viewed more as the gift of being and less as a meaningful, existential mode of *Dasein*'s being-in-the-world. As such – and in contradistinction to Pinker's view of language as a tool that the human being utilizes to survive – it is this gift that allows the human being to dwell in being at all. Thus Heidegger shares the view of Hegel before him that language plays a much more essential role in human existence. In the dialectic of Hegel language is shown, not as a way that the human being survives in the world, but as the way that human being moves through history and thereby makes concrete the truth of the world as ultimately rational. Similarly, Heidegger thinks that language is how human beings *are* essentially, how they have a world and how they come to be alongside other beings, and so why they are concerned for their own existences. However, Heidegger differs from Hegel insofar as he claims that there can be certain ruptures in meaning, ruptures which render language properly historical to the extent that it is able to 're-establish' a people's relation to being. This leads him to argue that a new view of language is required, one through which *Dasein* is able to listen to language as to the call of being, as it is in the word that *Dasein* is first called to its world and its existence. Heidegger argues that such a view can be sought through a renewed reflection on the nature of language and its poetic essence, to which we shall now turn.

## Language as the advent of being

Language is subject to the scrutiny of Heidegger's thought in much of his published works: from *Being and Time* to the *Four Seminars*, with notable stops along the way at 'The Origin', 'Letter on Humanism' and *On the Way to Language* as well as in his many lecture courses. In none of these works, as John T Lysaker points out, does Heidegger put forward a radical new view of language, an alternative theory of language that is more or less convincing than previous ones.[5] Instead, Heidegger insists that we should try to dwell in language, that is, that we should attend to our experience of language. This begs two questions. Firstly, what does Heidegger have in mind specifically when it comes to how we experience language? Is he thinking of speech, of thought, of the written word or all of these and more? Further, is Heidegger claiming that we do not properly experience language despite our near saturation in language in our everyday existence?

A provisional interpretation suggests that by language, what Heidegger has in mind is speech: 'To reflect on language means – to reach the speaking of language in such a way that this speaking takes place as that which grants an abode for the being of mortals' [PLT 190]. Thus Heidegger suggests that *language* speaks, but also that there is more to speaking than simply the spoken word. Through speech we find the granting of the abode of being for human being, which brings being to language and so allows mortals to dwell in being's openness. As such, speech is the way that language makes beings manifest through the word, so that not only speech but thought, reading and writing and any manner in which we are taken up with beings in our day-to-day existence is essentially speech. That Heidegger thinks speech in this way is because he thinks that we always, in some sense, find ourselves within language. Or perhaps it might be better to say that we always find ourselves within a world that is given to us through language as it is brought to light in the utterance of the word. In Heidegger's words, that human being finds itself *in being* is due to the fact that through its being 'language speaks' (*die Sprache spricht*) [PLT 195].

In light of this latter statement, it is clear that Heidegger thinks that we do not properly reflect on the nature of language, that we do not, so to speak, listen attentively enough to hear what is spoken in language. To say that language speaks is an intentionally provocative statement by Heidegger, seeming to diminish the role played by human being in bringing language to utterance and so situating being as such. According to Heidegger, that this is the case is due to the fact that language conceals itself insofar as it is essentially a pointing (*Zeige*) out of things. Language reveals beings in their presence in such a way that it points away from itself in bringing these things to light. Consequently – thanks to our general tendency to treat language as something that is just given over to us, that is *just there* for us as and when we need to talk or to think about something – we do not properly give ourselves over to what Heidegger terms the mystery (*Geheimnis*) that lies at the heart of language, that language speaks *through* human being and so 'solely and solitarily with itself' [BW 397]. In other words, language claims human being for itself, to such an extent that we are consequently 'within language, at home in language, prior to everything else' [BW 398]. Thus language is not to be thought traditionally, as an activity of the human being; rather, it is the very essence of what makes up the being of humanity. To this end Heidegger says:

> Nor is the capacity to speak merely *one* capability of human beings, on a par with the remaining ones. The capacity to speak distinguishes the human being as a human being. Such a distinguishing mark bears in itself the very design of the human essence. Man would not be man if it were denied him to speak – ceaselessly, ubiquitously, with respect to all things, in manifold variations, yet for the most part tacitly – by way of an "It is." Inasmuch as language grants this very thing, the essence of man consists in language.
>
> [BW 398]

We have just noted that for Heidegger language is essentially speech in the sense that it grants an abode for the being of mortals, and in so doing opens up a world in which human beings dwell. But the above quotation intimates that it is impossible to take up a position on how language functions from without language, as language is not one thing amongst others that the human being does but is rather that which constitutes the very essence of humanity. Thus the question arises as to how Heidegger is able to arrive at this interpretation of language if he thinks that we do not properly experience language at the culmination of the history of metaphysics. We get a hint here of what WS Allen means when he says that Heidegger, as his thought develops, is not so much after an understanding of language as it represents the world as he is in pursuit of an experience of the mystery of language – of something meaningful coming to presence in the utterance of the word.[6] Hence Heidegger's thought is increasingly concerned with opening up a genuine encounter with language in an attempt to hearken to what it has to say to us and so find an appropriate and perhaps transformative response to it.

In a lecture from 1959, in which Heidegger gathers together *in nuce* much of his later thinking on language and which was published as 'The Way to Language', we see Heidegger struggling to reveal this sense of mystery in language, to show that something is at stake in the word. This struggle unfolds in the problem that Heidegger sets himself in the text: how does one approach language so that one can somehow get to its essence, that is, how does one make language appear as language? Although this will take some explaining, Heidegger's central claim is that speech (as language) is the way in which language (in essence) forges a path (as *Dasein*) through the openness of being as the way in which being comes to light in the sounding of the word. Heidegger even suggests that an approach to the heart of language may not actually be possible, given that in seeking out a path to its essence, we are seemingly 'already at the place to which it is supposed to lead us' [BW 398]. This state of affairs is redolent of Heidegger's notion of the 'hermeneutical circle'. In 'The Origin' Heidegger raises the difficulty of how we are able to *distinguish* what an artwork is. That is, how do we know what an artwork is without having a prior understanding of art? And how can we have any understanding of art without having first experienced it in the artwork? This is what Heidegger refers to as a hermeneutical circle, the type of circular argument in the face of which logic flees.⁷ What Heidegger suggests, however, is that since we are compelled to follow the circle what we need to do is enter the circle in the right manner. And as art 'essentially unfolds in the artwork', and as we already have an understanding of what an artwork is, it is to the artwork itself that we should turn. Thus in seeking to approach art in a meaningful way, Heidegger tries to circumvent the fruitless entanglements in logical circularities that seek knowledge of the nature of the work of art whilst simultaneously trying to ground this knowledge in certainty. Instead, Heidegger begins his investigation of art by approaching that wherein art can be seen to actually occur – namely, the work of art. Hence, by analogy, it is not a question of finding a logical approach to the question of language. That we already find ourselves 'at home in language' means that Heidegger finds the most appropriate place from which to start an examination of language is with speech.

Significantly Heidegger, on his own account, must avoid approaching speech as an object of philosophical consideration. Speech (not to say language in general) is always for Heidegger fundamentally a way of revealing things, a way of addressing things through the word which essentially points away from itself and towards that which is revealed in the naming-power of the word. If this referential aspect of language is not accounted for, then any examination of speech, and by extension language, will be reduced to little more than an analysis of the functioning of phonemes.

In 'The Way to Language', Heidegger begins his investigation into the nature of language by stating his aim in the following formulation: 'to bring language as language to language' [BW 398]. This is a tripartite formulation which Heidegger uses in much the same way he does the notion of being-in-the-world in *Being and Time*, as a way of talking about a singular phenomenon by breaking it down into its inner relations. And Heidegger is mindful of the reader going astray when he says that such a formulation is not intended as a way of imposing a structure onto language but is rather a path down which language will lead us if we allow it to guide us along its way. Bearing this in mind, Heidegger begins his examination of the nature of language with speech, as it is through speech that things come to light in their being as the word is spoken and the thing is named. But this turn to speech opens up language in a surprising way:

> Language speaks by saying; that is, by showing. Its saying wells up from the once spoken yet long since unspoken saying that permeates the rift-design in the essence of language. Language speaks by pointing, reaching out to every region of presencing, letting what is present in each case appear in such regions or vanish from them.
>
> [BW 411]

What should be noted immediately is that speech is thought in the sense of a saying (*Sage*). Heidegger chooses this word with care. *Sage* in German means myth, and in using this term Heidegger is hinting that saying is tied to the mythical language of a people, as that which gives form to reality by bringing forth that which lies concealed. Thus Heidegger seeks to distance saying from its commonly held understanding as discourse (*Rede*), as discourse may or may not be taken as significant in itself.[8] Rather, Heidegger reclaims for the notion of saying what he regards as its original meaning – namely, 'showing', the pointing-out (*die Zeige*) of that which has already revealed itself from out of itself as a way of bringing this something to language. Thus language does not bring beings into unconcealment as such, but brings them to light instead in the unique way that language is able to do this, through the word. As a result, it is through the word that beings are brought to language.

It should also be noted that the most unique of beings, *Dasein*, is called to language and so into the particular openness that language grants as the being that is directly addressed in the utterance of the word. *Dasein*, so to speak, bears witness to what is shown in the saying of the word that calls forth *Dasein* into the open and so into an encounter with beings as such. Consequently, Heidegger maintains, the word is not in the possession of *Dasein* but reveals *Dasein* as belonging to language, as the one who responds to the call of language through the utterance of the word in the saying of speech. And so speech, as the response of *Dasein* to the call of language, is revealed in a new light – speech is, essentially, a listening, a hearing. Heidegger further elucidates:

> Accordingly, we listen to language in such a way that we let it tell us its saying. No matter what other sorts of hearing we engage in, whenever we

hear something we find ourselves caught up in a hearing that *lets itself be told*, a hearing that embraces all apprehending and representing. In speech, as listening to language, we reiterate the saying we have heard. We let its soundless voice advance, requesting the sound that is already held in reserve for us, calling for it, reaching out to it in a way that will suffice.

[BW 411]

Hence to speak is to hear, and to hear is to respond to the call of language itself. Lysaker sees Heidegger's path of thinking here as a way of leading us back to where we already are, that is, as beings that dwell within language.⁹ As a result, the success of Heidegger's insight depends on him revealing language as essentially laying claim to the thought and speech of *Dasein* in a pre-thematic calling to the word. That is, Heidegger must show how language lays claim to *Dasein* whilst his examination of language must simultaneously avoid treating language as an object. Further, this calling to the word must not only reveal language as that within which *Dasein* already dwells, but further, as Heidegger tells us in his 'Letter On Humanism', it must show that 'language is the house of being in which the human being ek-sists by dwelling, in that he belongs to the truth of being, guarding it' [BW 254]. In other words, Heidegger must also show that *Dasein* not only dwells in language, but that it does so essentially in a corresponding relation to being, that is, that *Dasein* is called into language and thereby dwells *within* the unfolding event (*Ereignis*) of the truth of being.

To this end Heidegger says that to speak is to say and to say is to show. Consequently, the word brings forth beings into the open in the 'rift-design' (*Aufriß*) that is the essence of language, allowing what comes into presence and what withdraws into absence to shine forth to the extent that the 'saying joins and pervades the open of the clearing which every shining must seek, every evanescence abandon, and to which every presencing and absencing must expose itself and commit itself' [BW 414]. As such, the *Aufriß* is the breaking out of an outline that adumbrates language essentially; it is a 'point of gathering' at which speaker and speech, spoken and unspoken are called to bear witness to what is shown through the word.

Thus the saying is a gathering, which serves as a reminder of the original Greek meaning of *logos*, a more primordial understanding than is rendered in its modern manifestation as logic, the science of thought, which serves to determine being in terms of what is objectively present to the mind. Instead, Heidegger says that originally 'the opening up of beings happens in logos as gathering' and that 'gathering is originally accomplished in language' [IM 198]. This is to say that *logos* is thought originally in the sense of a *legein*, a laying-together or gathering, a lying-forth and sustaining in presence of both that which lies forth and that which lets lie forth.[10] This process is then essentially an emergence into the unconcealment of truth (*a-letheia*) from out of concealment and so a process by which beings come into their being by being let be. As a result, Heidegger takes *logos* to mean the ground, or the being (*Sein*) through which all beings are gathered together into the openness of unconcealment in their beingness. Such emergence, being aletheic and so historical (*geschichtlich*) in essence, means that beings are gathered together in a process by which their emergence and their grounding are intertwined.

This last point is important as it signals the role that *Dasein* plays in attending to being is founded on the gathering of *logos*, whereby *Dasein* is brought into direct relation to being as constituted in the gathering-point, in which beings emerge into unconcealment. As such, being receives its measure through *Dasein* to the extent that Dasein attends to the saying of language in the word, which gives a clearer picture of the claim that Heidegger makes in 'Letter on Humanism' when he says that *Dasein* 'is the shepherd of being'.[11] In 'ek-sisting', in standing out into the open through the call of language in the saying of the word, the human being steps into her responsibility to attend to the advent of being, to attend to the truth of being in the coming to presence of beings out of unconcealment and into the rift-design of language. In attending to being in this way, *Dasein's* responsibility is to submit to its destiny and so hearken to language as the way in which being happens, and thereby to try to come to terms with what is said in the word and not to subject language to its own will.

William S Allen notes that Heidegger's thinking here (as elsewhere) can be traced back to his early forays into phenomenology and the possibility of bringing the world to language without objectifying it.[12] Allen links these initial forays to a remark Heidegger makes in his final seminar in Zähringen in 1973 in which he says, 'I name the thinking here in question tautological thinking. It is the primordial sense of phenomenology. Further, this kind of thinking is before any possible distinction between theory and praxis' [FS 80]. Thus, *how* language *says* being has always been at the heart of Heidegger's phenomenological project. Consequently, in the general sweep of Heidegger's thought there is the 'need to find a means of approaching the complexity and ambivalence of our relation to being (whereby there) is a realization that philosophy itself may be part of the problem, and that other ways of thinking might be more appropriate'.[13] Thus, Allen argues, in thinking language in terms of how it does justice to being, we see Heidegger's focus shifts from one in which he seeks an understanding of how language works to one in which he seeks (in his later works) to involve his reader in an experience of language as actually *working*.[14]

Seen in this light, for Heidegger to assert that speech is saying and saying is hearing is to point out *Dasein*'s responsibility to attend to the word as the way in which being happens. To listen to language in this sense 'precedes all other instances of hearing, albeit in an altogether inconspicuous way' [BW 411]. 'Inconspicuous' because one is not trading observations in a conversation, but because one is responding to the call of language in the sense that one has already been claimed by language to bear witness to the advent of being as it is revealed in the word. *Dasein* hereby enters into its own essence as that being which stands in the openness of being (as granted by *logos*) and so encounters beings as they come into the unconcealedness of their essence through the word, due to which *Dasein* is able to attend to the emergence and withdrawal of beings.

One hesitates to say that in some sense Heidegger identifies being with language here, although such a claim has been levelled against him. Gianni Vattimo notes that this criticism is levelled particularly in relation to Heidegger's contribution to hermeneutic ontology, whereby being is approached as it unfolds in language.[15] In a much broader sense, one hesitates because in equating being and language one runs the risk of making equivalent the word and that which it reveals, as we see in the case of the thing as it is rendered in the hylomorphic conceptual schema outlined in 'The Origin'. Viewed in this light, it could be argued that Heidegger is in some sense conceding the idealistic nature of language which, following Platonic thought, regards the idea (the word, the concept) as that which is most in being, and consequently a way of determining being as presence, a criticism that Jacques Derrida will come to make in his *Of Spirit: Heidegger and the Question*, which he encapsulates in the term 'logocentrism'.[16] However, it should be borne in mind that as early as *Being and Time*, in which Heidegger addresses directly the consequences of the Platonic notion of language, he maintains that *logos* originally makes manifest in the word that which has already revealed itself as significant for discourse. Although *logos* is here limited to the essential nature of *Dasein* as such, it suggests that for Heidegger what is primary in being is named by the word and is not the word itself.

In his 1935 work *Introduction to Metaphysics*, Heidegger examines the notion of *logos* through its original determination in the thought of both Heraclitus and Parmenides, in which being is regarded as originating in terms of the unfolding disjunction (*Auseinandertretens*) between *physis* and *logos* (thinking), an unfolding that simultaneously unifies through this very opposition.[17] *Physis*, as has already been noted, is here for Heidegger the self-revealing of being through the coming-to-presence of beings out of concealment. And truth, thought aletheically, lies at the heart of *physis* as the way in which beings are unhidden. Seen in this light, *logos* is the active gathering of beings into the truth of being as the way that beings reveal themselves in their unfolding coming-to-presence: it is the site at which *Dasein* comes into its history. That is, it is the site at which lie the origins of that path through which *Dasein* makes its way within being as a questioning into being. To this end Heidegger says:

> Only where being opens itself up in questioning does history happen, and with it that being of *the human being* by virtue of which the human being ventures the confrontation with beings as such.
>
> [IM 153]

Thus it is through the word that *Dasein* is appropriated (*ereignet*) into the openness of being, and thereby *how* truth is able to occur by allowing beings to come forth into the openness of being in relation to *Dasein*. But this occurrence of truth, this openness to being, remains open only so long as *Dasein* engages with being, so long as *Dasein* enquires into its nature. We can now see that this engagement or questioning is both dependent on, and concerns itself with, an understanding of the relation of *Dasein* to being as revealed through language, as the way in which a path opens up within the openness of being that allows for truth to occur historically. Thus the question into the meaning of being that motivates Heidegger's work becomes increasingly a question about language insofar as it allows beings to dwell within being. Moreover, it is also a question of how *Dasein*, as that being which finds itself called into the truth of being, and so responsible for maintaining the openness within being, attends to this responsibility. Viewed from this perspective, *Dasein*'s task is revealed in its attentiveness to its own being insofar as it concerns the '*Sein*' of *Da-sein*, the being of what is discovered 'there' in the openness of being, of how it is appropriated into the 'appropriating event' (*Ereignis*) of being which bestows the essential nature of truth, of how it comes to be in language as called into this truth through the original naming-power of the word.

Hence, to regard Heidegger as conflating being and language into some form of ideality would be wholly to misconstrue the essential nature of his approach to language. What Heidegger seeks to reveal, rather, is that language in some sense grounds being as truth. This is not, as we might now imagine, the stable ground of a logic that determines something as either true or false, but is rather *logos*, the lying-forth and sustaining in presence within which beings are gathered together upon an historically unfolding path, a path that unfolds and sustains itself within and in relation to the openness of being itself.

What is striking here is that language seems to function in a way similar to the work of art in Heidegger's thinking but, instead of the artwork, it is the word that sets forth an historical world in which *Dasein* comes to be itself, no doubt through certain key terms in a way similar to those traced by Heidegger from the origins of metaphysical thinking in the ancient Greeks. Indeed, Heidegger tells us in 'The Origin' that not only is art the 'setting-into-work of truth' and that 'art happens as poetry', but that 'language itself is poetry in the essential sense' [BW 199]. I shall return to this point below, when I come to discuss specifically the poetic word. However, having just argued that Heidegger understands language as grounding and sustaining *Dasein* in history, and in the knowledge that Western history ends in nihilism, the question arises as to the essence of language, as to *how* language calls us into history in such a way that being is hidden rather than made manifest. Or to put it another way: why do we no longer hear the call of language? If the essence of language can be ascertained (and we must be minded that essence is, for Heidegger, a *way*, not something objective), then the possibility will also present itself to Heidegger of returning us to the ground of human existence as the site at which language makes manifest being.

## Language as the ground of historical Dasein

Robert Bernasconi notes that Heidegger, in his 'On the Way to Language', makes use of what Heidegger calls a *Leitwort* or guiding-word in using the formula 'the essence of language: the language of essence' (*Das Wesen der Sprache: Die Sprache des Wesens*) [OWL 94]. Bernasconi maintains that in using this *Leitwort* Heidegger – in seeking to force us to undergo an original experience of language – could be thought to be indicating that at the end of metaphysics any reflection on the essence (being) of language becomes a question about the language of essence (being).[18] However, Bernasconi observes that there is more going on here than the simple reversal of terms. Instead, there is something transformative happening, which can be witnessed in a general trend in Heidegger's thought that seeks to bring to language the turn (*die Kehre*) in the history of metaphysics that signals the possibility of a new beginning. Consequently, Bernasconi draws parallels with a statement Heidegger makes in an essay from 1949 in which he states that 'the essence of truth is the truth of essence' (*Das Wesen der Wahrheit ist die Wahrheit des Wesens*) [PM 153], with the intention of using an exploration of the latter *Leitwort* to throw light on the former.

What allows Bernasconi to claim a more pronounced correspondence between the two statements is the way in which Heidegger brings into question what is meant by the word 'essence' (*Wesen*) in both cases. As we shall see, the question of essence brings us directly into the sphere of the question of being, as the essence of a thing is, for Heidegger, the sense in which that thing occurs, of how that thing *is*. In fact, the correspondence between the two is such that it might prove beneficial for the reader, at this particular juncture, to think of

Heidegger's use of the term 'essence' as synonymous with the term 'being', and this in relation to his struggle to make being question-worthy once more.

Bernasconi says that in Heidegger's proposition 'the essence of truth is the truth of essence' what we are witnessing is no straightforward reversal of terms.[19] What Heidegger argues, according to Bernasconi, is not that the question of the truth of essence arises out of the question of the essence of truth, but vice versa. This is significant as it means that in saying that the question of the essence of truth arises out of the question of the truth of essence Heidegger is not simply shifting the priority of his focus from the essence of truth to the truth of essence (significant though this is), but that he is also indicating the change of meaning that takes place in these terms once the end of metaphysical thinking comes into sight.

Moreover, Bernasconi suggests that, as a result of revealing a historical dimension to our understanding of how truth functions, Heidegger is able to draw to our attention a transformation in the meaning of truth that takes place at the culmination of metaphysics, and alongside it a transformation in Western thinking itself. This transformation, however, is not to be thought of, for example, in a Cartesian sense, in which there is a conscious attempt to place truth on a new footing.[20] The historical (*Geschichte*) nature of truth Heidegger has in mind here – in which being gives rise to truth through an unfolding relation (*Ereignis*) with *Dasein* – does not allow for the mere willing of truth that would be implied in the Cartesian sense. Instead, Heidegger thinks this transformation in the sense of recognizing that in its primordial conception – the ancient Greek *aletheia* – truth is thought privatively. And, as I have already noted, it is the notion of *aletheia* that Heidegger thinks is fundamental to understanding all Greek thought.

This privation that lies at the heart of the original experience of truth, and is referred to as the 'non-essence' (*Un-wesen*) of truth by Heidegger, not only goes un-thought by the Greeks, it is indeed forgotten and so lost to the Western tradition until this tradition reaches its terminus in modernity. Indeed, the whole metaphysical tradition can be seen to be founded on – and unfolds as a result of – the self-concealment of that which goes unconcealed in this history, along with a failure to recognize this to be the case. And although, as Michel Haar points out, Heidegger vacillates as to exactly when this metaphysical tradition commences (which in itself begs the question as to where the line between the inside and the outside of this history may be drawn – Haar settles, perspicuously, for defining it as 'enigmatic'), it takes place as a growing oblivion of the concealment that lies at the heart of the truth of being.[21] It ends in the reign of a technological thinking through which everything that is *is* in the sense of being present as a resource to be exploited, including *Dasein* itself.

Given the fresh impetus that Heidegger's insight into the nature of truth gives us, we can now read the phrase 'the essence of truth is the truth of essence' as indicating a transformation in what we recognize as the essence of truth. The first part of the phrase can be read in a traditional sense, that is, nominally, whereby essence is 'whatness' (Latin *quidditas*) and so the essence of truth is 'what can be known' – what stands present in unconcealment and can be an object of knowledge. Due to our transformed understanding of the primordial basis of truth as the coming-to-presence of beings from out of concealment, essence in the second part of the phrase is to be read verbally. Thus we have essence in the sense of 'essencing', of how truth is thought, and so the truth of essence becomes 'the way truth – as that which conceals the hiddenness of being in its unconcealment – is thought'. We can now see the full significance of Heidegger's proposition. The first part of the proposition is to be read metaphysically, insofar as the essence of truth involves the concealment of being as this essence. The second part, ushering in the possibility of a second beginning, reveals this concealment of essence as determining the history of metaphysics. The proposition therefore reveals the essence of truth as unfolding historically from the concealment of the hiddenness that lies at the heart of being to its revelation as doing so, and therefore essence thought in the sense of a permanent whatness dissolves into essence thought in the sense of an unfolding, thinking relation to the truth of being.

Yet what bearing does this have upon the nature of language and how it functions for Heidegger? In what sense is this proposition properly transformative, so that it points to the possibility of a transformation of our relation to language and does not just signal a change in Heidegger's viewpoint on the nature of being? And in what sense does this proposition convince us that this transformation tells us something about how *Dasein is*, and does not simply indicate how *Dasein* has been, but no longer is?

A good place to turn is to the actual proposition itself, to see how it works. 'The essence of truth is the truth of essence', as I have noted, is a *Leitwort*, a word or phrase that calls us to what is truly essential in what is to be thought. In a broad sense, what is to be thought is the saying of the turn in the history of being and is touched upon by Heidegger in 1946 in his 'Letter on Humanism'. At one point in this essay Heidegger refers to what he is trying to do in his 1930 essay 'On the Essence of Truth', stating that his intention is to try to think the truth of being from out of the experience of the oblivion of being, and this specifically in terms of how to approach the problem of thinking beyond the end of metaphysics from within the language of metaphysics itself.[22] To put it more plainly, Heidegger asks: how does one allow being to claim thinking, leaving aside any notion that it can simply be willed? Heidegger's first step is to attempt to shift thinking from its metaphysical foundations by subjecting his reader to an experience of language that is other than the traditional preoccupation with a subject and its predicate, to which end he employs the *Leitwort*. How, then, does this *Leitwort* work?

Bernasconi makes a convincing case for regarding the *Leitwort* (although he does not refer to it specifically by name) as paradigmatic of the 'speculative proposition' that GWF Hegel employs, with the intention of challenging the domination of the assertion as it is used in philosophical writing.[23] The speculative proposition is an attempt by Hegel to confound the reader's familiarity with the usual move from the subject to the predicate of an assertion. How the speculative proposition works is that what is predicated of the subject does not turn out to be an attribute of the subject. Instead, the reader discovers in the predicate the essence of the subject and so is disorientated, undergoing an experience of language – as Hegel sees it – that is properly philosophical. In other words, the reader is unable to move on from the content of the philosophical statement because the subject *is in* the predicate. Therefore, all that is left to the reader is to think through the philosophical content of the statement, to dwell on what is essential, rather than becoming embroiled in disputation.

Although ultimately the starting point for each philosopher differs (Hegel's philosophy starts out from the premise that the whole content of history, and so thought itself, finds its grounding in *Geist*, whilst Heidegger employs the *Leitwort* to undermine the notion of an absolute grounding, and starts out instead armed only with the guiding sentence itself), both use a form of speculative proposition in the attempt to leave behind the subjective point of view.[24] However, when seen from Heidegger's standpoint, Hegel's thinking springs from the notion of the movement of absolute spirit into its full disclosure as truth, and so any transformation that Hegel effects takes place solely within THE bounds of metaphysics, as a movement towards the absolute presence of spirit as the ground of truth. Heidegger, on the other hand, does not seek to move from one place to another (i.e. from one basis of thinking to another, through which what was once the basis for truth *is* no longer) but seeks to dwell instead within language itself, as that which grants the truth of being. In other words, Heidegger seeks to return thinking to where it already dwells but in which it fails to be at home.

Seen in this light, the *Leitwort* 'the essence of language: the language of essence' does not direct us towards a definition of what language is, but towards the question of how language can speak being, and, by implication, to the question of how *Dasein* comes to being through language. In other words, the *Leitwort* does not tell us *what* language is, but instead allows us to undergo an experience of language that reveals language as the way that being emerges. Thus language is experienced as motive, it moves being through the word, and in doing so it also brings the human being to language, and thereby brings thought to being. Thus language is essentially how being happens, and as such it is a portal into the openness of being.

We can now grasp more clearly that Heidegger uses the *Leitwort* as a way of trying to move away from our current metaphysical, conceptual notions of language and towards a more thought-worthy, open engagement with being. In terms of both the essence of truth and the essence of language, Heidegger seeks to open us up to an experience that reveals *Dasein* as thoughtfully dependent on its unfolding relation to being as the way that it (*Dasein*) *is* and how being happens. Specifically in the case of language, our attention is drawn to how being happens through the word, of how language calls *Dasein* to the word and so to the site of the happening of being. That is, language is revealed as calling *Dasein* to its (*Dasein*'s) world. Hence, in pursuing the essence of language we find ourselves involved in the language of essence, that is, we involve ourselves in an experience of language that does not name, dispute or communicate, but reveals *Dasein* as that being that *is* in language. Hereby the *Leitwort* is revealed as a way of emphasizing that language is not a 'whatness' but the path through which being comes to light in its truth and where *Dasein* essentially *is*.

Of course, we have already said that Heidegger, following Hegel, uses the *Leitwort* as a way of getting beyond the metaphysics of the subjective proposition. However, I have also just argued that the *Leitwort* is used by Heidegger as a way of enabling his reader to undergo an experience of language that returns the reader to the heart of language as that in which she dwells. But does not the notion of 'experience' itself suggest something subjective, something metaphysical?

Bernasconi thinks that such a criticism can be made, and in particular with regard to the whole tenet of 'On the Way to Language' as what Heidegger calls a 'matter of experiencing that unbinding bond in the weft of language' [BW 399].[25] This criticism arises if one gives Heidegger's text a 'Derridian' reading. Citing in particular Derrida in *Of Grammatology*, Bernasconi argues, amongst other things, that the idea of experiencing language carries with it, from Derrida's viewpoint, the whiff of privileging presence over absence. The implication is that any experience of language that *Dasein* undergoes is necessarily temporally grounded, that is, it has to take place in the present. Yet in naming what is present language cannot grasp the temporal flux of being *as it is given* because for this to be the case language would have to be spontaneous. But for language to work at all it must consist in, fundamentally, repeatable characteristics or forms. Language must be able to grasp hold of any given experience to the extent that it can both recall and repeat that experience in the word, a thought Heidegger himself gives voice to as early as 1925 when he says: 'We do not say what we see, but rather the reverse, we see what *one says* about the matter' [HCT 56]. So, on Derrida's account, the essence of language is not simply present but essentially absent, in the sense that language, in naming the present experience, simultaneously points both to the past and to the future in the word. Therefore in any given experience of language – an experience that cannot but take place in the present, as it is *an experience* – what is experienced is not experienced as present in the word, but is mediated through the word which transcends the present insofar as it is a mode of non-presence.

Of course, we are familiar with the idea that metaphysics can be determined in terms of thinking being as presence from Heidegger's own work, to which Derrida is himself indebted. Further, as Bernasconi points out, this Derridian reading of the experience of language in Heidegger would not be a direct criticism so much as showing that a metaphysical interpretation can be read into Heidegger's text, nor would this reading be complete without an alternative reading standing alongside it.[26] Yet this is no merely heuristic exercise. Why such a criticism could not confidently be levelled at Heidegger is because when he speaks of an experience of language, he does not seek what is present in such an experience but what is absent – namely, a word for being at the end of metaphysics. This is revealed, as we have seen, insofar as Heidegger fails to find a name for either the essence of truth or the essence of language. In both cases language is no longer able to mediate the experience of being (as this has happened in its metaphysical forms from Plato and Aristotle's *ousia* to Nietzsche's *Wille zur Macht*) and instead modern *Dasein* is left to face the groundlessness of being as given over to the silence of language.

Seen in this light, we can now grasp more clearly Heidegger's words in his 1955 essay that was written in honour of Ernst Jünger and eventually published as 'On the Question of Being' in which, in the context of attempting to delineate what nihilism means, Heidegger questions even if it is possible to attribute any definitive meaning to the word 'being', speaking of the difficulty in the following terms: '*The question concerning the essence of being dies off if it does not relinquish the language of metaphysics, because metaphysical representation prevents us from thinking the question concerning the essence of being*' [PM 306]. Hence Heidegger, in questioning into the essence of language, is testing the waters with regard to the possibility of opening up a new relation to being from within language. This new relation is to be one in which *Dasein* is not seen to ground being through language in a knowing relation, but instead sees *Dasein* as appropriated through language into its ownmost being through the call to the word which reveals language as the house of being. It is only at the end of metaphysics that language is thus revealed as the way in which being happens as the unfolding event of the truth of beings (*Ereignis*).

It is important, finally, not only to see that language is the site of the happening of being, but also to get a clearer view of *how* being comes to language so that

*Dasein* is able to articulate the truth of being. It is important not only in terms of where we stand in relation to being at the end of metaphysics, but speaks also to where we see ourselves with regard to what Heidegger refers to as another beginning (*anderer Anfang*) and for which we must prepare ourselves. With this in mind we can see that in speaking of the essence of language we can no longer approach language in the sense of how we can systematize it or how we can have knowledge of it – language cannot now be thought in any sense of standing objectively before us. Instead, we have to look to the way that language is claimed by and claims being to itself. In doing so, we do not so much fix our attention on how meanings are conveyed in the word, but rather on how the word brings beings into the openness of being. This language achieves through the power of the sounding of the word that calls *Dasein* into the mystery of language. As Heidegger says in 'On the Way to Language':

> What language properly pursues, right from the start, is the essential unfolding of speech, of saying. Language speaks by saying; that is, by showing. Its saying wells up from the once spoken yet long since unspoken saying that permeates the rift-design in the essence of language. Language speaks by pointing, reaching out to every region of presencing, letting what is present in each case appear in such regions or vanish from them. Accordingly, we listen to language in such a way that we let it tell us its saying. No matter what other sorts of hearing we engage in, whenever we hear something we find ourselves caught up in a hearing that *lets itself be told*, a hearing that embraces all apprehending and representing. In speech, as listening to language, we reiterate the saying we have heard. We let its soundless voice advance, requesting the sound that is already held in reserve for us, calling for it, reaching out to it in a way that will suffice.
>
> [BW 411]

This is what the *Leitwort* is intended to reveal that the fundamental experience of language requires of us a way of responding to the word by listening to what it has to say to us, which means allowing ourselves to belong to language as the way in which being is revealed. What Heidegger has in mind here is summed up with great clarity by Michel Haar when he says that 'to speak is to listen to language; it is to repeat (*nachsagen*) its speaking (*Sage*); it is to speak out loud, to make resonate what language says in secret'.[27] The key word here is 'secret', for what is secret in language is its lack of essence, its lack of anything substantial that allows us to see it for what it is. This is to say that language speaks out of silence and is grasped only insofar as it illuminates that which it is not. To undergo an authentic experience of language is therefore to be able to hear what language has to say in bringing being to light, in bringing into the truth of the word that which *is*. For *Dasein* to undergo such an experience of language it must be given over to language as that through which being happens, to experience what Heidegger terms *Ereignis*.

Earlier in this chapter I suggested that Heidegger speculated as to whether we could ever find a way to the essence of language, as we were seemingly 'already at the place to which it is supposed to lead us' [BW 398]. As is usual with Heidegger, such a gambit is a way of leading his reader beyond the metaphysical presuppositions that prevent a traditional philosophical enquiry from gaining an undistorted view of the matter at hand. Heidegger does this by confronting these presuppositions and working through them – as has been seen in this text with regard to traditional notions of truth and language, for example. Heidegger's use of the *Leitwort* in 'On the Way to Language' follows this pattern, leading us from the stance in which we view *Dasein* as that being that is distinguished by language (the *zoon logon echon* as it is traditionally rendered), to that being that finds itself at home within language, that is, within the unfolding coming-to-presence of being in the saying of the word. In other words, *Dasein* does not possess language, *Dasein* '*is*' through language.

It is easier now to understand the formulation that Heidegger gives to the task he sets himself in 'On the Way to Language' – namely, 'to bring language as language to language'. This can now be reformulated in the following way: *to bring language* (in its essence) as the way in which being is brought to the site of its truth; *as language* (as saying) through the pointing out of the happening of the truth of being; *to language* (to the word) through the call of language from out of the silent realm and to which *Dasein* responds, attending to its mysteriousness, to the secret that lies at its heart. We can see then that language is not so much an object for thought as the site at which *Dasein* exists thoughtfully, to the extent that Heidegger can claim that *Dasein* dwells within being as that being who is 'needed and used for the speaking of language'

[BW 423]. As such 'we human beings, in order to be who we are, remain within the essence of language [...] we can therefore never step outside it in order to look it over circumspectly [...] we catch a glimpse of the essence of language only to the extent that we ourselves are envisaged by it, remanded to it' [Ibid].

We are human to the extent that we are given over to language, and we are given over language in such a way that whatever 'shows up' in being is revealed in and through language. Thus,

> language was once called the "house of being". It is the guardian of presencing, inasmuch as the latter's radiance remains entrusted to the propriative showing of the saying. Language is the house of being because, as the saying, it is propriation's (*Ereignis*) mode.
>
> [BW 424][28]

Language was once called the house of being in 'Letter on Humanism' and is regarded as such by Heidegger because it is what is ownmost to being – it is what allows being to be revealed in its most appropriate way. As such, it is also what is ownmost to human being, as human being belongs to language (has it as its own) as language is the essence of what it is to be a human being. Thus any transformation in historical *Dasein*'s relation to being is afforded through a transformed relation to language. Such a transformation is in turn dependent on our relation to language as it is 'determined in accordance with the sending that determines whether and in what way we are embraced in propriation by the essence of language, which is the original pronouncement of propriation' [BW 425], that is, the way that language calls to us as the way that we are originally appropriated to language. Hence, any notion that our relation to language can be transformed by concocting neologisms or 'novel phrases' is deemed inappropriate. A transformed relation to language requires of us a step back into the way that language appropriates us most fittingly for the unfolding of being, a task that cannot be willed. To this end Heidegger says:

> Perhaps we can in some slight measure prepare for the transformation in our kinship with language. The following experience might awaken: Every thinking that is on the trail of something is a poetizing, and all poetry a

thinking. Each coheres with the other on the basis of the saying that has already pledged itself to the unsaid, the saying whose thinking is a thanking.

[BW 425]

Hereby Heidegger points us towards poetic thought as perhaps that fruitful mode of language which would allow us a view of what is ownmost to us in the way we are with language, of how to properly respond to language and to which we shall now turn.

## The poetic word as the ground of being

Truly poetic projection is the opening up of that into which human being as historical is already cast. This is the earth and, for a historical people, its earth, the self-secluding ground on which it rests together with everything that it already is, though still hidden from itself. But this is also its world, which prevails in virtue of the relation of human being to the unconcealment of being. For this reason, everything with which man is endowed must, in the projection, be drawn up from the closed ground and expressly set upon this ground. In this way the ground is first grounded as the bearing ground.

[BW 200]

It is not difficult to surmise, given what Heidegger has to say above, that what he seeks in poetry and the poetic differs widely from that which is sought by the average literary critic. Timothy Clark, a scholar whose interests cover both the literary and the philosophical, puts it most emphatically when he says that anyone 'who reads Heidegger and the monumental issues in his texts interested only in extracting some new method of reading to be added to the stockpile of literary criticism – this might be a good definition of an idiot'.[29] Although such an emphatic assertion may strike us initially as amusing, it should nonetheless put us on our guard when it comes to how we approach Heidegger's thinking with regard to both the literary and the poetic.

In 'The Origin' Heidegger views an aesthetic understanding of art as metaphysical. This is because aesthetics views art as a cultural phenomenon that gives expression to human experience, seeking its understanding in the pleasurable effects of the artwork or the intentions of the creator of the work. As Clark indicates above, Heidegger also eschews any idea of a 'poetics', if we mean by this a particular theory as to the form and content of poetic expression, or even a theory of poetic theory as such. In Heidegger's case, such a theory might be referred to as an 'ontological' reading, an all-consuming, standardized and topical interpretation in which the singularity of the genuinely poetical work is lost to an objectifying and institutionalized system of evaluation. But this, for Heidegger, would be to treat the poetic as 'literature' and so as part of the 'literature industry', which would render it the 'object of literary history'. Rather, Heidegger thinks of the poetical in terms of *Dichtung*, a German word that is translated into English as 'poetry' but which does not find its equivalence in this word. *Dichtung*, as the essence of art, is 'founding, [...] (the) instigation of the strife of truth' [BW 201]. Thus poetry and literature cannot be differentiated simply in terms of their formal aspects, as the poetic is not limited to verse but can also include other literary works of art, such as the novel, insofar as the poetical means the grounding of truth.

One way of bringing into relief Heidegger's thinking on the difference between a work that belongs to 'literature' and one that belongs to *Dichtung* is to situate each work in its distinct relation to history, and this relation as thought in the terms that Heidegger uses in *Being and Time* to distinguish between the ontic and the ontological determinations of history – namely, as the difference between *Historie* and *Geschichte*.[30] A work belonging to the former is one that exhausts itself in the context of its time. As a work it is an artefact, an object determinable and determined in its being (through the prevailing standards of hermeneutical exegesis) as holding significance in terms of how fully the social context out of which it arises can be reconstituted (by the literary critic). This means that the work is understood in terms of the prevalent values and concerns of society that obtain when it is originally created.

On the other hand, a work belonging to the latter notion of history thought as *Geschichte* resists such reconstitution. As a work it is not easily historically classified, as rather than belonging to history it gives rise to the very projection of history itself – to the happening of history as *Ereignis*. Consequently, the poetic work – as Heidegger tells us in 'The Origin' – is the 'opening up or disclosure of that into which human being as historical is already cast' [BW 200]. Hereby Heidegger not only signals the distinction between literature and *Dichtung* but also reveals a shift in his thinking of *Geschichte* itself. From *Being and Time*'s focus on the fundamentally temporal nature of *Dasein* in its particularity, we see *Geschichte* thought in the much broader sense of the fate of the West in general.

In light of this broader context the genuinely poetic work takes on considerable significance, to the extent that Heidegger says in 'Poetically Man Dwells' that poetry 'is what first brings man onto the earth, making him belong to it, and thus brings him into dwelling' [PLT 216]. Indeed, Heidegger says that dwelling (*Verweilen*) means to rest in the poetic (*dichterisch*); it is to pay heed to the poetic as that which gives measure to being.[31] Yet it is a measure that is in no sense calculative, insofar as it would allow what is unknown to become known. Instead, the poetic gives measure to that which is mysterious, to that which in coming to light simultaneously refuses to let itself be known, to what is referred to by Heidegger in 'The Origin' as the earth – or the abyssal ground of being. Hence, the obfuscation of being at the end of metaphysics becomes, increasingly for Heidegger, Western humanity's inability to dwell poetically, to attend to its ontological status as being essentially homeless (*Unheimlich*), that is, to attend to itself as a people whose essence is always in question.

We can see now that what Heidegger calls literature lacks content and is understood only in terms of *that which it is not*, what we call its historical 'context'. Contrarily, the poetic work (*Dichtung*) demands our attention as that which gives measure, as that which gives *Dasein* the historical dimension in which it is able to dwell and attend to 'a letting come of what has been dealt out' [PLT 222]. In other words, the poetic work gives form to the occurrence of being in such a way that it allows being to come forth in all its mystery. Hence what is to be sought in the truly poetic work is not knowledge of its historical context but measure (*Maß*) as that which is 'the original dimension of dwelling' [PLT 225]. We can see the way that Heidegger thinks measure here is of a more primordial nature than that in which it is normally held, as the ordering and quantifying of that which already exists. Instead, measure is a way of allowing that which comes into being to do so whilst simultaneously revealing itself as having something mysterious attached to it essentially, and suggests that Heidegger has given further thought to the idea of *Riß* (rift) that he speaks of in 'The Origin' (as the struggle between earth and world). To this end Heidegger says that the poetic saying (which speaks in the image, as that which lets something be seen) 'gathers the brightness and sound of the heavenly appearances into one with the darkness and silence of what is alien' [PLT 224]. This means that the word of the truly poetic work, especially in an age that is essentially unpoetic (*undichterisch*) – i.e. that does not recognize what is strange in the familiar – should be heeded (if, indeed, it can be heard at all), as this is the one way we have of discovering how to dwell in language.[32] Thought in this way the poetic word, to borrow a phrase from WS Wurzer, is 'the only hope after […] the end of metaphysics'.[33] The strangeness of saying that the poetic is the 'only hope' for Western civilization certainly deserves further examination, and I shall address this point now.

## The poetic as ethical

Michael E Zimmerman makes an interesting observation with regard to this latter issue. Referring, in particular, to Heidegger's 'Letter on Humanism', and this in relation to Heidegger's thinking in the 1930s and 1940s in the sense of its political implications, Zimmerman views Heidegger's turn to the poetic in terms of a search for the possibility of setting Western thought on a new *ethical* footing.[34] This need arises, to use Heidegger's own words, at a time when 'technological man, delivered over to mass society, can be kept reliably on call […] in a way that corresponds to technology' [BW 255]. In other words, the question of the ethical arises out of the perplexity of humanity in the face of its diminution to its usefulness (or lack thereof) for the waging of wars, consuming of goods or any other myriad ways in which it can be considered solely in terms of being a resource. Yet Heidegger's ontological response to this situation (what Zimmerman is here calling the ethical *in terms of* the poetic) has not received universal approbation.

In much secondary literature, Heidegger has been referred to as being both politically unethical and a philosopher who shows little or no interest in the ethical questions that confront modern Western humanity.[35] The former has much to do with the fact of Heidegger's involvement with the National

Socialist Party in the 1930s, an involvement referred to by John D Caputo as 'scandalous',[36] and one which Heidegger himself puts down to his assumption of the role of rector of Freiburg University in 1933 as a way of protecting the university's academic freedom.[37] The latter criticism is based on Heidegger's own words. In *Being and Time* Heidegger says that his ontological method and the intention that lies behind the text 'is far removed from any moralizing critique of everyday *Dasein*' [SZ 167]. Further, in his 'Letter on Humanism', Heidegger responds to a request that he should write an ethics by arguing that such a task rests on firstly thinking the question of being as the basis from which any notion of ethics can be properly viewed. Otherwise, if we think ethics in isolation from the question of being we run the risk of 'elevating man to the centre of beings' [BW 255].

Consequently, any notion of setting Western thought on a new ethical footing cannot be viewed in terms of what is traditionally understood as 'ethics' – namely, a set of rules as to how humanity should live. This view is metaphysical insofar as it makes humanity what is central to being, hiding from humanity what is ownmost to it – that it belongs to being and should attend to it thoughtfully. How, then, does Heidegger respond to the call of humanity at its darkest hour?

Heidegger's response is to seek a new *ethos* for the West in the sense taken from the way the Greeks originally thought it as the abode or dwelling place of the human being. To this end Heidegger cites a phrase from Heraclitus, which he sees as appositely bringing to light the essence of *ethos* by rendering *ēthos anthrōpōi daimōn*, which is usually translated 'a man's character is his demon' as 'the (familiar) abode of man is the open region for the presencing of god (the unfamiliar one)' [BW 258].[38] Heidegger uses this phrase to make the case that originally the *ethos* of the human being is to be at home (be familiar) within being *as that which is unfamiliar*, and that therefore *ethos* should be understood as more primordial than both ethics (which does not address being as such) and ontology (which is not concerned with the truth of being, but rather the being of beings) as *ethos* speaks to the abode of the human being. In other words, ethical concern is not originally a branch of philosophy, but is the enquiry into the truth of being (as the abode of the human being), and so is concerned with humanity's coming to be at home in what is unfamiliar, namely being.

Moreover, ethical thinking understood in this way can no longer be confined (as it tends to be, understandably, in discussions on the role of ethics in *Being and Time*) to the question of the authenticity (*Eigentlichkeit*) and inauthenticity (*Uneigentlichkeit*) of *Dasein*. To live an authentic existence (and so to live ethically) insofar as it can be accounted for in *Being and Time* is given over to *Dasein* in terms of the possibility of its dislocation, at any given moment, from its traditional, everyday ethical life, a life of shared values in which 'one' (*das Man*) acts in accordance with one's community's ideals.[39] As such, dislocation (as the interruption of *Dasein*'s everyday shared existence by the individuating thought of its own mortality) is important for Heidegger insofar as it allows for the possibility of freeing the individual from the prevailing metaphysical determinations of its own being. This happens when *Dasein* is revealed to itself as finite, and so as differing from itself as determined in terms of the 'one': as finite, as a being that has as its utmost possibility its own death; it cannot be sustained in its being by notions of the ideal.

At best, this affords *Dasein* the possibility of a thoughtful preparation (*Vorbereitung*), a waiting on the destining of being that Heidegger refers to in his 1966 interview with the German magazine *Der Spiegel*, subsequently published as 'Only a God Can Save Us' in which he responds to the prompting of the interviewer as to what philosophy and the individual are capable of by saying: 'This preparation of the readiness, of keeping oneself open for the arrival or the absence of the god. Moreover, the experience of this absence is not nothing, but rather a liberation of man from what I called "fallenness amidst beings" in *Being and Time*. A meditation on what *is* today belongs to the preparation of the readiness we referred to' [HC 108].

In other words, at the end of the history of metaphysics, *Dasein* is free to meditate on the nihilism that engulfs it but is unable to break free from it. Yet this does not mean that *Dasein* is impassive in its being; rather, it is free to reflect on the absence of a meaningful relation to being and on the primordial reasons for this that lie in the ancient Greek determination of being as presence, which in turn allows for a 'thinking through of the questions which are still unasked since the time of Greek philosophy' [HC 109]. But any possibility of another beginning is dependent on the appearance of a new God, of *Dasein* finding itself at home in being in such a way that what comes to be does so in light of that which refuses to do so. And at the risk of repeating myself *Dasein* is not free to will this new God into existence but must thoughtfully await its arrival. Hence Heidegger's statement that 'man is the shepherd of being' and not its master.

This is an important point when we come to think of much of the criticism levelled at Heidegger's preoccupation with the thinking of being. This comes to the fore particularly concerning the period when Heidegger's thinking becomes increasingly preoccupied with the poetic and the possibilities it holds for setting the West on a new footing. It is both the ethical and political implications of Heidegger's poetic thought that receive most of the criticism, which is encapsulated in the words of John D Caputo, who says:

> Heidegger is led by the inordinate valorising of the *Wesen* of being and truth (and of history, technology, art, dwelling, etc.) into the most radical insensitivity toward the exigencies of "factical life". The transformation of the question of being from a hermeneutics of facticity to an "essential thinking," from facticity to *Wesen*, is accompanied by an ominous, unearthly indifference to concrete historical life.[40]

What Caputo's criticism amounts to is that Heidegger, in his turn from looking to the exigencies of the individual *Dasein* to a concern for *Dasein* thought of collectively and historically, reveals a complete lack of sensitivity to the suffering of individual people as a result of a war instigated by the German people. Thus Heidegger's increasing concern with the poetic essence of language as a way for Europe to move beyond technological mobilization and the suffering it is able to inflict on great swathes of people passes over individual suffering, silently. Contrarily, I think it is true to say that Heidegger's relation to the ethical and political questions of the 1930s and 1940s shows a change from what Jacques Derrida rather over-emphatically calls the 'massive voluntarism'[41] of his 1933 Rectorial Address to the self-professed confrontation (*Auseinandersetzung*) with National Socialism in his Nietzsche lectures over the years 1936–1944,[42] a change that reveals at least a certain sensitivity to the prevailing exigencies of the German people (and by inference all the peoples involved in the conflict in Europe). Another point that needs to be taken into consideration is that in 1936 in 'The Origin of the Work of Art', the founding of truth (and so the opening up of another beginning) is possible not only through art and thought, but also through 'the act that founds a political state' [BW 186], a notion that is completely missing from his lecture series later in the 1930s.

Now, although some critics impute this distancing of Heidegger from National Socialism during the 1930s to the failure of his rectorship at Freiburg University, it is my contention that something more fundamental is happening within Heidegger's thought, a contention that is shared by Slavoj Žižek.[43] Žižek maintains that it can be argued by any Heideggerian that far from Heidegger's 'valorizing' of the essence of being and truth leading him to overlook or ignore the excesses of National Socialism, National Socialism itself provided the ontological insight necessary for Heidegger to recognize the modern guise of nihilism in technology. Although this argument could be dismissed as viewing Heidegger's engagement with the National Socialists as in some sense a-political, the engagement itself makes Heidegger's ontological insight significant to the extent that he could not (and did not) walk away from its ontical consequences, as Caputo claims.

More importantly for this study, however, is Žižek's insight that there is for Heidegger's thought a major difficulty, a theoretical impasse that Heidegger finds difficult to resolve between the ontic and the ontological, between how one is and what one does, that suggests his engagement with National Socialism is a way of breaking out of this deadlock by way of an act of revolution. This is to say that Heidegger's engagement with the National Socialists has little or nothing to do with National Socialism, and everything to do with resolving the deadlock that lies at the heart of his own thinking in the 1930s. Yet, even if we do not agree with Žižek, Heidegger's philosophical engagement with the 1930s and beyond betrays a philosopher very much alive to the ethical and political significance of both his thoughts and actions. Furthermore, what is problematical for Heidegger at this time – the inextricable relation of the ontic and the ontological – is a difficulty he consciously wrestles with and is evidenced in his work both before and after the period in question.

It is, however, not surprising that when it comes to the question of what one is to do in the face of nihilism, it is ontological considerations that prove decisive for Heidegger. For our current purposes, this is the reason that

Heidegger is concerned with ethical thought in terms of *ethos* (of how we are at home in being), rather than ethics (in the sense of what we should do), as the latter is dependent on the former. This is because what we do is dependent on how we see ourselves in an ongoing relation to being. At the end of the history of metaphysics this relation is nihilistic, its modern guise technology, and any chance of founding a new *ethos*, of founding a new historical dwelling place for *Dasein*, is purely providential – it is dependent on being calling *Dasein* into a new abode within language, and on *Dasein* harkening to this call. In other words, it is dependent on poetic revealing, on *poiesis* as the revelation of truth and perhaps, more specifically, on the 'bringing forth of truth into the beautiful' [BW 339]. But what if modern humanity is deaf to the call of being? What if it is blind to poetic revelation? What if our technological age is the age in which being finally and forever ceases to be question-worthy?

To conclude, as the history of metaphysics draws to a close it is to language thought as essentially poetic that Heidegger turns, seeing in it the possibility of the most fundamental saving power emerging. This is because, according to Heidegger, language is not first and foremost a means of communication but that which claims *Dasein* for being insofar as it gathers beings into the openness of being through the word. This allows Heidegger to claim that 'language is the house of being' in which human beings come to dwell in being. However, as we can no longer be said to dwell within language at the end of metaphysics, Heidegger suggests that we turn to the poetic word as it holds out the possibility of transforming our relation to language and thereby opening up a dimension within being that would allow *Dasein* to be at home within its openness. It is with this thought in mind that we now turn to Heidegger's engagement with the poetry of Friedrich Hölderlin.

# 4
# *Hölderlin and the possibility of poetry*

## Why Hölderlin?

Unlike Hegel, Heidegger does not think that in turning to art as a way in which truth is established he is necessarily involving himself in something whose significance lies in the past. For Heidegger, the 'death' of art as a way in which truth happens can be pronounced only when art is viewed from within the realms of metaphysical thought (although this is not to say it is a view universally held within aesthetics). When the certainty of metaphysical thought is undermined, that is, when truth as the correspondence of a thing and its correct representation in thought is revealed to be founded on the more primordial notion of truth thought aletheically, then we stand in a transformed relation to metaphysics which allows us to meditate on our relation to being and the possibility of renewing this relation. It is the function of art, Heidegger consistently maintains, that allows for the possibility of such renewal to be established. Yet this possibility lies only with great art (*grosse Kunst*), with art that sets truth to work and thereby calls for a decision of historical significance.[1]

Moreover, as the history of metaphysics draws to a close, any possibility of renewal, any thought that Western humanity can be set on a new path, has to be considered purely providential. It is dependent on being calling *Dasein* into a new abode within language, and on *Dasein* responding to this call. Hence, any notion of a new beginning opening up at the close of metaphysical history is dependent, according to Heidegger, on poetic revelation bringing historical being into the word. And yet one has to ask: at a time when Nietzsche's pronouncement of the death of God casts its shadow over European thought; in the face of the increasing domination of Western life by technology; at a point when Western humanity is on the precipice of a Second World War; or to use Heidegger's own words, in a 'destitute time', why does Heidegger turn to the enigmatic Romantic poet Friedrich Hölderlin?[2]

This is a question that Julian Young asks, going on to make the more general point that modern art (poetic or otherwise) cannot meet the Greek 'paradigm' of great art that Heidegger sets for the establishment of a new truth, whereby art has a communal role, preserved as it is by an entire people, and sustaining this people in its historical being.[3] Young goes so far as to say that in turning to Hölderlin, Heidegger's position is self-contradictory, as not only is there nothing communal about modern art (an essentially private phenomenon) but that this is particularly the case in Hölderlin's work – a man whose poetry is a 'byword for hermetic obscurity'.[4] Young attributes this contradictory element to Heidegger's early approach to Hölderlin, whereby the poet is treated ostensibly as a thinker rather than as a poet.[5] Thought in Heideggerian terms, Young's criticism is that Heidegger initially approaches Hölderlin as a thinker of being, as someone who thoughtfully pursues that which withdraws from thought, and not as a poet, as someone who establishes truth in the word as that which is to be thought about. It is only through his ongoing engagement with Hölderlin, Young suggests, that Heidegger eventually comes alive to the importance of Hölderlin as a poet and is able subsequently to escape the 'tyranny' of the Greek paradigm and to develop a new approach to art in which the poet is seen as preparing the way for the overcoming of metaphysics.

Such tyranny, I think, can be put down to the fact that in 'The Origin' Heidegger turns to Greek art as an example of art that pre-dates aesthetics. It is a time, in fact, when what we now call 'art' is not known as art but is, rather, an essential way that the Greeks come to see the truth about themselves and as such calls upon them to make decisions about what it means *to be* a people. Hence, for Heidegger, Greek art serves as a template for the way that great art is able to open up the history of a people into its truth but is not necessarily paradigmatic of the way that all great art can happen. Seen in this light, Heidegger's turn to Greek art proves not to be as tyrannical as Young suggests, allowing as it does for the development of Heidegger's thought on the possibilities inherent in art for a more open relation to being. Yet this does not bring us any closer to answering the question as to why Heidegger turns to Hölderlin as a way of seeking to establish a renewal of Western history.

Dominique Janicaud anticipates Young's criticism when he argues that Heidegger initially approaches Hölderlin's poetry with the intention of revealing the fundamental determination (*Grundbestimmung*) of a particular poem ('Germanien') as metaphysical, and consequently serving as a paradigm for the determination of any given poem, and so poetry as such.[6] Janicaud goes on to argue that by the time of the *Ister* lecture course in 1942, some seven years later, Heidegger locates Hölderlin's poetry outside metaphysics, as founding a new epoch. However, in revealing how Heidegger's view of Hölderlin's poetry changes from the lecture courses of the mid-1930s to the mid-1940s, Janicaud is also able to bring to light that which remains unchanged and so essential to Heidegger's engagement with Hölderlin – namely, a radically new experience of what it means to dwell poetically. Janicaud emphasizes the point with a quotation from Heidegger's 1934/5 lecture course on Hölderlin's hymns *Germanien* and *Der Rhein*, which I shall repeat here:

> One considers Hölderlin historiographically and one fails to recognize the only essential point: his work – which has not yet found its time and space – has already overcome our historiographical embarrassment and has founded the beginning of another history, that history which starts with the contest concerning the advent or the vanishing of God.
>
> [GA 39: I][7]

That Heidegger seeks in the poetic word a way of escaping the language of representation should not come as a surprise, given what I have argued in the last chapter. That he is able to take from an experience of reading Hölderlin's work what he views as the grounding of a new history, however, is not only a bold claim on Heidegger's part but something that will only make sense once we have examined Heidegger's engagement with Hölderlin, to which we shall now turn after a few preliminary biographical remarks on Hölderlin in order to give a little historical context to his work.

Hölderlin was born in Germany in Lauffen am Neckar, north of Stuttgart, in 1770 and died in Tübingen, in 1843. As a young man he was a fellow student and friend at Tübingen University of GWF Hegel and FWJ Schelling (both of whom would go on to be leading figures in German Idealist philosophy) and his work shares with theirs the struggle to come to terms with the then prevailing Enlightenment ideals that stressed the pursuit of human freedom through rationality.[8] He also bore witness in his youth to the effects that the French Revolution had directly on Germany as well as the rest of Europe, both in terms of its ideals (Liberty, Equality and Fraternity, ideals borne out of Enlightenment thinking) and in terms of what immediately became of these ideals in the ensuing Terror, as well as at the hands of Napoleon Bonaparte. Such details are important, David Constantine suggests, insofar as 'real places, real people and real events are the foundation of Hölderlin's idealism, in Tübingen as also later',[9] an idealism that *essentially* informs Hölderlin's poetry. Thus, it can be claimed that Hölderlin's poems reveal the struggle between freedom and tyranny, honesty and untruth, simplicity and corruption, and most decisively as Hölderlin's poetry matures, there is the increasing preoccupation with an irretrievably lost past. This maturation, however, was cut short when in 1806 Hölderlin succumbed to the madness that was to assail him until his death, some thirty-seven years later.

So much for the man: wherein lies the significance of Hölderlin's poetry? Heidegger, towards the end of his life, says of Hölderlin admiringly:

> My thinking stands in a definitive relationship to the poetry of Hölderlin. I do not take Hölderlin to be just any poet whose work, amongst many others, has been taken as a subject by literary historians. For me Hölderlin is the poet who points to the future, who expects god and who therefore may not remain merely an object of Hölderlin research and of the kind of presentations offered by literary historians.
>
> [HC 112]

Certainly, regarding Heidegger's definitive relation to Hölderlin's work, we see evidence for this in the fact that after Nietzsche, Hölderlin's work is given more coverage than any other thinker in Heidegger's texts. Moreover, Heidegger's engagement with Hölderlin's work is at its most intense from the mid-1930s to the mid-1940s, a time when Heidegger is consciously distancing himself from a purely philosophical engagement with thought (and this mainly with Nietzsche's thought and his notion of *Will to Power*) and is instead turning to an investigation of thought that is other than metaphysical. In fact, Heidegger was so taken with Hölderlin's work that he goes as far as to state at one point that on reading Hölderlin's poetry as a student it hit him 'like an earthquake'.[10] Yet all of this only tells us that Hölderlin's work was significant for Heidegger, and not why. In point of fact, the idea that Hölderlin's poetry hit Heidegger and his fellow students like an earthquake so long after his death suggests a poet who had not dominated the German intellectual landscape of the time in the same way as Goethe or, to a lesser extent, Schiller had, writers and poets who were contemporaries of Hölderlin in the latter part of their lives. Indeed, German philosopher Hans-Georg Gadamer, a former student and colleague of Heidegger's, suggests that the high rank accorded to Hölderlin's poetry was only recognized during his and Heidegger's own lifetimes, and that belatedly.[11] Heidegger was not oblivious to this fact, nor to the conclusions that might be drawn from it. At the beginning of his essay 'Hölderlin and the Essence of Poetry', published in 1936, Heidegger says:

> Why choose *Hölderlin's* work if our purpose is to show the essence of poetry? Why not Homer or Sophocles, why not Virgil or Dante, why not Shakespeare or Goethe? Surely the essence of poetry has come to rich expression in the works of these poets, more so indeed than in Hölderlin's creation, which broke off so briefly and abruptly.
>
> [EHP 52]

Thus Heidegger demonstrates that it is not the stature in which Hölderlin's poetry is held that is its chief attraction. Nor is it, for that matter, how 'accomplished' Hölderlin's work appears. For Heidegger, what is decisive is the *essentially poetic* nature of Hölderlin's work.[12] Further, this poetic nature is not to be understood in terms of how Hölderlin employs imagery and symbol, allegory and metaphor in his work, but in terms of the privileged mode of *poiesis* that takes place there. This privileged mode is revealed in the power of the poetic word to name the 'essential', to bring what *is* into the open in such a way that it founds both a new truth and thereby a new historical epoch. This is why Heidegger does not resort to a 'comparative study', whereby a variety of poets and their poems would be examined in order to distil a universal essence of poetry from them. The essence of poetry cannot be thought in a universal sense for Heidegger, as such a thought would miss what is truly essential in the poem, i.e. that the poem is a singular event which gives rise to its own context, to the extent that only the poem itself can reveal its own nature.

It is in the poetry of Hölderlin, Heidegger maintains, that *poiesis* in its essential nature happens, that is, as the power of the poetic word to name the essential. Hence, it is with this in mind – and noting that what occurs essentially in Hölderlin's poetry must necessarily be singular – that any analysis of Heidegger's approach to Hölderlin's poetry should be understood. To this end, Heidegger says:

> I do not choose Hölderlin because his work, as one among many, realizes the universal essence of poetry, but rather because Hölderlin's poetry is sustained by his whole poetic mission: to make poems solely about the essence of poetry. Hölderlin is for us in a preeminent sense *the poet's poet*. And for that reason he forces a decision upon us.
> 
> [EHP 52]

What Heidegger is suggesting here is that in Hölderlin's poetry what is happening *in the poems* is the call for a decision to be made about the essence of poetry, about whether poetry is able to ground truth in the word and so open up a new history, a 'new time', or whether poetry is simply 'harmless and ineffectual'. For Heidegger, therefore, what is at stake in Hölderlin's poetry is nothing less than the possibility of establishing a new relation to being in which language is brought forth as other than the calculative determining of metaphysical thought.

If we note the above citation, Julian Young points to Heidegger's use of the definite article here as indicating a *singular* essence, suggesting that for Heidegger there is only *one proper measure* for authentic poetry, i.e. the Greek paradigm, whereby poetry is able to found a 'world'. Whilst such an interpretation has some merit (given 'Hölderlin and the Essence of Poetry' is written around the same time as 'The Origin', and given the latter essay's concerns (both stated and un-stated) with the possibility of founding a new history for Germany and the West), it views Heidegger's approach to the work of Hölderlin in the mid-1930s as content-led.[13] This is to say, according to Young's account, Heidegger is seeking out in the poetry of Hölderlin *that which is stated*, in other words, a meaning, rather than attending to the fact that what is said *is said poetically*. Indeed, as Joseph J Kockelmans originally notes, Heidegger treats Hölderlin – in Hölderlin's poetising of the essence of poetry – as he would any great thinker of the past, viewing what is said poetically by Hölderlin in the same way as he views what the great thinker thinks philosophically.[14] What is more, Kockelmans also notes that Heidegger fails to thematize the difference between thinking and poetry at this juncture, only hinting at it here and there, and that it is not until much later that Heidegger is able to bring any clarity to the issue.[15]

However, if we contrast Heidegger's meditative engagement with Hölderlin and compare it to his critical disengagement with Nietzsche, as George Pattison suggests, then although we see similarities (Heidegger cites his engagement with both men as evidence of his intellectual resistance to Nazism and therefore part of his confrontation with planetary technology) there are also some pronounced differences.[16] Not least amongst these differences is Heidegger's approach to each of them. In the case of Nietzsche (as the voice of nihilism) Heidegger adopts an increasingly critical role, attempting to distance his own thought from the danger inherent in the thinker that is 'closest to us'. In his approach to Hölderlin, as the harbinger of a new beginning, Heidegger tries a more positive appropriation, one that points away from metaphysical thought and promises the possibility of being able 'to stand in the domain of poetry' [39: 19].

We go astray, then, if we view Heidegger's initial forays into Hölderlin's poetry as in some sense the pursuit of the content of the poems or the thoughts of Hölderlin. It should be recalled that in 'The Origin' (just to re-emphasize, written contemporaneously to the period to which Young refers)[17] Heidegger makes the case for a re-thinking of language, seeking to reinstate the poetic as its most privileged form. This conception views language aletheically, in terms of a projective saying, which 'brings what is, as something that is, into the open for the first time' [BW 198]. This conception, in turn, depends on an experience of language as the 'happening' (*Ereignis*) of this saying. Thus even if, as Jacques

Taminiaux suggests, Heidegger's first approach to Hölderlin in the winter semester of 1934 is with an eye to the political (in a move away from the authentic *Dasein* of *Being and Time* to an authentic German people (*Volk*) or community), it is not because of what Hölderlin thinks or says.[18] It is, rather, because of what *happens* in the poetry of Hölderlin, of what originates in his poetic word. Heidegger's claim is that in Hölderlin's poetry we witness the instituting of the fundamental mood of the German people, which gathers this people into its unity by revealing in the 'sacred mourning' of Hölderlin's poetry the absence of the gods, which in turn brings into relief the task of the German people as preparing the ground for the return of the gods. In other words, Hölderlin is the poet of modernity, revealing the destitution of our times through that which stands outside of thought, by sensing the prevailing mood of the times (*Grundstimmung*) and so bringing it to light in the essential word of his poetry. Thereby, Hölderlin's work brings historical *Dasein* into a more thoughtful relation to being, a relation that opens up being to the scrutiny of the thinker.

Thus, what is significant for Heidegger in Hölderlin's poetry is not its content, which sees its meaning as something which can be assimilated and communicated, but rather the possibility of an engagement with language by which we come to 'dwell' within it. Bearing this in mind, and that what is essential to this poetry is to be properly established by the thinker, it should come as no surprise that Heidegger insists, in his 1951 'Introduction' to the second edition of a collection of essays on Hölderlin published as *Elucidations of Hölderlin's Poetry*, that 'these elucidations belong within the dialogue of thinking with a form of poetry whose historical uniqueness can never be proved by the history of literature, but which can be pointed out by the dialogue with thinking' [EHP 21]. Hence, whilst a thoughtful engagement with a thinker like Nietzsche seeks to discover what goes unsaid in what he says, that is, how he thinks being, what thinking seeks in engaging with poetry is that which withdraws from it, namely, being itself. Thus, it is in the hands of the thinker to properly appropriate what is most singular and essential in Hölderlin's poetry, and thereby bring to light modern humanity's historical task. But what is most singular to Hölderlin's poetry cannot be conveyed through assertions and must be experienced thoughtfully in an engagement with the poetry itself, an engagement that seeks to discover how Hölderlin's poetic word reveals its epochal truth.

This begs three questions. To begin with, how does one approach Hölderlin's poetry so that one is able to experience the happening of truth there? The modern reader, it must be recalled, carries with her the baggage of metaphysical thinking, approaching the artwork as an object of aesthetics, with a form and a content that stimulates the senses or the intellect. For Heidegger, however, the artwork is singular; thus, any reading of it must also be singular and dependent on what happens in the work itself. Thus we will need to examine how Heidegger confronts the poem, to which I shall turn presently. There is also the question of *how* Hölderlin is able to establish a 'new time', i.e. how his poetry is able to ground truth as the opening up of a new history. To answer this question I shall analyse Heidegger's claim that in Hölderlin's poems the essence of poetry is to be discovered. This means that Heidegger has to show that in the experience of engaging with Hölderlin's poetry truth can be revealed as actually happening. Finally and directly related to how we answer this question, we must ask: *what form* does this truth take? That is, what does Hölderlin's poetry tell us about our world and our historical existence that it calls us into a new relation to being?

## How does one approach Hölderlin's poetic word?

In 'Hölderlin and the Essence of Poetry', Heidegger examines the following lines from a preliminary draft of Hölderlin's poem 'Celebration of Peace', entitled 'Conciliator, you that no longer believed in … '

> Much has man undergone/Has given name to many of the heavenly ones/ Since we have been a conversation/And able to hear from one another.[19]

A literalist interpretation of these lines might render them as the melancholy reflections of a Romantic poet. Yet Heidegger sees in these few lines from Hölderlin something beyond the merely subjective yearnings of a young poet, he sees something coming to light that speaks to the essential being of humanity – namely, that 'We – human beings – are a conversation' [EHP 56]. There is something both familiar and unfamiliar here. In the first instance, Heidegger is maintaining that language is not simply a tool that the human being possesses (as I have already argued). Rather than *having* language, the human being is to be discovered within language. But Heidegger also sees something telling about the nature of language in Hölderlin's notion of a conversation (*Gespräch*), suggesting that the human being is not only grounded in language, but that 'language is essential only as conversation' [Ibid]. What is it for human being *to be* a conversation?

We must be careful how we tread here. For Heidegger it is no simple matter of trying to discover in Hölderlin's use of the word 'conversation' what the poet means by this word, i.e. what is re-presented in the word. The poetic word does not *stand in for* something else. As Heidegger tells us in 'The Origin', what is brought to the fore in the poetic work (as the happening of truth) 'can never be proved or derived from what went before [...] (as this is) refuted in its exclusive reality by the work' [BW 200]. What happens in the poetic word – and we should be minded that Heidegger is here talking about poetry in the sense of *Dichtung* (the instigation of the strife of truth) – is that something new is brought forth that can be approached only in terms of the poetic word itself. Further, and as Heidegger says most clearly in 1957 in his *On the Way to Language* (in which he is discussing Stefan George's poem 'The Word'), 'we must be careful not to force the vibration of the poetic saying into the rigid groove of a univocal statement, and so destroy it' [OWL 64]. That is, in Heidegger's view, rather than attempting to render intelligible what the poet has to say, we would be better served if we simply attended to the call of the poetic word insofar as it reveals that which it names singularly. Notwithstanding this singularity (in 'The Origin', Heidegger calls this a 'self-sufficient presencing' [BW 154]), in the naming of the poetic word there resonates a plurality of meaning, a plurality that resists easy definition and invites thoughtful engagement. The poetic word draws our attention to itself as language, to language as that which has mystery attached to it – the mystery of the naming power of the word, of the essence of language as a calling into being.

Heidegger continues:

> But Hölderlin says, "Since we have been a conversation and able to hear from one another." Being able to hear is not merely a consequence of speaking with one another, but is on the contrary the presupposition of speaking. But even being able to hear is itself in turn based upon the possibility of

the word and has need of it. Being able to talk and being able to hear are co-original. [...] We are a conversation, that always also signifies we are *one* conversation. [...] Conversation and its unity support our existence.

[EHP 57]

For Heidegger, the truly poetic awakens in us an experience of language as a propriating event (*Ereignis*). That is, the poetic word, as it is rendered in the poem, invites the reader into a relation with the language of the poem that is both singular and open. The poem does this because in its essence it 'brings what comes to presence (in the word) out of its propriety to a kind of radiance; it lauds what comes to presence; that is, allows it in its own essential unfolding' [BW 424]. Timothy Clark clarifies this point when he says that in using the poet's own terms to 'internally translate' the poem, Heidegger seeks to move beyond a point at which poetic words are viewed as objects and instead tries to *think through* these very words, and consequently deliver us over into the open realm as it is opened up within the poem.[20] This is what Heidegger has in mind when he says that the poem can be only properly understood in its own terms, through a process in which the ultimate task of any interpretation of the poem 'consists in disappearing, along with its elucidations, before the pure presence of the poem' [EHP 22].

Heidegger's interpretation of Hölderlin's lines is certainly compelling, appearing to interpret Hölderlin's words in their own terms. To this end Heidegger sees in the line 'Since we have been a conversation' the unsaid basis that gives rise to its expression, that *the word founds our world* and so a relation both between ourselves and within being. That is, insofar as *we are*, we are a conversation – we are called into being by the word and come to be who we are through the word. We thus get a sense of the power of the poetic word to draw attention to itself as that which grounds being. And this drawing attention to itself is also what attracts the thinker into a thinking relation with the poem. Although the relation of thinker and poet is somewhat ambiguous in Heidegger's writings of the 1930s and 1940s (as already noted), it is always the case that being is opened up to question in the genuinely poetic, and that the thinker is the one whose task it is to respond thoughtfully to being thus opened up. Further, the thinker always responds to the singularity of the poetic word through an attentive hearing, a hearing which requires of the thinker a 'leap' into thought, 'to where everything is different, so different that it strikes us as strange' [WCT 12]. Thus the thinker renders the singularity of the poetic word in the singularity of her response through a leap into thought, a leap that cannot of itself guarantee the essential nature of the word, as it is fundamentally a leap into the dark, into groundlessness.

Véronique M Foti takes issue with Heidegger on this point. She sees in Heidegger's engagement with Hölderlin the totalizing tendency of a thinker who appropriates the poem to his own thought as the mythologizing of Western history (as the oblivion of being).[21] Heidegger does this, she claims, through his 'insistence on the essential unsaid as the unitary source of textual configuration'.[22] Foti is here adverting to the fact that Heidegger views the poetic word as drawing us into thought by pointing out being as that which is to be thought about. And what thought is drawn towards, as Heidegger tells us in *What Is Called Thinking*, is that which 'turns away from man. It withdraws from him' [WCT 8]. Moreover, it is the poetic word which brings this withdrawal into presence as an event which in fact

> may even concern and claim man more essentially than anything present that strikes and touches him. Being struck by actuality is what we like to regard as constitutive of the actuality of the actual. However, in being struck by what is actual, man may be debarred precisely from what concerns and touches him – touches him in the surely mysterious way of escaping him by withdrawal. The event of withdrawal could be what is most present in all our present, and so infinitely exceed the actuality of everything actual.
> [WCT 9]

In Hölderlin's poetry the withdrawal of that which is to be thought about is brought forth in the word. However, it is not so much that which withdraws, but withdrawal itself which comes to presence in the word as a drawing away. Subsequently, the poet, as exemplar of the human being, acts as a sign but in such a way that the 'sign stays without interpretation' [WCT 10]. This is not to say that the sign signals nothing, however, but that it opens up a space for thought. Indeed, what is opened up here is what Heidegger refers to as 'food for thought', and what is explained at the conclusion of *What Is Called Thinking* in the following manner:

> The essential nature of thinking is determined by what there is to be thought about: the presence of what is present, the being of beings. Thinking is thinking only when it *recalls* in thought the ἐόν, that which this word indicates properly and truly, that is, unspoken tacitly. And that is the duality of beings and being. This quality is what properly gives food for thought. And when it is so given, is the gift of what is most worthy of question.
> [WCT 244]

In other words, in the poetic word of Hölderlin the question of being is opened up to thought in such a way that we are involved in a particular form of 'hearing', one in which we must attend to the poetic word as that which draws us into 'a way of thought that tracks in thought what is most thought-provoking' [WCT 12] – namely, being.

It is with this in mind that Foti claims Heidegger sacrifices what is singular about poetry on the altar of his own philosophical concerns. Regarding Hölderlin's poetry this means that, according to Foti (and despite his best efforts), Heidegger is unable to account for singularities such as the ultimate sense of loss and irremediable danger that Hölderlin's poetry contains. Implicit in this criticism is a much broader issue, namely, that Heidegger misses the singularity of any text, due to the fact of his preoccupation with the question of being, through which he interprets and understands the whole of Western history, from the ancient Greeks to the modern technological age. This in turn, Foti thinks, leads to a thematizing of history on Heidegger's part that prevents him from acknowledging the simple 'otherness' of any given text that he interprets, failing to see in the text that element which of itself eludes thought.

Foti is not alone in seeing this thematizing tendency in Heidegger's engagement with Hölderlin. Prior to her Otto Pöggeler asked in this relation: 'Is not even Hölderlin's poetry turned into its opposite by the use Heidegger makes of it?'[23] It has also been argued that Heidegger de-contextualizes Hölderlin's poetry from its own historico-political concerns, i.e. those that arise out of the French Revolution, to the extent that he either ignores the political concerns that come to the fore in Hölderlin's poetry (as being little better than humanism), or mentions them only to dismiss them as untimely with regard to the concerns of Germany in the 1930s.[24] It should also be noted that what can be counted as singular to the poem and yet unessential to its historical significance are certain emotions that are not in themselves fundamental attunements (*Grundstimmungen*), that is, emotions that are not 'world' disclosive. This would include emotions such as loss or compassion, both of which are emotions that nevertheless permeate Hölderlin's poetry. This begs the question: can Heidegger's turn to Hölderlin's poetry as a way of opening up being to questioning be reduced to little more than a philosophical doctrine that thematizes alterity, and in doing so fails to account for that which refuses itself to thought?

Before giving an alternative reading of what Heidegger might be doing here, I shall address the notion that there is a 'totalizing tendency' in Heidegger's reading of Hölderlin, which is summed up succinctly by William S Allen.[25] Allen suggests that in perceiving Heidegger's encounter with Hölderlin we need to think of it with regard to its textuality and rhetorical *praxis* and not in the sense that it is another piece of Heidegger's thinking that needs explicating or that it is a case of Heidegger simply appropriating the language of poetry for his own ends. In the former, exegetical readings (to which this thesis belongs), Allen sees a tendency to spend too little time trying to understand Hölderlin's work on its own terms and in the latter there is a tendency to damn Heidegger too quickly for his insensitivity. In both cases, however, Allen sees the same problem at work: the relation between Heidegger and Hölderlin has already been decided beforehand, whilst the reading itself only takes seriously one side of the relation. Subsequently, the totalizing tendency that some see in Heidegger's readings of Hölderlin's texts can be viewed as not doing justice, in equal measure, to both thinker *and* poet.

There is, of course, the possibility of an alternative reading of Heidegger's engagement with Hölderlin, one in which this totalizing tendency disappears in the face of a genuine experience of the poetic word. It could be argued that, far from closing his eyes to that which refuses itself to thought, Heidegger's engagement with Hölderlin's poetry has the effect of opening up to thought that which in fact eludes its grasp and always will elude it. This is because in focusing on Hölderlin's poetry, in *engaging with* its language, Heidegger is able to show that the original essence of language, as given in the poetic word, bears little resemblance to language understood in terms of the calculative word of everyday discourse, the language of representation. In experiencing language in Hölderlin's poetry as essentially founding truth, Heidegger is able to make the claim that language is 'the basic capacity for human dwelling' [PLT 226], that is, it allows for unconcealment to happen. Conversely, such an experience allows us to see that Western humanity currently dwells 'unpoetically', as the calculative word – through which language is reduced to little more than the exchange of information – does not allow for an experience of language as revelatory. As such, the importance of language – that we are able to experience a world through it, and that this is fundamental to how we understand this world – fails to come into view.

In contrast to the language of everyday calculation, Heidegger shows, through his engagement with Hölderlin, that the essential language of poetry draws attention to itself as question-worthy, both in terms of its significance as belonging 'to the closest neighbourhood of man's being' [PLT 187] and as that which 'gathers poiesis under a holy compulsion' [EHP 219]. That is, poetic language reveals the fundamental nature of language as that which originates truth and draws *Dasein* into this truth. This in turn opens up language to a questioning that the narrow confines of its everyday use do not allow. Language thought poetically is revealed as situating the human being historically within language, as transporting *Dasein* ecstatically towards the uncertainties of its own fate. Thus the question of language opens up the question of being and what it is *to be* as a being in being. Far from failing to account for that which refuses itself to thought, Heidegger's engagement with Hölderlin seeks to open thought up to that which in its essence is always out of the grasp of thought.

We can say, then, that in approaching Hölderlin's poetry we are able to experience the happening of truth therein due to the singularity of the poetic word and its self-contained capacity for the unconcealing of being (and that this comes to the fore due to the thinker's direct engagement with the poem). We should keep this in mind now that we come to the point at which we look to how Heidegger thinks Hölderlin's poetry is able to establish truth, whatever this truth turns out to be. For in the singularity of Hölderlin's poetic word, whatever truth is established can be established only insofar as it is the opening up of the possibility of a new relation to being as one that has attached to it the withdrawal of being. This means that in Hölderlin's poetry truth must be not only experienced as the establishing of *Dasein* on a new historical path, one that is brought about through Hölderlin's poetic word as that which draws *Dasein* into the essence of language, but also one that brings *Dasein* into an authentic, poetic relation to being.

## Poetic revelation as the grounding of the history of *Dasein*

In his treatment of some lines from Hölderlin's hymn 'Remembrance' (*Andenken*), written in 1942, Heidegger draws to our attention the power of poetry to speak the essential word and to bring into question both our relation to language and how language itself functions. These lines are as follows:

> But someone pass me/Full of dark light/The fragrant cup/So that now I may rest, for sweet/It would be to slumber in the shade.
>
> [EHP 141][26]

The significance of these lines, however, only fully comes to light when they are viewed in the context in which they occur in the poem, a context which I shall sketch out in order to reveal the full significance they have for Heidegger. The lines appear at a point in 'Remembrance' when the poet, in Heidegger's reading, seeks the clarity of sobriety in order to open up himself to the call of what has been sent through language in the 'flaming light of the holy' [EHP 140]. In attending to what being sends in this flaming light, that is, in stepping out into the holy, the poet signals (acting as the sign) what is sent by being (through language) by bringing it to the word (for the people). Moreover, in stepping out into the holy the poet *becomes the 'between'*, that is, the poet stands in the realm which obtains between gods and human beings, allowing language to speak through him and thus calling a people into its historical ground. As Heidegger puts it in 'Hölderlin and the Essence of Poetry', referring directly to what he terms the hints of the gods as the ground on which the poet founds being:

> The poet's saying is the intercepting of these hints, in order to pass them on to his people. The intercepting of hints is a receiving, and yet at the same time, a new giving; for in the first "signs" the poet catches sight of what has been completed, and boldly puts what has been seen into his word to foretell what is not yet fulfilled.
>
> [EHP 63]

Hence the poet steps out into the holy and thereby steps out into his fate as mediator between the gods and the people. In doing so, the poet acts *as a sign*, or perhaps more properly *is* as a sign. As a sign, the poet can be read in two distinct but interrelated ways: as that being which is distinguished in its being by *being in language*; as that being which *originates the truth of being insofar as it is given over to language*. To repeat myself, these two aspects are brought together in the figure of the poet, who serves thereby as an exemplar of the human being in its fundamental linguistic nature as that being which is able to transcend itself ec-statically. Ecstasy is here thought in the original Greek sense of the word as a 'standing outside' oneself, and points to the temporal nature of the human being as a being that is able to go beyond itself as a merely *present* entity.

This account of ecstatic transcendence is significant for Heidegger in two ways. In the first instance, it allows him to indicate where a positive appropriation of truth may be located in the face of the prevailing subjectivist account that can be traced from Descartes but crystallizes in Leibniz, Hegel and Husserl. Indeed, a most striking difference is marked here in the different phenomenological approaches of Heidegger and his one-time colleague and mentor Edmund Husserl, the philosopher who introduced Heidegger to the possibilities of phenomenology. For Husserl, the subjectivist account of truth is one in which the human being, thought essentially in terms of a transcendent consciousness, stands in opposition to its object and thereby provides the conditions by which this object is determined. Thus, the subject provides the basis for objective truth, which is constituted in and through subjective acts of consciousness. For Heidegger, the problem with this picture is that it does not account for the disclosure of beings that forms the basis for the very possibility of this opposition between subject and object, which in *Being and Time*, for example, Heidegger thinks in terms of being-in-the-world.[27] What is more, Heidegger thinks transcendence in terms of *ekstasis*, in the sense of a stepping forth in which *Dasein* projects itself towards it past, present and future, thereby making temporality the basis for the possibility of being-in-the-world. Thus truth is fundamentally temporal in nature. Consequently, in the ecstatic transcendence that language accords the human being, Heidegger sees a way of accounting for the temporal nature of truth in terms of a happening (*Ereignis*) in which *Dasein comes forth into an open relation* to the presencing of beings and thereby being as such. Further, it is through language, as made evident in the poetic word, that Heidegger brings to light *Dasein*'s predisposition to transcend its own subjective presence and return it to the ground of its own existence, pointing to the human subject as essentially going beyond itself as a being that is merely present and into the open region of being as the ground of its historical unfolding.

And yet, for Heidegger, we only come to discover the poet *as* sign and language as humanity's domain within being through the power of the poetic word. Moreover, this is only brought to light insofar as the poet is seen to be called to her historical task, to the extent that being is both delimited and thus brought forth for the questioning gaze of *Dasein* in the poem as a happening that is experienced through the poetic word. This has serious implications for Heidegger's interpretation of Hölderlin. If, as Heidegger maintains, the poem gives measure to the historical ground on which *Dasein* stands, then the poet's vocation is to ready this ground in the sense that 'the homeland is first prepared as the land of the nearness to origin' [EHP 47]. Consequently, Hölderlin's poetry must in itself give shape to this homecoming in much the same way that we see the Greek temple do in Heidegger's 'The Origin', whereby it 'first gives to things their look and to men their outlook on themselves' [BW 168]. In other words, Hölderlin's poetry must ground a new history, must open up a new truth and must also be able to be experienced as doing so in his poetry as such. How does Heidegger make good this claim?

On the basis of what I have just outlined it can be seen that, in Heidegger's view, Hölderlin – by stepping out into 'the flaming light of the holy' – ecstatically transcends himself as a human being by stepping into a poetic existence (within the parameters of his poetry). Hence, in the poem, the poet is seen to dwell poetically, and as such, gives measure to what *is* in his employment of the poetic word. Hölderlin's poetry gives this measure not by calculating, reckoning or any other form of grasping, but 'rather in a letting come of what has been dealt out' [PLT 222] by being. In doing so, his poems are able to bring together the 'brightness and sound of the heavenly appearances into one with the darkness and silence of what is alien' [PLT 224], and in doing this his poems 'first of all admits man's dwelling into its very nature, its presencing being' [PLT 225]. Thus, the question arises immediately as to what is revealed of modern *Dasein* in the figure of the poet as he stands in Hölderlin's poetry.

Insofar as the poet comes to dwell in the poem, we can see that the poet is called by being into language in order to give measure to that which *is*. In being given measure, that which is comes forth in its strangeness as that which has attached to it an element that resists fully coming into presence – what is brought to light comes forth from the shade. Viewed in this way, in the figure of the poet *Dasein* (in its modern guise) is revealed in Hölderlin's poetry as a being who dwells unpoetically. This comes to light in the poem by way of an experience of the contrast between how the reader stands in her own existence and how the poet stands within the poem. As Heidegger tells us, to dwell unpoetically means that *Dasein* must in essence dwell poetically, and this 'we can in any case learn only if we know the poetic' [PLT 226].

How exactly is such truth revealed in Hölderlin's poetry? We see it in the ecstatic transcendence of the poet in language, due to which he harkens to the word that is sent to him from out of being, which in turn sees him – to lend a phrase that George Pattison employs to great effect – give himself over to 'relative non-being'.[28] This is what Heidegger is adverting to in the earlier citation from Hölderlin, where the poet says, 'But someone pass me/Full of dark light/The fragrant cup'. In going beyond himself into the flaming light of the holy, the poet is not seeking the clarity of reason, 'because its brightness leads to the illusion that in its appearance alone there can be sight' [EHP 141]. This is why the poet seeks out the 'fragrant cup' that is full of 'dark light', although not so that he can cancel out the clarity of the brightness by calling for the 'fragrance which anesthetizes one into forgetfulness and for the inebriating drink which makes one lose consciousness' [Ibid]. What the poet seeks in the dark light is not loss of awareness. Rather, the dark light

> lets one's meditations pass beyond that mere illusion of clarity which is possessed by everything calculable and shallow. [...] Its work is not to make one inebriated, but it does nevertheless make one intoxicated. The intoxication is that sublime elevation of mood wherein that single voice can be heard that sets a tone, and where those who are attuned to it may be led most resolutely beyond themselves. [...] This intoxication lifts one into the illuminating clarity in which the depths of the concealed are opened up and darkness appears as the sister of clarity.
>
> [EHP 142]

This is how truth happens in the poem. The poet, in composing the poem, hands over herself to the poetic word of language and in doing so steps beyond herself as a merely present human subject and into an open relation to being. In stepping beyond her own subjectivity, the poet finds herself in the realm that lies between the gods and the people, and thereby the poet is able to attune herself to the prevailing, fundamental mood (*Grundstimmung*) of being. It is in the fundamental mood that the world is disclosed in light of *Dasein*'s attunement to being. This attunement, which in *Being and Time* is thought in terms of anxiety (*Angst*) and is limited to the individual human being, becomes, in Heidegger's later work, the historical disposition of an epoch and is revealed in Hölderlin's poetry in the sense of the loss (*Fehl*) of the gods.[29] The fundamental mood reveals the modern Western world as one that is abandoned by being, given over to an inauthentic existence of calculation and adventure. In Hölderlin's poetry, however, the world is also marked as a beginning or a possibility for *Dasein*, as made evident in the poet's giving himself over or being appropriated into the occurrence of being (*Ereignis*) through poetic language. The poet thereby acts as a sign, a sign that points out *Dasein* as standing in an open relation to being which at the same time is revealed as that which withdraws from *Dasein*.

All of this comes to the fore for the reader in the poem's fundamental tone.[30] The tone of the poem is not, therefore, primarily conjured up from the mind of the poet but nonetheless resonates throughout the poem, lending it a wholeness or coherence that in some sense delimits being in the very self-sufficiency of the poem itself. To this end, Heidegger says in his first lecture course on Hölderlin, given in the winter semester of 1934–5, that 'the poet speaks from out of a tone ... this tone we call the fundamental tone of poetry ... this fundamental tone gives us the world, which is delimited in its being by poetic language (*der Dichter aus einer Stimmung spricht ... Diese Stimmung nennen wir die Grundstimmung der Dichtung ... die Grundstimmung eröffnet die Welt, die im dichterischen Sagen das Gespräge des Seyns empfängt*)' [GA 39: 79].

It is the notion of *Stimmung* that allows Heidegger to avoid the idea of the muse or divine inspiration being the 'cause' of the poem, and of the poet as somehow being involved in a causal nexus. Instead, our focus shifts to the poet's passive attunement to being, due to which the fundamental mood of the poet's relation to being is disclosed in the fundamental tone of the poem, to which the reader is able to attune herself. It is this notion of tone that Heidegger draws to our attention in his essay 'Homecoming/To Kindred Ones', written in 1943, where he says that 'Joyfulness is composed into the poem. The joyful is tuned by joy into joy. In this way it is what is rejoiced in, and equally what rejoices. And this again can bring joy to others' [EHP 34]. In other words, in the tone of the poem 'Homecoming', Hölderlin (as poet) is revealed as given over to the joy of what it is to be a poet in the very composing of the poem, as in its composing the poet is brought into proximity with being, is attuned to being joyfully. This joyful attunement is brought forth in Hölderlin's poetic word, to which he is called and which he brings forth in the poem as a way of dwelling in being.

A question that immediately springs to mind is which arises first, the fundamental attunement to being or the poetic word that delimits it? In Hölderlin's poem 'Homecoming', for example, is it the joyful attunement (as revelatory of the poet's being as given over to a world that is abandoned by being) or is it the poetic word that gives voice and limit to this attunement? The answer is neither, as this would be to lapse into thinking about the poem as if it were part of a causal nexus. For Heidegger, both the attunement to being *and* the poetic word that delimits it arise simultaneously and stand in a fugal rather than a linear relation, a point to which I shall return when I come to discuss Heidegger's notion of the *Geviert*.

For the reader, then, it is in the tone of the poem that the world is revealed anew and revealed not so much *in* the poetic word as *through* it, which is to say that the language of the poem does not set the poem's tone – rather, the tone gives rise to the arrangement of the words in the poem. This is important insofar as it signals that poetic revelation cannot be reduced to what the poem means, to what is represented in the language of the poem (as that which is already in the world), because what is given rise to in the poetic word, i.e. through the tone, comes to the fore only insofar as it is arises in the singularity of the poem. We get a sense of what Heidegger is driving at here in his description of another type of artwork in 'The Origin' – namely, a painting by Van Gogh of a pair of peasant's shoes. There, Heidegger accounts for the truth of the shoes purely in terms of how they *occur in the painting* and not by referring to the 'real' shoes in the 'real' world and how they are represented in the work.[31] Similarly, it is in the singularity that the poem's true significance similarly comes to light, giving rise to the possibility of the reader's re-attunement to being. The poem does this by unsettling the reader's normal attitude to language by drawing her into the poem as a form of language that directly addresses her, seeking her active engagement in language as the revelation of being. This is because the tone of the poem reveals language as essentially the opening up of a meaning that it names but cannot contain, and thereby the opening up of new possibilities for *Dasein* as that being that is essentially in language. It is, therefore, the singularity of the poem that draws attention to language as the attunement of human beings to being in language, and to language as the opening up of a place to dwell within being as such, of the possibility of experiencing being as a happening, an unfolding – in short, as historical. Language here cannot be considered as a means to an end, but as the opening up of the possible in relation to what is named, that is, being. And, as Heidegger tells us as early as *Being and Time*: 'Higher than actuality stands *possibility*' [BT 63].

One final point needs to be raised here. In the poem, the poet is involved in the possibility of an essential naming (i.e. of originating truth and thereby of giving rise to a world and opening up a new historical epoch). I say the possibility of an essential naming as language is, and as Heidegger reminds us (in citing a letter of Hölderlin's) 'the most dangerous of goods' [EHP 54]. What does Heidegger mean by this? He says in 'Hölderlin and the Essence of Poetry':

> It is the danger of all dangers because it first creates the possibility of danger. Danger is the threat that beings pose to being itself. [...] Language first creates the manifest place of this threat to being, and the confusion and the possibility even of the loss of being, that is – danger. Language is charged with the task of making beings manifest and preserving them as such – in the linguistic work. Language gives expression to what is most pure and most concealed, as well as what is confused and common. Indeed, even the essential word, if it is to be understood and so become the common possession of all, must make itself common. [...] The word as word never offers any immediate guarantee as to whether it is an essential word or a deception.
>
> [EHP 55]

This is significant not just insofar as it points to the role that language plays in the unfolding of truth (*aletheia*) as an historical event (*Ereignis*) whereby the poetic word grounds truth in being and thereby opens up being to questioning, as it also opens up being to the possibility of its own oblivion. In Heidegger's view, as we are aware, the history of the West attests to the oblivion of being as it stands within modernity. However, the threat to being that results in its oblivion is implicit in the poetic word as such, and so stands over any possible future history for *Dasein*. This is due to the fact that language intrinsically threatens being insofar as it delimits being in the word, it gives measure to being in *logos*, which in turn can lead *Dasein* astray. As the site at which being is brought to measure in *logos*, *Dasein* holds sway over being as the rational being that secures truth and so can be led easily into thinking that as a being it secures all that comes into being. Further, language, as essentially poetic, i.e. as founding being,[32] is capable of a 'falling away' in which what is founded in the original naming power of the word disappears from view in the day-to-day commerce of language. Heidegger reveals this in his own retrieval of what he sees as the essential words of the Western tradition, a retrieval that seeks to uncover the original relation of language to being in ancient Greece and how this relation is subsequently covered over by the tradition.

Hence, Heidegger does not draw our attention to the dangers inherent in language simply for the sake of pointing out what has already happened to the West, but as a warning as to what the future might hold. It is a warning to those of us who are potential hearers of Hölderlin's poetic word, and therefore potential thinkers and questioners of what this word tells us about being. It is a call to be on our guard in the way that we approach the poetic word and its facility for revealing the open region of being. It is a pointing out of the fact that 'Metaphysics belongs to the nature of man' [EP 87]. Seen in this light, it can be viewed as Heidegger's call to modern humanity to think being in terms of *Gelassenheit* (releasement), the authentic attunement of *Dasein* to being whereby 'the nature of thinking, namely, releasement to the open-region (*Gegnet*),[33] would be a resolve for the coming forth of truth's nature' [DT 81, trans. mod.]. In other words, *Gelassenheit* signifies a form of calmness or restraint in the face of that which comes into being. Yet this is no passive restraint that Heidegger here has in mind, and *Gelassenheit*, as Bret W Davis argues, is not a straightforward notion but functions in such a way in Heidegger's thought that it has more than one phase to it.[34] It is – and as I have already noted in relation to Nietzsche's thought – a twisting free of *Dasein* from a willing relation to being into one in which a 'letting be' of being takes place. But it also has a more positive aspect, one in which one is not simply released from willing but one is released *for that which is sent* (by being, in the word). As Heidegger puts it, 'authentic releasement consists in this: that man in his very nature belongs to the open-region, i.e., he is released to it' [DT 82, trans. mod.]. Thus *Dasein*, in the attunement that is *Gelassenheit*, takes up a resolute openness (*Entschlossenheit*) to what is sent by being, which amounts to a thoughtful standing within the openness of being (as it unfolds) in order to properly appropriate it. In other words, *Dasein* becomes properly historical (*Geschichtlich*).

Jennifer Anna Gosetti-Ferencei sees a problem in Heidegger's readings of Hölderlin that arises out of his retreat from what would be an acutely phenomenological approach to the poems in favour of viewing them as founding a new history of being (*Seinsgeschichte*).[35] Gosetti-Ferencei argues, rightly, that Heidegger's *seinsgeschichtliche* approach to Hölderlin, which leads him to view the poet as a 'sign', means that Heidegger 'desubjectifies' the poet and so reduces him to the role of mediator of poetic language (as the saying of being). Problematically, Gosetti-Ferencei maintains, this means that Hölderlin, in undergoing a poetic experience in the poem, simply disappears. Consequently, as there is no place for the 'I' in the poem (i.e. no factical content) as far as Heidegger is concerned, then there is no individual that undergoes the poetic experience, there is only the poetic as such – that is, historical happening.

Viewed in this light, Gosetti-Ferencei argues, Heidegger disregards an essential element of Hölderlin's poetry – namely, the struggle of the 'poetic self'. Here, the self is not to be understood in terms of the human subject as the referential centre of beings, but as the disjointed and distressed being of a self, 'theoretically ungraspable, but factically and politically "real"'.[36] This element, which Gosetti-Ferencei takes mainly from Hölderlin's philosophical and theoretical writings, reveals a poetic corpus that is concerned with the poet transcending his own rational subjectivity through the poetic word in the hope of opening up a new relation to the world, and thereby opening up the question of being in terms of what it means to be an 'I', in notions such as the soul, the spiritually real, 'real' life, experience, feelings etc., as well as the nature of the poetic. Gosetti-Ferencei goes so far as to suggest that 'the elusiveness of being is discovered as the point of departure for a subjectivity not left behind but unravelled, not irrelevant to poetry but rather poetized'.[37]

Such a reading is important insofar as Hölderlin's poetry is revealed as the attempt of the human subject to seek unity with being - a (ultimately impossible) unity that stands as a lack at the heart of human subjectivity – through the poetic word. This task, not dissimilar to Heidegger's insofar as it seeks to undermine the metaphysical opposition of the subject and the object through a 'poetological' access to being, leads to a very different interpretation of how Hölderlin's poems function. The elements of Hölderlin's poetic composition, for example the use of metaphor, allegory and syntax, are on this account essential to the poem's composition. These formal characteristics, which for Heidegger have a derivative significance given that what is essential to the poem concerns its ontological, rather than its philological significance, become key on Gosetti-Ferencei's account insofar as they are constitutive of a poetic experience in which human subjectivity is transcended through the elevation of the poet to the poem, a moment in which the human subject is 'obliterated'.

What I think Gosetti-Ferencei's account overlooks, however, is that for Heidegger the lack of a subject does not mean the lack of a 'self'. And a self, to be sure, is never essentially an 'I' but is conceived as *a way of being* for *Dasein*. Heidegger says as early as *Being and Time* that we should refrain from treating *Dasein* as a subject and that any 'apprehensiveness however which one may have about this gets its nourishment from the perverse assumption that the entity in question has at bottom the kind of being which belongs to something present-at-hand, even if one is far from attributing to it the solidity of an occurrent corporeal Thing. Yet man's "*substance*" is not spirit as a synthesis of soul and body; it is rather *existence*' [BT 153]. In other words, the human being is essentially ecstatic for Heidegger, it finds its 'I' in what it does and what it does is to give itself over to the happening (*Ereignis*) of being. It is in this happening (and we are talking here about *Dasein* at its most authentic) that the 'I' is discovered as the 'self', understood purely in terms of its experience of its existence insofar as it relates to other beings. This means that in the case of Hölderlin he is at his most authentic when he is *as* a poet, for when he is given over to his poetry he is given over to the happening of being as it relates to beings.

Michael E Zimmerman raises a familiar point about a Heidegger reading with regard to Hölderlin in his *Heidegger's Confrontation with Modernity*, but it is one that is worthy of a little deeper scrutiny in this case. Zimmerman says of Heidegger's reading that 'one is never sure whether Heidegger or Hölderlin is speaking, although Heidegger would have asserted that "the matter itself" (*die Sache selbst*) was speaking'.[38] Zimmerman speaks of Heidegger's commentaries on both Nietzsche and Hölderlin, referring to them in terms of the complexity and violence they do to the texts of both thinkers. The key to these readings, however, is that both thinkers' thought is what Heidegger terms untimely (*unzeitgemäß*), that is, their thought is attuned to being in such a way that it is properly historical (*Geschichte*). In being properly historical, thought gives measure to time rather than finding a direct resonance (*Widerklang*) in its own time, it is never *essentially* fashionable, but it can find an inner harmony with the history of a people or even give rise to it.³⁹ Zimmerman's point is that in a Heideggerian reading there is a thoughtful confrontation in which thought itself happens as a means in which being itself is brought forth through and for thinking. This can lead, Zimmerman says, to a reading that is 'at times selective and idiosyncratic, refracted through the optic of Heidegger's specific philosophical and political concerns'.⁴⁰

These concerns lead Heidegger, in the case of Hölderlin, to treat the poems as the happening of language as the revelation of being, whereby it is only the poem itself that can tell us what it means. And we should be minded at this point that poetry and philosophy are not the same. If the history of Western thought reveals anything to the scrutiny of the watchful eye, it is the univocity of philosophical thinking, which sees language as a means to an ends, as a way of communicating (meaningful content). Poetic language differs – it is the happening of the essential word. Indeed, it is the singularity of a call to language and into an open relation to being which in itself cannot be contained in the word, but which can only be approached through the poetic saying. Thus truth in the poem essentially goes unsaid, but is brought to light in the poetic saying, and thereby opens up being to the scrutiny of the thinker.⁴¹

Bearing this in mind, it is not difficult to see why Heidegger gives selective and idiosyncratic readings. As Timothy Clark points out, it also explains the resistance of Heidegger's readings of Hölderlin to any broad re-reading or generalization that can be reduced to something that the reader already understands, i.e. it cannot be 'decoded'.⁴² Heidegger's readings of Hölderlin's poetry are dependent on the *happening* of the essential word, in which what is named is not objectified but is a path for thought to follow, and the poet is revealed (as sign) not simply as a subject but as standing in a non-subjective relation to being. Thus Heidegger does not talk of the poet as transcending his subjectivity in terms of existing between being and beings, but in terms of the poet existing between the gods and mortals, called into the openness of being. Being itself is revealed, in the naming of the poet, as 'the holy', to the extent that a 'brightness extends into the solitary souls of those poets who are embraced by the holy and belong to it' [EHP 86]. The site between the gods and mortals is termed the 'between', and names the point of transcendence in which the poet (and therefore the human being) stands in the openness of being. The between is also the river that allows man to dwell on earth, and the *stay* in time that allows that which comes into and goes out of being to come to presence. It is the here and now in which the hints of the gods are heard, and the poet names these in his essential word, thereby founding truth and sending forth an historical fate. Thus, a Heideggerian reading resists the reduction that is common to modern philosophical and aesthetic analysis which tries to extract a content that then can be easily assimilated into a categorical schema. Instead, a Heideggerian reading points to an engagement with the poem as singular and so to that which can only be understood in terms of itself. As a result, any interpretation will be singular.

One final point that is worth noting is raised by Gosetti-Ferencei. She suggests that Heidegger's analysis of how truth functions means that the poetic word is capable of founding both truth and error. This is because truth, for Heidegger, is thought aletheically, that is, as the disclosure of being which is intrinsically bound to the withdrawal of being. Hence, truth is a twofold structure of disclosure and withdrawal – of truth and error intertwined. This means that if Hölderlin's poetry founds a new truth and so a new history, then the decision that this opens up for historical *Dasein* (i.e. whether or not to submit to a departure from metaphysics as announced by the poet) is also *essentially* prone to error. Gosetti-Ferencei's main concern in raising this point is to see if it is possible to locate an ethical content in the occurrence of error and to assign responsibility for individual errors – given error is only part of the occurrence (*Ereignis*) of disclosure, which in turn renders silent any specific factual content.[43]

Whilst Gosetti-Ferencei's concerns and conclusions do not specifically interest us here, she does bring to light an important point regarding Hölderlin's poetry as the point at which a new beginning to Western history is claimed on Heidegger's part. This lies in the revelation that Hölderlin's poetry is a form of remembrance (as shall be shown below) in which *Dasein*'s metaphysical relation to being is revealed in its historical origins as finite. As such, the founding of truth is revealed – as I have just noted – as consisting in both disclosure and hiddenness. Truth, therefore, is revealed in its historical unfolding as a relation to being whereby being is revealed in a way that has error as an essential part of this unfolding. This means that the possibility for a new beginning or history is originated in a way that being is necessarily opened up and sustained in this openness in a question-worthy way – the question of being becomes the question of the meaning of being as that which simultaneously conceals itself in its unconcealment.

## Hölderlin's word as the fate of the West

If, as Heidegger maintains, language is revealed in the poem as the way in which being comes to presence *as* that which exceeds language, and if thereby the human being is revealed as standing in an open relation to being, then the poem reveals language as the site in which the human being dwells. As the site of human dwelling language is thus seen to involve *Dasein* in the happening of being as the unfolding of truth (in an ongoing tension between what presences and what refuses to presence). Hence, the poetic word reveals language as the way in which being occurs historically (*Geschichtlich*). History, here understood in the sense of *Geschichte*, is not only the fundamental happening of the history of a people in relation to being (in distinction from *Historie* as an account of the manifestation of this history), it is also a destiny (*Geschick*) that is sent to a people when a new relation of *Dasein* to being is opened up, a destiny that in itself is not wholly given to a people but only gradually comes to light as it unfolds historically. The question is, as a poet who speaks the essential word of being, in what way does Hölderlin's poetic word open up such a relation – that is, in what sense does it originate a destiny for the West? Heidegger writes:

> Hölderlin puts into poetry the very essence of poetry – but not in the sense of a timelessly valid concept. This essence of poetry belongs to a definite time. But not in such a way that it merely conforms to that time as some time already existing. Rather, by providing anew the essence of poetry, Hölderlin first determines a new time. It is the time of the gods who have fled *and* of the god who is coming. It is the *time of need* because it stands in a double lack and a double not: in the no-longer of the gods who have fled and in the not-yet of the god who is coming. […] The essence of poetry

which is founded by Hölderlin is historical in the highest degree because it anticipates a historical time. As a historical essence; however, it is the only true essence.

[EHP 64]

As I have noted already, the essential word of the poem creates its own context. What it makes manifest in the word is the fundamental attunement of the poet to the historical destiny of being as it relates to *Dasein*, and as such, it speaks not only out of the past but brings what has been into the present and consequently speaks to the future. It does this because the poetic word is the *essential* word, it speaks of essence, and in Hölderlin's poetic word this essence is revealed in the fundamental tone of his poems through what George Pattison refers to as the 'elegiac mood'.[44] In poetry, the elegiac mood speaks of a sense of loss and is pitched in a tone that is both mournful and wistful. The sense of loss that is to be found in Hölderlin's poems speaks of the loss or absence of the gods, an absence that Jacques Taminiaux suggests is Heidegger's way of revealing the truth of the German people in the mid-1930s, a way that also opens up the German people to a decision about its historical destiny.[45] This sense of loss, however, can only be understood properly in relation to Hölderlin's ongoing dialogue with the ancient Greeks, a dialogue that is marked by Hölderlin's reverence for them as the initiators of Western thought, a dialogue that is as important for Hölderlin as it is for Heidegger.[46]

Briefly, this is brought into relief particularly if we compare Heidegger's engagement with Hölderlin alongside his engagement with Nietzsche, both of which are at their most intense from the mid-1930s to the mid-1940s. Of course, Nietzsche's thought was also greatly concerned with the ancient Greeks, which is evident from as early as his first book *The Birth of Tragedy from the Spirit of Music*. Here, Nietzsche locates in the movement from the Greek tragic view of life to the philosophical thinking of Socrates (and Plato) the origins of a falling away from the strength and creative power of the Greek world to that of the present world as one dominated by a kind of enervating rationalism. But whereas Nietzsche turns to the ancient Greeks in order to retrieve a sense of truth as essentially tragic and does so by conceiving of the

Greek god Dionysos as a kind of trans-historical creative life force that has disappeared from view in modernity, for Hölderlin, the absence of the Greek gods is a decisive point in Western history. This is why Heidegger's thought turns increasingly from an appropriation of Nietzsche's as still allied to the history of metaphysics, to an appropriation of Hölderlin's thought as freeing itself from this history and so genuinely pointing out the possibility of a new beginning, of a new historical epoch. This is because as far as Hölderlin is concerned, the Greek gods have fled; they are no longer within reach, which interestingly enough for Heidegger means that in Hölderlin's poetry the gods are present as 'having-been'.

As this brings us to the essential word of Hölderlin's poetry, it is a good point at which to note what Heidegger means by 'essence'. From the past participle of the German verb 'to be' (*sein*) we get *gewesen*, which in turn gives us the German philosophical term for essence (*Wesen*) that is sometimes translated as 'being'. Hence, for Heidegger, essence is what has-been (*das Gewesene*). What has-been is not, however, simply something that has happened in the past. As that which is essential, what has-been also has a fundamental bearing on that which is yet to come, on the future. Thus, it would be more correct to say that essence, for Heidegger, names that which is passing (in its having-been and its yet-to-be), and that what is passing is essentially brought to presence in Hölderlin's poetry as the absence of the gods. Why is this significant? Why should we be concerned with the absence of the ancient Greeks gods? It is because, as Heidegger says in the late 1930s in his *Contributions to Philosophy*: 'God is so far removed from us that we are incapable of deciding whether it is moving toward us or away from us' [C 17]. In other words, the absence of the gods reveals modernity as a time that has no measure, no history – no essential truth to guide it. All that *is* is reduced to that which is the case and nothing more, i.e. positivism. Hereby, the revelation of the absence of the gods in Hölderlin's poetic word speaks to the future by founding a new time, 'the time of the gods who have fled *and* of the god who is coming'.

Moreover, that the poet speaks of the absence of the gods means that the poet involves himself in a form of remembrance or recollection (*Andenken*). According to Heidegger, 'poetry is remembrance. Remembrance is founding'

[EHP 172], and as a founding, Heidegger argues, remembrance must therefore be a form of 'thinking of' (*Andenken an*) something. Remembrance as a form of 'thinking of' something, however, must not be mistaken for thinking as a way of clinging to the past. Instead, 'thinking of' here indicates a way of thinking about what is yet to come, to which end Heidegger says that '"thinking of" what is yet to come can only be "thinking of" what has been, which, in distinction to what is simply past, we understand as what is still coming into presence from afar' [EHP 109]. Consequently, in recollecting the Greek gods and so making them present in their absence, Hölderlin's poetic word brings forth the origins of *Dasein*'s metaphysical relation to being as the origins of being's occlusion in modernity. Heidegger's point here is not, of course, to draw to our attention some idyllic time when *Dasein* was 'at one' with being. Rather, Heidegger's point is that Hölderlin's poetry reveals the finite nature of the metaphysical history of *Dasein*, and in so doing opens up a relation to being that offers more thoughtful, historical possibilities for *Dasein* to be.

In accordance with what I have just said, Heidegger thinks that in determining a new time by standing out into the not-yet and the no-longer, Hölderlin opens up a space in being which allows for a decision (*Entscheidung*) to be taken about being. Such a decision is in no sense determined by Hölderlin's work but rather, as Heidegger tells us in 'The Origin', decision 'is grounded in something that cannot be mastered, something concealed, something disconcerting. Otherwise it would never be a decision' [OBT 31]. The decision that Hölderlin's work opens up for modernity is the decision about a new beginning, about whether or not to take a stance outside of metaphysics, about opening up future possibilities in which *Dasein* will be able to stand in relation to being – a relation that is revealed in Hölderlin's poetry as destinal, rather than determinate. And it is through the notion of decision that Heidegger can make the case for distinguishing the difference between the poet and the thinker. If the poet partakes in the opening up of a new destiny for humanity, then it is the thinker's task to make sense of what this destiny means, i.e. to think being and the possible ways that *Dasein* can be. Yet the idea of decision here excludes any notion of choice – nothing here is predeterminable, that is, one does not simply choose from the options on offer in the certainty of what the outcome shall be. The thinker stands in the openness of being tasked with deciding what it is that is *essentially founded* in the poetic word. As such, the matter of making a decision is, for the thinker, permeated with difficulty as it belongs to the historical unfolding of truth. This means that *Dasein* is unable to guarantee the outcome of its decisions as they are taken against a background in which being, as that which is brought to the essential word of the poet, mysteriously draws away from its essential naming. Consequently, what is left to *Dasein* as it stands in modernity is to turn towards what is referred to by Bret W Davis as an 'attentive waiting (which) is a thoughtful remembrance, a restrained comportment, an indwelling forbearance, which steadfastly stays within being as the open region or "abiding expanse" that requires our thoughtful participation for the appropriating events of its clearing of truth'[47] – that is, *Gelassenheit*.

Talk of the presence and absence of the gods brings to mind Véronique M Foti's criticism of Heidegger's interpretation of Hölderlin's poetry as rejecting outright 'allegory, symbol, simile and example as attesting to representational thinking (whilst) his own reading tacitly avails itself of these interpretive structures,'[48] citing Heidegger's *Hölderlin's Hymn 'Der Ister'* [GA 53: 16] in evidence. Yet whilst it is true that Heidegger rejects such notions as belonging to the work of art thought aesthetically, that is, as something sensuous that 'stands in' for something else, it is also true that for Heidegger the absent gods of Hölderlin's poetry are not symbolic images standing in for something that has a 'higher' or 'deeper' content. What is required here is an ontological, rather than a philological interpretation of Hölderlin's poetry. To this end it can be said that speaking strictly in a symbolic sense, the Greek gods of Hölderlin bring to the word the sensuous image of something that in itself is non-sensuous, i.e. it indicates a meaning that is not to be found in the work of poetry itself. This non-sensuous element is further defined by Heidegger as pointing towards 'a spiritual content' and thence the framework for the distinction between the sensuous and non-sensuous elements of the artwork, elements 'which are normative for the Western world, (and which first) occurred in Plato's thought' [GA 53: 18].

Hence, the symbolic is located within the distinction between the sensuous and the non-sensuous, a distinction that Heidegger views as originating in Platonic thought, in which the world of lived experience has less reality, less being, than that of the Ideal realm, the former only making sense in terms of the latter. Hence, the Ideal realm is where unchanging truth is to be found, and the changing world of experience (in which things are not truly what they appear to be) is only true in relation to this realm. This structure of understanding being, which lies at the heart of metaphysics, eventually reveals itself as what Heidegger terms 'ontotheology'. Ontotheology is Heidegger's interpretation of metaphysics as that by which being (*Sein*) is understood in terms of a highest being (*ein höchstes Seiendes*) whose being determines the being of beings (*das Seiende*).[49] For our current purposes, this means that the non-sensuous, symbolic god of artistic representation is nothing less than the attempt to make manifest that which explains the mysteriousness that lies at the heart of being – it is the metaphysical drive to grasp the ungraspable by bringing it to presence.

On the other hand, for Heidegger, the absent god comes to presence in Hölderlin's poetry in terms of the hint (*Wink*) to which the attentive poet is called and responds with his essential word. However, in responding to the hint the poet does not represent the god in his word, nor does he symbolize or make present that which is hinted at. Instead, Hölderlin names in his essential word 'the last god' (*der letzte Gott*) which 'has its *essential swaying* within the hint, the onset and staying-away of the arrival as well as the flight of the gods who have been, and within their settled and hidden transformation' [C 288]. In other words, the last god consists in the hint – is hinted at in the poetic word – and as such the last god *is* only insofar as it is a 'passing by' (*Vorbeigang*), i.e. essentially ephemeral. This is significant as it allows Heidegger to distance the notion of the god in Hölderlin's poetry from that of the Christian god of symbolic art. Whereas the Christian god is infinite and consequently gives meaning to the finite, Hölderlin's god is significant insofar as it comes to presence in the poem as that which is fleeting and ungraspable. As such, the last god is revealed as finite and does not come to a rest in presence but instead remains hidden from *Dasein*, revealing only a trace of itself in the poetic word. The question arises, from where does this last god hint, to what realm does it belong?

Heidegger's answer is that we get a hint of the gods from the realm of the holy (*das Heilige*), the seriousness of which he conveys in the 'Letter on Humanism':

> How can the human being at the present stage of world history ask at all seriously and rigorously whether the god nears or withdraws, when he has above all neglected to think into the dimension of the holy, which indeed remains closed as a dimension if the open region of being is not cleared and in its clearing is near to humans. Perhaps what is distinctive about this world-epoch consists in the closure of the dimension of the hale [*das Heilen*]. Perhaps that is the sole malignancy [*Unheil*].
>
> [PM 267]

And yet the god sends hints from the dimension of the holy. How can this be? The hint that the poet brings to the essential word 'beckon(s) us toward that from which they unexpectedly bear themselves toward us' [OWL 26]. That is, the hints of the god are sent from and reveal that which is concealed, that which refuses to presence but which reveals itself in this refusal – namely, the holy. The poet is able to attune himself to the hints and thereby brings to light the holy in its absence. As such, the poet brings into relief the holy as that which makes possible the appearance of the divine but which is simultaneously beyond the grasp of calculative thinking. It is the hinting of that which refuses to presence that draws the poet into a relation to the (absent) god and thereby reveals that which is absent as the ground for the appearance of the god and *Dasein* in a mutual relation. On the other hand, the revelation of the mutual relation in which *Dasein* stands towards the absent god speaks of the inability of modern humanity to experience the holy as that which grounds this relation. What does this mean for the function of the god in Hölderlin's poetry?

Heidegger's view of the last god does not mean he sees it in the sense of the final one of a series of gods, but it is rather 'meant as the allusion to the undecidability of the being of gods' [C 308]. Heidegger thus speaks to the historical finitude of god, of a god that does not stand over the history of being (as its creator) but instead is subject to this very history. This, in turn, points to the lack of an experience of the holy, to the absence of a space in which the gods can appear. Consequently, Heidegger tells us that

> the holy, which alone is the essential sphere of divinity, which in turn alone affords a dimension for the gods and for God, comes to radiate only when being itself beforehand and after extensive preparation has been cleared and experienced in its truth.
>
> [PM 258]

Thus the last god speaks to the future as well as the past. It reveals a decisive moment in history in which the question of the passing of god comes to light as the question of the meaning of being. It is a question about whether a god can arise once more and, if so, in what relation it would stand to *Dasein*. In turn, this suggests the possibility of a new relation to being as the hints of the gods are suggestive of something that lies beyond that which is merely present to calculative thought, namely, the holy. Thus the last god of Hölderlin's poetry calls *Dasein* into a thoughtful relation to being as the preparation for the possibility of the arrival of a new god.

We can see then that - far from being a symbolic representation that points to something that is absent from the poem – Heidegger views Hölderlin's god as opening up an historical possibility for *Dasein*. That Hölderlin's poetry is able to do this is due to its fundamental tone, to its elegiac mood as one of loss or of 'holy mourning', in which a world is opened up for thoughtful decision insofar as it speaks of the absence of the holy and an open relation to that which refuses to come to presence.

## The *Geviert*

To conclude, we come to Heidegger's final conception of the occurrence of truth, what he calls the *Geviert* (the fourfold). The *Geviert* is a concept that is built up over time in Heidegger's thought through his engagement with the work of Hölderlin, but it is one that is based on another of Heidegger's fundamental concepts, *Ereignis*, a concept we have already met in various guises throughout this text. *Ereignis*, as a concept, is first used by Heidegger as early as 1919,[50] but is only fully worked out by Heidegger during the 1930s, and is given its fullest account in his *Contributions to Philosophy*, a work finished in 1938 but not published until 1989. *Ereignis* is the happening of being as the historical unfolding of truth, to which *Dasein* is appropriated as to its ownmost, that is, to the disclosure of that which is as it *is*. As such, it is a way of experiencing truth in modernity as the oblivion of being. As we now recognize, the oblivion of being is not recognized as such by *Dasein*, and in modernity *Dasein*'s technological experience of being, *Gestell*, covers over this abandonment in its disclosure of being as the presence of beings as standing reserve. However, there are certain individuals who are able to experience this abandonment, and Hölderlin in particular brings this experience to light in his poetry as the absence of the gods.

Thus Hölderlin, in giving measure to the oblivion of being in his poetry, steps out into the holy and thereby becomes the 'between', the mediator between the gods and *Dasein*. In stepping into the between and acting as mediator, Hölderlin is able to bring *Dasein* and the gods (the latter *as* absent) into a mutual relation so that the truth of being is experienced (and thus *happens*) as the loss of being. As such, the gods hint to *Dasein* as something that lies beyond the merely present. This, of itself, opens up the possibility of a new beginning for *Dasein* (*Einsprung in das Dasein*) – not in the sense that *Dasein* undergoes an experience of truth – but to the extent that truth is opened up to thought as an historical happening.

Heidegger, in his later thought, goes on to envisage a possible happening of truth as it is founded in Hölderlin's poetry as what he calls the *Geviert*. The *Geviert* is Heidegger's vision of a fourfold happening of truth to which the poetic word gives measure or gathers together not only the divinities (present in remembrance) and mortals (*Dasein*) but also earth and sky. Together, these four amount to what Heidegger calls 'world'. As such, the *Geviert* is what allows beings to appear although neither in the sense of self-contained beings that are merely present, nor as links in a causal chain. Beings are here construed in their being as the fugal articulation[51] of the fourfold of earth, sky, divinities and mortals:

> Earth and sky, divinities and mortals – being at one with one another of their own accord – belong together by way of the simpleness of the united fourfold. Each of the four mirrors in its own way the presence of the others. Each therewith reflects itself in its own way into its own, within the simpleness of the four. This mirroring does not portray a likeness. The mirroring, lightening each of the four, appropriates their own presencing into simple belonging to one another. Mirroring in this appropriating-lightening way, each of the four plays to each of the others. The appropriative mirroring sets each of the four free into its own, but it binds these free ones into the simplicity of their essential being toward one another.
> 
> [PLT 177]

Thus the notion of the *Geviert* gives form to the possibility of how *Dasein* might come to dwell openly in being. It is world thought as the happening of truth in the sense of a new beginning. It is language thought essentially as a saying that points out beings (and so being) as 'food for thought'. As such, the *Geviert* names the intertwining of *Dasein* as the mortal who dwells on the abyssal ground of the earth, and earth as that which bears this dwelling. Further, this dwelling happens beneath the vault of the sky as that which brings to light this dwelling and so brings those who dwell face to face with the gods who (in their absence) hint at something mysterious that lies beyond the *Geviert*.[52] This something mysterious is what calls for decision, it is what allows *Dasein* to step out into the openness of being and question what it is to be.

What is more, in world thought in terms of the happening of truth as the *Geviert*, beings no longer appear as wholly present in themselves. Rather, beings show up as finite, they come to presence in the gathering of the fourfold which limits them to an ongoing articulation that obtains between the elements of sky, earth, mortals and gods. As gathered into the fourfold of these elements, beings cannot but show up as tied to the world, and that in such a way that any being is always related to something which lies outside itself. This is because what unifies the being in its essential coming to presence is also the source of its disunity – the fact that it is given over to that which lies beyond itself, to the happening of being as world as the interplay of sky, earth, mortals and gods. This means that beings are never self-identical, are never limited in their being in the sense that they come to an end. Instead, beings are now thought in terms of a coming into their own, as being set free to become what they are.

This is an appropriate juncture at which to raise a question to which Jeff Malpas gives voice, a question that is raised in much secondary literature on Heidegger with regard in particular to his engagement with Hölderlin, but also with his later thinking in general – namely, is what Heidegger is doing any longer philosophy?[53] Heidegger himself would not view such a question as in any sense a form of censure on his work. After all, Heidegger eventually comes to equate philosophy with metaphysics, and metaphysics as a mode of thinking that leads to nihilism and ends in the technological age's most extreme possibility as cybernetics.[54]

What is more, Heidegger does not involve himself in furthering any philosophical doctrine or building any philosophical 'system' around which other philosophers can take sides. Heidegger's thought is rather the task he sets for himself of attempting to lead Western thought out of metaphysics by returning to its origins to see if there is a possibility for thinking in a way that is other than metaphysical, 'a possibility from which the thinking of philosophy would have to start out, but which as philosophy it could nevertheless not experience and adopt' [TB 59]? Such a task leads Heidegger to view the origin of metaphysics as borne out of truth thought aletheically, that is, as the unconcealment of beings that has attached to it an essential concealment, a concealment that was not thought by the Greeks. This latter point means that philosophy, for Heidegger, is still worthy of thought as what goes unsaid in philosophy, what does not to come presence in metaphysics, is that on which what comes to presence rests. Seen in this light, Heidegger's turn to the poetic can be seen as borne out of his original philosophical task of questioning into the meaning of being.

# *Conclusion*

What I have tried to trace in the preceding chapters of this text is the movement in Heidegger's thought from the mid-1930s to the early 1940s. It is a movement that can be traced in the critical distancing of his own thought from that of Nietzsche's (as the thinker of nihilism, the last metaphysician) and in his positive appropriation of the poetry of Hölderlin (the poet whose word lies outside of metaphysics and thereby offers us the possibility of founding a new history). What underlies this engagement with the question of our historical destiny is Heidegger's struggle to free his own thought from the metaphysical traces he detected there in *Being and Time*. To this end Heidegger tells us in his 'Letter on Humanism' (written in 1947) that the third division of the first part of *Being and Time* (to be entitled 'Time and Being') was held back because language failed to think what Heidegger was trying to bring to light there. And what Heidegger wanted to say there is that the truth of *Dasein*'s being can only be thought in terms of its coming to be from out of the unfolding of being as such, and so talking about this phenomenon in terms of a temporal horizon of being runs the risk of making this horizon into an object for thought, making *Dasein* into a thinking 'subject' and thereby thinking *Dasein* and being from out of the traditional language of metaphysics.

What was needed was a new approach to thinking being and the point at which this thought occurs is revealed in Heidegger's *Black Notebooks*. In a note from 1932 Heidegger says:

> Today (March 1932) I am in all clarity at a place from which my entire previous literary output ... has become alien to me. Alien like a path brought to an impasse, a path overgrown with grass and vegetation – a path which yet retains the fact that it leads into Da-sein as temporality. A path whose

edges stands much that is contemporary and mendacious – often in such a way that these 'path markings' are taken as more important than the path itself.[1]

This sounds like an epiphany of a sort. That is, it sounds like Heidegger has come to a point in his thinking in which he recognizes that perhaps a trace of the metaphysics of presence still attaches itself to his thought and yet he is on a path that is still somehow worth pursuing. But what form his thought should take at this point Heidegger seems to be at a loss to pinpoint, concluding his quotation with the plaintive 'Yet why still record this, since to me myself the question is becoming ever more problematic'. However, only a few weeks later we get an idea of what this thinking might consist in when Heidegger says that 'the task is now: to win back the beginning – to question again within its most intrinsic questions'.[2] And then a little later still he says that this winning back of the beginning involves thinking in a struggle 'over the grasp of the beginning and over the acknowledgement of the unavoidableness of the act of beginning and thereby over the theme of a distant injunction – the catching up of the latter'.[3]

We can see in what Heidegger has to say here the rudimentary moves in a stepping back into a properly historical thinking or what Heidegger will come to refer to as a being-historical thinking (*Seinsgeschichtliches Denken*). Heidegger's recognition that his thought needs to take this turn means that he tries to work out what form his thinking should take throughout the rest of 1930s (and beyond) by thinking through *Dasein's* relation to being in a way in which being itself becomes more prominently focused on as the location of *Dasein* coming into the truth of its being (and so its historical situatedness) and *Dasein* itself moves increasingly out of focus and is thought more in terms of Da-sein (in which the emphasis is on how the human being belongs to the unfolding truth of being *and* how being is dependent on the human being for this truth to unfold).

This way of thinking human being's historical relation to being is most strikingly seen to develop in Heidegger's *Contributions to Philosophy* (1936–8) (which, it has been argued, is his second major work after *Being and Time*)[4] as well as in his texts *Mindfulness* (1938–9) and *The History of Beyng* (1938–40).

Here Heidegger's thought develops along a path that introduces the historical notions of a first and an other beginning (as already noted) in which he tries to render a non-traditional experience of thinking being. It is an experience of thinking which leads us away from the idea of being as an horizon towards which *Dasein* transcends and towards the idea of being as a 'happening' (*Ereignis*) that provides the possibility for *Dasein* to make decisions about its own historical destiny. Further, such a happening should be understood in terms of a turning (*Kehre*) that takes place *within being* itself. This turning reveals *Dasein* in its being as thrown into the truth of being (thought in terms of an open relation to things), a thrownness for which Dasein must take responsibility (in terms of keeping open this relation to things). Hence the truth of being is seen as arising through *Dasein* as that being which allows for this truth to come into the open (and to which *Dasein* belongs). In the interplay between the two (which necessarily involves, amongst other things, an ongoing hiddenness and unhiddenness of the truth of being itself) history itself is able to arise and unfold. And it is the hidden possibilities that lie within this occurrence of history that Heidegger seeks to bring to light in thought.

Having outlined the trajectory of Heidegger's thinking from the mid-1930s to the early 1940s what I intend to do now is examine how – despite seeking to distance his own thought from that of Nietzsche's through his positive engagement with Hölderlin from the same period – Heidegger's thought can be seen to be indebted to Nietzsche's and is presented in an increasingly similar and fragmented fashion. We shall begin by looking at what is going on with Nietzsche's texts.

## Nietzsche

*The effectiveness of the incomplete.* – Just as figures in relief produce so strong an impression on the imagination because they are as it were on the point of stepping out of the wall but have suddenly been brought to a halt, so the relief-like, incomplete presentation of an idea, of a whole philosophy, is sometimes more effective than its exhaustive realization: more is left for the beholder to do, he is impelled to continue working on that which appears before him so strongly etched in light and shadow, to think it through to the end, and to overcome even that constraint which has hitherto prevented it from stepping forth fully formed.[5]

Here Nietzsche, in his *Human, All Too Human* (1878) marks the transition from his earlier philological work to his much more experimental sojourns into philosophical observation and insight. As such, it gives us a clue as to how Nietzsche's philosophical mission will unfold in his so-called 'middle' and 'later' writings.[6] These texts will increasingly seek to view existence from the perspective of life (and thereby speak from out of and to our historical situation) and they will try to provoke a response in the reader (to this historical situation). To this end Nietzsche's texts give rise to thoughts and ideas that are not fully rationalized but instead confront the reader with a bluntness and singularity that seeks to shock her out of her everyday way of (metaphysical) thinking. Thus Nietzsche seeks to confront his reader in such a way that she has to respond to his thoughts from out of the singularity of her own lived experience.

That Nietzsche's texts seek to do this should come as no surprise at this point. We have already examined Nietzsche's notion of nihilism as defining our current historical situation as one in which finally the 'highest values devaluate themselves'.[7] What this amounts to is that the values that the West currently lives by and which arose historically in ancient Greek philosophy and Christianity have finally proved ruinous to this life itself: 'the desert grows' as Nietzsche warns us in his *Zarathustra*. This is because the values that have been placed on life take a detached, God-like perspective. Whether this is in terms of the search for universal truths or even the concepts we employ to have knowledge of the world, these values are applied to life from outside life itself – that is, they view life from the point of view of death. But as Nietzsche observes these values arose originally *out of lived experience* and can only properly be understood insofar as they are either beneficial or deleterious for life itself. And thus it is life itself that forms the basis and allows us the perspective from which any value can be properly evaluated.

It is with this in mind that Nietzsche turns to the more experimental forms of expression he gives to his thoughts as they unfold, either in the form of aphorisms, fragments, extended fragments, the allegorical and even poems.

The fragmentary nature of his thoughts, as they are grounded in life and therefore history, suits these more finite forms of expression. We can best see just how effective Nietzsche is in grounding his thoughts historically by looking to a couple of his most profound thoughts, the first of which is taken from a fragment from *The Gay Science* that we have already met with in Chapter 1:

> The madman jumped into their midst and pierced them with his eyes. "Whither is God?" he cried; "I will tell you. *We have killed him* – you and I. All of us are his murderers. But how did we do this? How could we drink up the sea? Who gave us the sponge to wipe away the entire horizon? What were we doing when we unchained this earth from its sun? Whither is it moving now? Whither are we moving? Away from all suns? Are we not plunging continually? Backward, sideward, forward, in all directions? Is there still any up or down? Are we not straying as through an infinite nothing"?[8]

Here we see Nietzsche – in stepping back from using the rational, neutral thinking of metaphysics – grounding his thought in life and so the flux of history. God is dead. This speaks directly to the present historical situation of the Western human being as living in the shadow of nihilism. Further, this is a truly historical thought as it understands our situation as having been arrived at from out of the flux of our historical past as it originates with the ancient Greeks. And it also speaks to the future as being directionless as a result of this historical unfolding. Indeed, one could say that Nietzsche here does not simply reflect on our historical situation but actually gives form to it, giving rise to a thought that actually effects our historical situation. This historical motivation can be seen in the way Nietzsche confronts his reader here. This is not systematic thinking but an historical thought expressed in a way that confronts the reader with a bluntness that not only provides food for thought but which seeks to elicit from the reader a direct response (to her current historical situation). There is something meaningful at stake here and Nietzsche seeks to stimulate the reader to look to her own life as a way of responding to this very situation.

As we can see, Nietzsche does not set out his thought that God is dead in terms of a persuasive argument but in terms of provocative imagery. The horizon has gone, the earth is detached from its sun, one wonders if there is any longer an up or down. All these images are intended to unsettle the reader from her everyday mode of thinking, to confront her with her historical situation and prompt her to a response. Sadly, for Nietzsche, the paragraph that follows this in his text shows the fundamental problem for a properly historical thinker as his audience is unable to hear what he has to say; it is still tied to the metaphysics of representational thinking. But Nietzsche has a response to this situation of his own:

Behold, I teach you the overhuman
The overhuman is the meaning of the earth. Let your will say: The overhuman *shall be* the meaning of the earth!

I entreat you, my brothers, *remain true to the earth*, and do not believe those who speak to you of superterrestrial hopes! They are prisoners, whether they know it or not(trans. mod.).[9]

The overhuman is Nietzsche's response to the death of God and opens up a future path for thought to travel along. The overhuman is a properly historical thought insofar as, to quote Ullrich Haase, it 'picks us up and moves us somewhere else'.[10] This kind of movement is not conveyed by systems or rational arguments but is a movement that is experienced in the whole of our being and is revealed, in the case of *Zarathustra*, in an allegorical tale steeped in the depths of history thought as the Eternal Return of the Same. What Nietzsche wants to do is prompt us to will the overhuman as the meaning of the world as the self-overcoming of the human being. This is because with the death of God that space beyond life towards which it directs itself and which gives life its meaning has disappeared. To give life back its direction means we must find this direction out of life itself – thus Nietzsche's thought of the overhuman is a future possibility towards which the human being can strive.

That Nietzsche is often criticized for not giving a clear conception of what the overhuman looks like shows the historical nature of this thought. As a historical thought the overhuman is also a finite thought. To make positive claims about the future would be to represent this future now – that is, it would be to make present something that has not yet become present. Thus the overhuman does not so much serve as a fixed goal for the self-overcoming human being but opens up a path whereby the human being can actively try to determine itself into the future.

Nonetheless (and as I have argued), Heidegger views Nietzsche's thought as historical insofar as it brings the history of metaphysics to a conclusion. Nietzsche's thought cannot escape this history as his notion of the overhuman, based as it is on being thought as the *Will to Power*, places a value on being as such and so the question of being itself disappears from view. However, a historical thinker whose thought Heidegger does think resides outside the history of metaphysics is Hölderlin. So we will turn briefly to see the positive influence his poetic word had on Heidegger during this period insofar as the latter steps back from metaphysical thinking (in distancing himself from Nietzsche) and into a being-historical thinking.

## Hölderlin

In *Contributions to Philosoophy* Heidegger has this to say about his philosophy and its relation to Hölderlin's poetic word:

> At present and in the future the essential grasping of the concept of philosophy ... is *historical* grasping ... "Historical" here means: belonging to the essential swaying of be-ing itself, enjoined unto the distress of the truth of be-ing and thus bound into the necessity of that decision which on the whole has at its disposal what is ownmost to history and its essential swaying. Thereupon philosophy is now primarily preparation for philosophy in the manner of building the nearest forecourts in whose spatial configuration Hölderlin's word becomes hearable and is replied to by Da-*sein* and in such a reply becomes grounded as the language of future man. It is only in this way that man enters the next, steady, and narrow walkway to be-ing. [C 258]

Thus Heidegger's thought regarding the opening up of an other history is seen to be directly tied to Hölderlin's poetic word as the founding of a new time which is, as has already been noted, 'the time of the gods who have fled *and* of the god who is coming' [EHP 64], a time which lies beyond the history of metaphysics. Indeed, Heidegger sees in Hölderlin's poetic word a properly historical dimension of thought: it reveals the past in the form of the absent gods; it shows us our current historical situation as one in which we are no longer at home within being and it is suggestive of the future as the opening up of a space within being for the preparation of a new god. Hölderlin's word is properly historical because it has a dimension that is missing from that of metaphysical thought: it reveals being as emerging into to the light *from out of the dark*. Hence being, in its unhiddenness, is revealed as having an element of hiddenness attached to it. Further, Heidegger argues that Hölderlin's poetry is able to open up a new time to the extent that he is able to intercept the hints (*Winke*) of the absent gods, hints which in themselves suggest the mystery that lies beyond that which is merely present. Moreover, beings themselves show up in Hölderlin's poetry aletheically, that is, not as things that are simply on-hand but in the way that they actually *are* – as strange, as unfamiliar, as having darkness attached to them. In this way Hölderlin, according to Heidegger, opens up our historical situation as one which requires a decision with regard to the following: what kind of relation shall we sustain within being?

What we get a glimpse at from this analysis is that there is something going on with Hölderlin's poetry that is akin to Heidegger's notion of *Ereignis* to which Heidegger responds in his *Contributions to Philosophy*, *Mindfulness* and *The History of Beyng*. Indeed, according to Heidegger, the thinker responds to the singularity of the poet with a singularity of her own by taking a leap into (non-metaphysical) thought that does not guarantee the essential nature of the word as it is a leap into the abyss, into groundlessness. We can see this response in all three of the works just mentioned and I will now outline three important ways in which I think Hölderlin's poetry influences Heidegger's texts in a positive way.

To begin with, we see in Heidegger's attempts to step out of metaphysical thinking and into a being-historical thinking an attempt to decide, and to respond to, what is essentially founded in Hölderlin's poetic word. Thus the time of the absence of the gods that is given rise to in Hölderlin's poetry becomes for Heidegger a time of startled dismay (*Erschrecken*) at having been abandoned by being. Nonetheless, this is a distress that is historical insofar as it is transformational of our current historical situation.

Furthermore, there is something poietical going on with these texts as Heidegger seeks to think being in a non-representational way. That is, Heideggger seeks to think being not in the sense of a being but in the sense of it being no-thing (*das Nichts*). Thus being cannot be approached in any direct manner and so Heidegger instead seeks to make his reader undergo a genuine experience of language as that which allows being to be unconcealed in a way that reveals being as having concealment essentially attached to it. Thus Heidegger's singular use of language in these texts seeks to bring his reader into a situation in which being becomes question-worthy once again. It is really a poietic way of re-attuning his reader to language as an essential happening in which being is attended to instead of grasped, in which being is brought forth and simultaneously withdraws and so is a way of opening up being to thinking.

Finally, there is also something aletheic about these texts. In seeking to plunge himself and his readers into the essential sway of language Heidegger tries to bring forth being in a way that being emerges as essentially mysterious. What is more, the reader herself undergoes a strange experience in which she finds herself on uncertain and unfamiliar ground insofar as she engages with these texts in which being is suddenly question-worthy. This speaks to the task Heidegger sets himself in these texts which is for the reader to undergo an experience of being (through language) opened up as *Ereignis* in which the reader experiences herself as somehow given over to the sway of being insofar as she is able to catch a glimpse of the truth of being as being enowned by being.

Thus in moving away from Nietzsche as thinker and towards Hölderlin as poet Heidegger's own thought is transformed in such a way that it seeks to induce a properly historical experience of language (as a way of bringing to light being as *Ereignis*) in its readers. But what I now wish to draw attention to – and despite his movement away from Nietzsche in this period – is the indebtedness to Nietzsche of Heidegger's thought insofar as it seeks a properly historical grounding, insofar as it seeks a response to this grounding in its reader and even to the extent of the increasingly fragmentary way his thought is presented to its readers in the three texts with which we are concerned.

## Heidegger

In *The History of Beyng*, Heidegger tells us:

> '*The History of Beyng*' is the name for the attempt to place the truth of being as event back into the word of thinking, and thereby to entrust it to an essential ground of historical human beings – to the word and its sayability. Whether the attempted saying itself belongs to the event and thereby participates in the stillness of that which *is* without having an effect or requiring an effectiveness can never be discerned by calculation. But the attempt would necessarily remain entirely outside of its realm, if it were not to know that it would more appropriately be named: "*To the very threshold.*" And yet this hint once more diverts us away from the issue and toward the attempt to approach it.
>
> The simple, mature conjoining of the *Contributions* and *Mindfulness*; the *Contributions* remain a framework, yet without structural articulation; *Mindfulness* is a middle, but not the source. [HB §1]

Firstly, here we witness Heidegger linking his three major works from 1936–40 in a way that shows their shared purpose – to step out of metaphysical thinking and to try to bring thought into an historical relation to being. This mirrors the movement in Nietzsche's thought insofar as he tries to step away from the metaphysics of representation and into thought grounded in life and therefore in history. For Heidegger, however, he seeks to bring to light the turn he sees taking place in our relation to being and instead of grounding thought in life seeks to situate it in a new historical relation to being thought as *Ereignis*. As we saw in Chapter 2, *Ereignis* is being thought as an unfolding event which gives rise to and unfolds *as* history in which being (*Seyn*) relies on *Dasein* in order to hold sway and *Dasein* belongs to being as that which allows being to hold sway. Thus history is understood here as unfolding through the constant interplay between being and historical *Dasein*. This, for Heidegger, is how truth occurs and is thought no longer in terms of a horizon towards which *Dasein* transcends but as an openness in which *Dasein* is given over to the happening of being. Thus at the end of the history of metaphysics the possibility opens up of a new experience of being in which the forgottenness of being (*Seinsvergessenheit*) is overcome by making being question-worthy once more. In order to do this, however, Heidegger turns away from the language of metaphysics, the language of representation and towards language thought poietically. This use of language can also be seen to be indebted to Nietzsche insofar as Heidegger's texts are presented to the reader in increasingly experimental ways (even to the extent that Heidegger follows Nietzsche in his *Mindfulness* text by presenting some of his thoughts as poems).

In the language (and form) that Heidegger presents his thoughts in *Contributions to Philosophy*, *Mindfulness* and *The History of Beyng* we see him making his first steps along the path that will eventually lead him to say that 'language is the house of being. In its home man dwells' [BW 317]. It is language, thought poietically, that allows being to be revealed and to which *Dasein* as such belongs. Language is thus the essence of the human being and any transformed relation to being depends on a transformed relation to language. An example of how Heidegger attempts this transformation is given in his *Contributions to Philosophy*, a text in which Heidegger expresses his thoughts in the following manner in a fragment entitled 'The Essential Swaying of Truth':

> A deciding question is whether the essential swaying of truth as clearing for self-sheltering-concealing is grounded on Da-sein, or whether this essential swaying of truth itself is the ground for Da-sein – or whether both are true? And what does ground mean in each case?
>
> These questions are decidable only if what is shown as ownmost to truth is grasped as the truth of be-ing and thus in terms of enowning.
>
> What does it mean to be placed before *self-sheltering-concealing*, re-fusal, hesitation, and to be steadfast in their *open*? [It means] *reservedness* and thus grounding-attunement: startled dismay, reservedness, deep awe. Such [is] gifted only to man – whenever and however. [C §215]

The singularity of Heidegger's language in this fragment has something of the poietic about it. Indeed, all the fragments that make up *Contributions to Philosophy* are expressed in such a way that they invite, and benefit from, repeated interpretation. And what strikes the reader as the strangeness of the language that is employed here can be viewed as an attempt by Heidegger to do two things: to allow being to reclaim language in such a way that being becomes question-worthy once more; to allow the reader an authentic experience of language that goes beyond the traditional subject and object structure of metaphysical thought. Hence these fragments are *food for thought*.

What we see in the above fragment is Heidegger seeking to show how language – in allowing us to leap into the essential sway of being – brings being to light in a question-worthy way. Specifically, Heidegger brings into question truth thought out of being understood as *Ereignis*. Thus we are not presented here with assertions but with perplexities. What *is* the truth of being understood in terms of a dynamic historical relation in which being and Da-sein rely on each other in their coming into the open? Rather than providing the reader with an answer Heidegger here seems rather to be trying to stimulate in his reader an experience of a fundamental attunement (*Grundstimmung*) that speaks to our current historical situation, one in which the gods have flown.

Thus these fragments are rather like paths that open us up to an experience of our historical situation and so allow thought the possibility of following these openings within being in order to think being more authentically – that is, that allows being to be. Hence we see Heidegger's indebtedness to Nietzsche here insofar as the former mirrors the latter to the extent that these texts seek to transpose the reader into her historical situation and thereby induce in her a response to this situation by making this situation question-worthy.

Iain D Thomson, for one, minds us to be wary of direct comparisons with Nietzsche's aphoristic style. Following Heidegger's suggestion that *Contributions to Philosophy* is made up of a series of interlinked jointures (*Fügungen*) Thomson suggests that what is actually going on this text is nothing less than the application of the musical model of the fugue to philosophical expression.[11] What this amounts to is that through a series of interlinked reflections Heidegger is able to explore 'the fullest possible resonances of the polyphonic phenomenon of enowning (*Ereignis*)' in a way that helps the transition from the first to the other beginning. Hence these fugally linked reflections allow Heidegger, in a non-systematic way, to let his thought to fully explore the notion of being as *Ereignis*. There is little to disagree with here, even insofar as Heidegger's *Mindfulness* and *The History of Beyng* become increasingly fragmentary.

However, and as Walter Kaufmann notes, Nietzsche is no system-thinker but a problem-thinker.[12] His aphorisms and fragments are experiments that attempt to get beyond philosophical preconceptions and to the root of problems themselves, which is to say, to try to understand these problems from out of life as such. So although Nietzsche's thoughts may seem somewhat disconnected and unendingly self-contradictory, this is simply part of a process in which he constantly thinks and re-thinks certain fundamental problems in terms of life itself. Consequently, in returning thought to life Nietzsche's finite, fragmentary attempts to get to the bottom of problems have a coherence that holds these thoughts together. Thus Nietzsche's experimental attempts to think historically out of life speak directly to Heidegger's experimental attempts to think historically out of being (thought as *Ereignis*).

# Notes

# Introduction

1 Jennifer Anna Gosetti-Ferencei, *Heidegger, Hölderlin, and the Subject of Poetic Language: Towards a New Poetics of Dasein* (New York: Fordham University Press, 2004), p 31.

2 As Louis P Blond notes, Heidegger from as early as 1927 makes the crucial distinction (which profoundly influences much of his subsequent thought) between the objects of the sciences and that of philosophy. The former is concerned with that which is positively given, namely beings, whilst the latter is concerned with that which eludes such a determination – namely being. Cf. Louis P Blond, *Heidegger and Nietzsche: Overcoming Metaphysics* (Continuum: London, 2010), p 32f. This is also the basis for Heidegger's ongoing criticism of metaphysics, according to Blond, which focuses on the being of that which is positively given and not on how beings come to be given in the first place. Indeed, we see a pronounced movement in this direction on Heidegger's part between 1927 and 1935. This movement loosely takes the form of viewing metaphysics as a branch of philosophy (*Being and Time*), to regarding it as practically equated with human being (*What Is Metaphysics*) to the clarity of seeing it as the history of Western thinking that needs to be overcome (*Introduction to Metaphysics*).

3 Gosetti-Ferencei, *op. cit.*, p 31.

4 Throughout this thesis I will be using the broader terms 'Western' or 'the West' in place of European or even German when reflecting on metaphysical thought as it is inclusive of all three.

5 Cf. Felix Ó Murchadha, *The Time of Revolution: Kairos and Chronos in Heidegger* (London: Bloomsbury, 2013), p 153.

6 I am indebted in the following analysis to Dorothea Frede in her 'The Question of Being: Heidegger's Project' in *The Cambridge Companion to Heidegger*, ed. Charles B Guignon (Cambridge: Cambridge University Press, 2006), p 42f.

7 Being is spelt in a variety of ways in order to convey a variety of meanings in many translations and much secondary literature, including the use of a capital letter 'B' at the beginning of the word. I shall normalize all these spellings into 'being' unless I specifically state otherwise.

8 I am indebted to Ullrich Haase for this translation of the term *Auseinandersetzung* in his 'Approaching Heidegger's History of Being through the Black Notebooks', *The Journal of the British Society for Phenomenology*, Vol. 51, 2020, pp 95–109. This term is translated in various ways in the secondary literature and I myself shall translate it with the term as 'confrontation' or even 'meditative engagement' where appropriate in this text. But in regard to Nietzsche this term seems most apt as Heidegger views the former as the thinker that is closest to us and thus the thinker from whom we need to distance ourselves as best we can.

9 Cf. GA 52: 55.

# Chapter 1

1 Conor Cunningham, *Genealogy of Nihilism: Philosophies of Nothing and the Difference of Theology* (London: Routledge, 2002), p 132.

2 The abandonment of being, which Heidegger also refers to as the 'disintegration of truth', is the state of distress the Western humanity endures in the age of nihilism, even if we feel a '*lack of distress in this distress*'. Cf. *Contributions to Philosophy*, §79.

3 Keith Ansell Pearson and Diane Morgan, 'Introduction: The Return of Monstrous Nihilism' in *Nihilism Now! Monsters of Energy*, eds. KA Pearson and D Morgan (London: MacMillan, 2000), p ix.

4 Cf. Gianni Vattimo, *The End of Modernity: Nihilism and Hermeneutics in Post-modern Culture*, trans. JR Snyder (Cambridge: Polity Press, 1988), p 19.

5 Indeed, even the very nature of nihilism being distilled in the notion of the death of God has been disputed. Michael Gillespie has argued that nihilism is not issued in by the death of God but by a transformation in idea of God to a God of the will. Cf. Michael Gillespie, *Nihilism before Nietzsche* (Chicago: Cambridge University Press, 1995).

6 Heidegger views the German term *Dasein* as being synonymous with the Greek term *psyche*. *Dasein* is a colloquial German word meaning 'existence' which also carries the literal meaning of 'there-being' as it is a compound of the words *Da*(there) and *Sein* (being). However, 'there-being' or 'being-there' does not adequately translate all that Heidegger intends with this word, as it suggests that *Dasein*, in some sense, is simply present in its being. Consequently, a more appropriate translation of what Heidegger means would be 'being-the-there'. Being-the-there implies that the very possibility that there is a 'there' (that there is an ontological relation between beings and that beings thereby manifest themselves in their being) rests with the ontological constitution of the human being. Thus, *Dasein* names the being of the human being as the possibility that *there is* something (in which beings come *to be*) rather than nothing.

7 It must be noted that Nietzsche actually calls himself 'the first perfect nihilist of Europe', although he does not mean this in the sense that he is the first to hold nihilism as a doctrine but rather in the sense that he has experienced nihilism fully and has left it behind. Cf. the Preface in Friedrich Nietzsche, *The Will to Power*, trans. W Kaufmann and RJ Hollingdale (New York: Vintage Books, 1968). I shall hereafter cite this text in the main body of the work as WTP followed by the section number.

8 With the notable exception of Karl Jaspers' general introduction: Karl Jaspers, *Nietzsche* (Berlin: de Gruyter, 1935), trans. as *Nietzsche: An Introduction to the Understanding of his Philosophical Activity* (Baltimore: Johns Hopkins University Press, 1997). Nonetheless, Georg Picht regards Heidegger's work as the first to show how to engage questioningly with Nietzsche's thought and Gianni Vattimo sees Heidegger as the first properly contextualized Nietzsche's notion of the *Will to Power*, perhaps Nietzsche's most fundamental thought, by reading Nietzsche's thought as the culmination of metaphysics. Cf. respectively Georg Picht, 'Nietzsche – Thought and the Truth of History', trans. Ullrich Haase in *The Journal of the British Society for Phenomenology*, Vol. 38, No. 1, January 2007, p 6 and Gianni Vattimo, *The Adventure of Difference: Philosophy after Nietzsche and Heidegger*, trans. C Blamires and T Harrison (Cambridge: Polity Press, 1993), p 85.

9 Cf. N4, p1. The following outline of the history of the concept of nihilism is indebted to Simon Critchley, *Very Little … Almost Nothing* (London: Routledge, 1997), Chapter 1.

10 See, in particular, IvanTurgeniev's *Fathers and Sons*.

11 As Eugen Fink notes, although to begin with nihilism is essentially worked out by Nietzsche as a problem of morality, but gains a much broader historical significance in his later work. Cf. Eugen Fink, *Nietzsche's Philosophy*, trans. G Richter (London: Continuum, 2003), p 140f.

12 Jörg Salaquarda makes the case that Nietzsche views the new secular ideas that spring up in the late nineteenth century as nothing more than new expressions of the old, traditional foundations of Western thought. That is, Nietzsche viewed these secular ideas in the same way that he did philosophical and traditional Western religious thought, as essentially systematizations of a deeply moral attitude. Cf. Jörg Salaquarda, 'Nietzsche and the Judeo-Christian Tradition' in *The Cambridge Companion to Nietzsche*, eds. B Magnus and KM Higgins (Cambridge: Cambridge University Press, 1996), p 102.

13 Friedrich Nietzsche, *The Gay Science*, trans. W Kaufmann (New York: Vintage Books, 1974), §125.

14 I shall return to this notion of Plato's thinking as giving rise to the history of the West in the next section of this chapter.

15 Friedrich Nietzsche, *Beyond Good and Evil*, trans. M Faber (Oxford: Oxford University Press, 1998), p 4.

16 John 8:12 'The New Testament' in *The Holy Bible* (London: Catholic Truth Society, 1966), p 95.

17 Eugen Fink notes that the opposition between being and becoming is the basic model that Nietzsche uses in his analysis of the history of the West thought metaphysically. Nietzsche thinks of being as the unchanging and timeless (which he associates with Plato's ideal realm) and becoming as the moving and temporal (that he associates with Plato's world of appearance). Cf. Fink, *op. cit.*, p 129f.

18 Cf. Walter Kaufmann, *Nietzsche: Philosopher, Psychologist, Antichrist* (New Jersey: Princetown University Press, 1974), p 101.

19 Cf. in particular the 3rd Meditation in René Descartes, *Mediations on First Philosophy*, trans. John Cottingham (Cambridge: Cambridge University Press, 1996).

20 Friedrich Nietzsche, 'On Truth and Lying in a Non-Moral Sense' in *The Birth of Tragedy and Other Writings*, trans. R Speirs (Cambridge: Cambridge University Press, 1999), p 145.

21 Thought as a physician, the philosopher helps the human being (in the era of nihilism) to move from passivity to activity, from taking a neutral stance on her existence to rolling up her sleeves and plunging into it. Although, it should also be noted, Nietzsche does not think that the philosopher-physician should tell the human being what to do with her life, only that she is ill. For a succinct analysis of Nietzsche's thinking on the philosopher-physician, Cf. Ullrich Haase, *Starting with Nietzsche* (London: Continuum, 2008), p 27f.

22 Nietzsche, *The Gay Science*, p 35.

23 Cf. Haase, *Starting with Nietzsche*, p 29.

24 Friedrich Nietzsche, 'How the "Real World Finally Became a Fable"' in *Twilight of the Idols*, trans. Duncan Large (Oxford: Oxford University Press, 1998), p 20. In this text Nietzsche outlines in six steps what he sees as the history of the West as the history of philosophical/metaphysical thought, that is, as the history of what he calls an 'error'.

25 Eugen Fink, for one, thinks that Nietzsche goes wrong in regarding Plato as holding a dualistic 'two world' theory, founding the ideal world to stand over and against the apparent world due a moralistic interpretation of being on Plato's part. Rather, Fink sees in Plato's positing of the ideal world in relation to the finite world as the beginning of the dissolution of an original cosmological conception that tries to reconcile the notions of the one and the many. Cf. Fink, *op. cit.*, p 130f.

26 Plato, *Republic*, trans. Paul Shorey (Massachusetts: Harvard University Press, 1930), 508d.

27 Plato, *Phaedo*, trans. Hugh Tredennick (Harmondsworth: Penguin, 1954), 61c.

28 Lee Spinks points out that the notion of (the) will to power has exerted a tremendous influence on how Heidegger's thought is perceived throughout the world, not least in Nazi Germany where his work was thought to lend credence to the use of physical force and violence. His defence of Nietzsche, however, that he did not publish the book when he was alive and that it is made up of many of his discarded thoughts, as well as

the question of unity of thought that the published work contains that is lacking in his other work, are not convincing. Heidegger, for one, sees a unity in Nietzsche's concept of *Will to Power* that makes it the central thought of his work, in his eyes (as we shall see). Cf. Lee Spinks, *Nietzsche* (London: Routledge, 2003), p 154.

29 Friedrich Nietzsche, *The Birth of Tragedy and Other Writings*, trans. R Speirs (Cambridge: Cambridge University Press, 1999), §2.

30 Lee Spinks suggests that it is difficult to say with any certainty whether *Will to Power* can be represented as a 'theory', an 'idea' or even a 'principle' given it is an attempt on Nietzsche's part to name a creative force that transforms any 'version' of reality that we encounter. Spinks argues that what Nietzsche is presenting here is a dynamic vision of life that can be experienced simultaneously in both a verbal and a nominal sense through which every aspect of existence is reinterpreted. Cf. Spinks, *op. cit.*, p 133.

31 Cf. Haase, *Starting with Nietzsche*, p 168.

32 To this end Nietzsche says in §335 of *The Gay Science*: 'We however, *we want to become those who we are* – human beings who are new, unique, incomparable, who give themselves laws, who create themselves.'

33 Cf. Kaufmann, *Nietzsche: Philosopher, Psychologist, Antichrist*, p 110f.

34 Friedrich Nietzsche, 'Ecce Homo' in *The Anti-Christ, Ecce Homo, The Twilight of the Idols and Other Writings*, trans. J Norman (Cambridge: Cambridge University Press, 2005), p 144.

35 Cf. Kaufmann, *Nietzsche: Philosopher, Psychologist, Antichrist*, p 111.

36 Friedrich Nietzsche, *Thus Spoke Zarathustra*, trans. RJ Hollingdale (London: Penguin, 2003), p 297. All future quotations will translate *Übermensch* literally as 'overhuman'.

37 Ibid., p 44.

38 Nietzsche says in *Thus Spoke Zarathustra*: 'I love those who do not seek beyond the stars for reasons to go down and to be sacrifices: but who sacrifice themselves to the earth, that the earth may one day belong to the overhuman' [Ibid].

39 As Ullrich Haase observes, for Nietzsche thinking is action, it picks us up somewhere and moves us somewhere else. Thus thought is movement, and movement in itself cannot be represented clearly and distinctly in thought. This is why Nietzsche has recourse to speaking in riddles as it hands us over to the movement of thought itself. Cf. Haase, *Starting with Nietzsche*, p 146.

40 Nietzsche, *Ecce Homo*, p 101.

41 Nietzsche, *Thus Spoke Zarathustra*, p 43.

42 Bernd Magnus and Kathleen Higgins note that much Nietzsche scholarship that is critical of Heidegger's readings of Nietzsche is based on the premise that Heidegger is motivated by the wish to do justice to his own philosophical perspective rather than Nietzsche's. They cite in this respect Heidegger's use of work that went unpublished

in Nietzsche lifetime but which Heidegger drew on in his own readings as Nietzsche's most important philosophy. Cf. B Magnus and K Higgins, 'Nietzsche's Works and their Themes' in *The Cambridge Companion to Nietzsche*, eds. B Magnus and K Higgins (Cambridge: Cambridge University Press, 1996), p 58. Heidegger deals with such criticism in his *What Is Called Thinking* when at a point in which he is discussing Nietzsche's work he says: 'But no thinker can ever be overcome by our refuting him and stacking up around him a literature of refutation. What a thinker has thought can only be mastered if we refer everything in his thought that is still unthought back to its originary truth. Of course, the thoughtful dialogue ... turns into a disputation of rising acrimony' [WCT 54].

43 Cf. Walter Kaufmann, *Discovering the Mind, Volume II: Nietzsche, Heidegger and Buber* (New Jersey: Transaction Publishers, 2009), p 189f.

44 This is summed up in Heidegger's notion of *Gelassenheit*, which will be addressed in the next chapter.

45 As Babette Babich notes, Heidegger's son is reported to have told the philosopher Hans Georg Gadamer that his father, towards the end of his life, was wont to state that 'Nietzsche ruined me', perhaps a reference to how Heidegger took on Nietzsche's problems as his own, with similar results. Cf. Babette Babich, 'Heidegger's Will to Power', *The Journal of the British Society for Phenomenology*, Vol. 38, No. 1, January 2007, pp 37–60.

46 Cf. Gianni Vattimo, *Dialogue with Nietzsche*, trans. William McCuaig (New York: Columbia University Press, 2000), p 182.

47 It has been argued that Nietzsche is here proposing that modernity should turn its back on rationality in favour of making all judgements aesthetic ones, or even of turning to conscious myth-making, given the more authentic nature of the Greeks (wherein lies the origin of Western thought) is tragic. However, this would suggest a decline of some sort that springs from the origins of the West, which in turn suggest some kind of goal has failed to be attained. As we have already seen, the idea of life having a goal for Nietzsche is equivocal, at least beyond the notion that the goal of life is to have a goal rather than attaining one. Cf. Alexander Nehamas, 'Nietzsche, Modernity, Aestheticsim' in *The Cambridge Companion to Nietzsche*, p 228f.

48 Nietzsche, *Thus Spoke Zarathustra*, p 297.

49 In *On Truth and Lying in a Non-moral Sense*, Nietzsche says: 'Truths are illusions of which we have forgotten that they are illusions, metaphors which have become worn by frequent use and have lost all sensuous vigour.' See Nietzsche, *The Birth of Tragedy and Other Writings*, p 146.

50 Vattimo argues that there is a distance between the two thinkers overlooked by many commentators, citing the fact that Heidegger regarded Nietzsche as profoundly remote from himself, as belonging to the history of metaphysics. Cf. Vattimo, *Dialogue with Nietzsche*, p 182f.

51 Cf. Ullrich Haase, 'Δίκη and *iustitia*or: Between Heidegger and Nietzsche', *The Journal of the British Society for Phenomenology*, Vol. 38, No. 1, January 2007, pp 18–36.

52 Cf. Eugen Fink, *op. cit.*, p 171f.

53 Cf. Ernst Behler, 'Nietzsche in the Twentieth Century' in *The Cambridge Companion to Nietzsche*, 1996, p 281f.

54 In *The End of Philosophy and the Task of Thinking* Heidegger equates philosophy with metaphysics as being understood as the grounding of beings in terms of presence. Cf. Heidegger, *Basic Writings* trans. & ed. David Farrell Krell (London: Routledge, 1993), p 432f.

55 Cf. Will McNeill, 'Traces of Discordance' in *Nietzsche: A Critical Reader*, ed. PR Sedgwick (Oxford: Blackwell, 1995), p 176f.

# Chapter 2

1 Cf. Michael A Gillespie, *Hegel, Heidegger and the Ground of History* (Chicago: Chicago University Press, 1984), p 133f.

2 'Be-ing' here translates the German word *Seyn*, an obsolete spelling of *Sein* that Heidegger employs in order to indicate the event of the inception of being rather than a particular sense of what it is to be.

3 Heidegger's idea is that it is the disclosedness (*Erschlossenheit*) of beings that marks the essence of truth. As such, Heidegger claims that the unhiddenness of beings (from out of hiddenness) forms the basic sense of truth from which our traditional conception of truth as correspondence is derived. In order to make good his claim, Heidegger investigates an ancient Greek conception of truth that is synonymous with disclosedness with the intention of retrieving what he thinks is truth's original essence. Truth, primordially, is *aletheia*. Cf., for example, *Being and Time* §44.

4 *Ereignis* is here translated as 'event' for the sake of clarity, but for Heidegger the word carries a much broader significance. Heidegger shows this by separating out the two components of the word. The prefix *er-* suggests the beginning of a motion whilst *-eignis* refers to the word *eigen* which can be rendered as 'own' as well as 'authentic'. This leads some scholars to translate *Ereignis* as 'event of appropriation' or 'appropriation' as well as the more uncomfortable 'enowning', as is given in the English text I am following here. For further analysis of Heidegger's use of this concept see Daniela Vallega-Neu, 'Ereignis: The Event of Appropriation' in *Martin Heidegger: Key Concepts*, ed. Bret W Davis (Durham: Acumen, 2010), p 140f.

5 *Wesen* is a complex word in Heidegger's thought which is generally translated as 'essence'. However, the richness of Heidegger's use of the word in *Contributions to*

*Philosophy* means the simplicity of 'essence' is likely to be misleading in most cases. I have used 'essential sway' here and in doing so follow the translators of the text as this translation renders both the vibrancy that Heidegger attaches to the word and a sense that this vibrancy is what is ownmost to what Heidegger wishes to say about being. Cf. *Contributions to Philosophy*, Introduction §3.

6   Cf. *Contributions to Philosophy* §132, in which Heidegger speaks of this problem as belonging to the notion of the 'ontological difference' as outlined in *Being and Time*.

7   Specifically, Polt is here suggesting that Heidegger's turn to the concept of *Ereignis* allows him to show the traditional ontological approach to being as one that is limited to the temporal notion that the world is that which is present. What it fails to reveal is the dependence of that which is present on temporality itself, i.e. what it fails to account for is how that which is present arises historically. Cf. Richard Polt, 'Being and Time' in *Martin Heidegger: Key Concepts*, p 75f.

8   As Thomas Sheehan notes, the translation of *Seinsgeschichte* as history of being does not quite hit the mark. It is rather a highly idiosyncratic history of ontology that argues for and presupposes Heidegger's unique view of being thought in terms of appropriated clearing. Cf. Thomas Sheehan, *Making Sense of Heidegger: A Paradigm Shift* (New York: Rowman & Littlefield, 2015), p 250.

9   In his *Contributions to Philosophy* Heidegger says that the fundamental attunement of modernity is one of deep foreboding (*Er-ahnen*), although the 'grounding-attunement of another beginning can hardly ever be known merely by one name – and especially in crossing to that beginning' [C 16]. As we are about to discover, one of the other names Heidegger gives it is 'startled dismay' (*das Erschrecken*), which forms a kind of unity alongside 'restraint' (*Verhaltenheit*) and 'diffidence' (*Scheu*).

10  Charles Bambach suggests that it is not only ontological considerations that motivate Heidegger's thinking here, but that an acute political awareness of Germany's political situation in the mid-1930s is at work. Cf. Charles Bambach, *Heidegger's Roots: Nietzsche, National Socialism, and the Greeks* (Ithaca: Cornell University Press, 2005), p 162f. Cf. also Bambach on how Heidegger opens up ethical considerations in his work on Hölderlin and his notion of poetic dwelling in the mid-1930s in 'Who Is Heidegger's Hölderlin', *Research in Phenomenology*, Vol. 47, No. 1, 2017, 39–59.

11  Heidegger distinguishes between the *Leitfrage* (guiding question) and the *Grundfrage* (grounding question) of philosophical enquiry as a way of opening up to question the essence of truth. His aim is to move the focus of the question of being away from the being of beings and onto the meaning of being as an historical event. Cf. N1, 67f and the first chapter of *Introduction to Metaphysics*.

12  Richard Polt points out that what we here call a beginning Heidegger himself prefers to refer to as an 'inception'. The difference lies in the fact that we are here dealing with being. A beginning merely points to a particular phase in a process, whereas an inception suggests that something new and eventful has taken place. Cf. Richard Polt, 'Being and Time' in *Martin Heidegger: Key Concepts*, p 76f.

13 Cf. ÓMurchadha, *op. cit.*, p 30f.

14 Cf. Bambach, *op. cit.*, p 191f.

15 See, for example, Bret W Davis, 'Will and Gelassenheit' in *Martin Heidegger: Key Concepts*, p 172f.

16 Cf. Babette Babich, *Words in Blood, Like Flowers: Philosophy and Poetry, Music and Eros in Hölderlin, Nietzsche and Heidegger* (Albany: State of New York Press, 2006), p 16f.

17 Cf. George Pattison, *The Later Heidegger* (London: Routledge, 2000), p 132. Pattison emphasizes in particular Heidegger's engagement with the pre-Socratic thinkers Parmenides and Heraclitus. For the sake of clarity and brevity I shall be focussing on one particular Greek concept that will serve the same purpose – namely, *physis*.

18 I shall return to the importance of language in allowing *Dasein* to dwell historically in the final two chapters of this study.

19 According to Heidegger, 'The decisive principle that guides Aristotle's interpretation of φύσις declares that φύσις must be understood as οὐσία, as a kind and mode of presencing' [PM 200].

20 Heidegger employs his method of philosophical *Destruktion* in order to reveal that the metaphysical tradition stems from a temporal determination of being, one in which being is thought of as a constant presence. To this end, in *Being and Time* Heidegger says: 'In line with the positive tendencies of this destruction (*Destruktion*), we must in the first instance raise the question whether and to what extent the interpretation of being and the phenomenon of time have been brought together thematically in the course of the history of ontology, and whether the problematic of temporality required for this has ever been worked out in principle or ever could have been' [BT 44].

21 For an interesting discussion of this matter see Mark Sinclair, *Heidegger, Aristotle and the Work of Art: Poiesis in Being* (New York: Palgrave Macmillan, 2006), p 22f.

22 For the traditional translation compare, for example, Jonathon Barnes, *Early Greek Philosophy* (London: Penguin, 1987), p 112.

23 Heidegger will later say with regard to the Greek notion of truth in *The End of Philosophy and the Task of Thinking* that: '*Alētheia*, unconcealment as the clearing of presence, is not yet truth. Is *alētheia* then less than truth? Or is it more, because it first grants truth as *adequatio* and *certitudo*, because there can be no presence and presenting outside the realm of the clearing' [BW 446]? Heidegger is here stating that whilst any claim that for the Greeks truth was understood aletheically would be erroneous (a claim Heidegger maintained for much of his philosophical life), it is only out of an experience of unconcealment that the Greek notion of truth can take hold. Thus it would be untenable to claim that there was a transformation in the Greek notion of truth from unconcealment to truth thought as correctness (*orthotēs*) of statements or representations.

**24** Cf. Ó Murchadha, *op. cit.*, p 8. Ó Murchadha makes the point that Heidegger's much criticized 'destruction' of other philosopher's texts has everything to do with his desire to wrest the truth from them, that is, what is most thought-worthy in them, and little to do with dismantling their doctrines.

**25** William J Richardson notes that Aristotle's use of the word *physis* is not always uniform. On the one hand it signifies the beingness (*ousia*) of beings as a whole and on the other hand that of the domain of natural beings only. The first use points to the future metaphysical tradition and the latter back to the conception of the early Greek thinkers. Thus Aristotle's thought stands in a transitional point between metaphysics and what went before. Cf. William J Richardson, 'Toward the Future of Truth' in *Heidegger and the Greeks: Interpretive Essays*, eds. Hyland and Manoussakis (Indiana: Indiana University Press, 2006), p 309f.

**26** Cf. Aristotle, *Metaphysics* Θ 6, 1048 b23 where he says: ὁρα ἁμα καί ἑώραχε.

**27** Heidegger speaks of this in his *Plato's Doctrine of Truth* where he says: 'In Greek, "visible form" is εἶδος or ἰδέα. In the "allegory" (of the cave) the things that are visible in the daylight outside the cave, where sight is free to look at everything, are a concrete illustration of the ideas' [PM 164].

**28** Richardson suggests that whilst Heidegger would presumably frown upon translating *steresis* as 'privation' given the Latin roots of this word, and given Heidegger's mistrust of Latin translations of important Greek concepts, it nonetheless conveys a good sense of absencing as belonging to the process of coming to presence. Cf. Richardson, *op. cit.*, p 312f.

**29** Heidegger says: 'The merely spatial image of a circle is essentially inadequate because this going-forth that goes back into itself precisely lets something go forth from which and to which the going-forth is in each instance on the way' [PM 224].

**30** Cf. *Introduction to Metaphysics*, p 18f, where Heidegger not only defines metaphysics as that which goes beyond natural beings but where he claims that, understood as such, metaphysics determines the essence of philosophy.

**31** Cf. Walter A Brogan, 'The Intractable Interrelation of Physis and Technē' in *Heidegger and the Greeks: Interpretive Essays*, eds. DA Hyland and JP Manoussakis (Indianapolis: Indiana University Press, 2006), pp 43–56.

**32** Cf. Aristotle's *Physics*, Γ I, 201 b4f.

**33** To this end Hans Ruin says helpfully that 'on the one hand, *techne* in the sense of the fabricated artefact functions from the inception of metaphysics as the matrix for thinking being as a disconnected entity, a metaphysical thinking that comes to the fore definitively in modernity, where the truth or event of being is covered over and domesticated in a representational and objectifying understanding'. Hans Ruin, '*Ge-stell*: Enframing as the Essence of Technology' in *Martin Heidegger: Key Concepts*, p 188.

34 Heidegger says, in *The Question Concerning Technology*, 'Technology is not equivalent to the essence of technology. When we are seeking the essence of "tree," we have become aware that what pervades every tree, as tree, is not itself a tree that can be encountered among all other trees. Likewise, the essence of technology is by no means anything technological' [BW 311].

35 Hans Ruin notes that Heidegger gathers various uses of the terms *Stellen* (placing, setting) that he employs in previous texts into the notion of *Gestell*. Noting that the '*Ge-*' can imply a 'gathering together' in German such as in the word *Gebirge* (mountain range), Ruin says that *Gestell* means for Heidegger the gathering together of the various forms of *stellen* to depict the way the world manifests itself in the technological age. Cf. Ruin, *op. cit.*, p 191.

36 Pattison, *op. cit.*, p 54.

37 In fact, Gosetti-Ferencei suggests that *The Question Concerning Technology* addresses two interwoven themes: the destruction of earth by technology and our failure to ask about the philosophical origins of this destruction. Both come together in the question of whether we are any longer able to question technology as such. Cf. Jennifer Anna Gosetti-Ferencei, *op. cit.*, p 145.

# Chapter 3

1 In his 'Letter on Humanism' Heidegger says, 'Language is the house of being. In its home man dwells. Those who think and those who create with words are the guardians of this home. Their guardianship accomplishes the manifestation of being insofar as they bring the manifestation to language and maintain it in language through their speech' [BW 217].

2 Heidegger thinks that originally discourse, like *logos*, is a way of making beings manifest in Greek thinking. One makes something manifest in talking about it, in bringing it into the open in the spoken word. Thus, discourse is a way that *Dasein* can *be*, a way that it can relate to beings. However, discourse has the potential to be either authentic or inauthentic. Consequently, beings can come forth into the word meaningfully as that which is talked about or they can be passed over in what Heidegger calls idle talk [*Gerede*] which is marked by an indifference to beings.

3 Steven Pinker, *The Language Instinct* (New York: Harper Collins, 2007), p 6.

4 Cf. Heidegger, *Zollikon Seminars*, trans. Franz Mayr & Richard Askay (New Haven: Northwestern University Press, 2001), p 326f.

5 Cf. John T Lysaker, 'Language and Poetry' in *Martin Heidegger: Key Concepts*, p 195f.

6 Cf. Allen, *Ellipsis: Of Poetry and the Experience of Language after Heidegger, Hölderlin and Blanchot* (New York: New York University Press, 2007), p 170f.

7   According to Françoise Dastur, the problem that Heidegger confronts in 'The Origin' is that of approaching the essence of the artwork in a way that moves away from the level of 'objectivity'. In recognizing the work of art as neither an object nor a product implies a prior understanding of what art is essentially. The only way to confront the circularity that results from this thinking (that we are looking for what we already know) is to enter into the circle at the right point in order to discover what exactly it is that we know already. Cf. Françoise Dastur, 'Heidegger's Freiburg Version of the Origin of the Work of Art' in *Heidegger towards the Turn: Essays on the Work of the 1930s*, ed. J Risser (New York: State University of New York Press, 1999), p 122f.

8   That is, as Heidegger says in *Being and Time*, discourse can either be authentic or inauthentic. Cf. *Being and Time*, p 55f.

9   Cf. Lysaker, *op. cit.*, p 196.

10  I am indebted to William J Richardson for the following analysis. Cf. Williamson, *op. cit.*, p 490f.

11  Heidegger, *Basic Writings*, p 234.

12  Cf. Allen, *op. cit.*, chapter 1.

13  Ibid., p 37.

14  Ibid., p 155.

15  Vattimo says in his *The Adventure of Difference* that this being-language nexus is problematical for Heidegger as 'the being-language nexus is always linked with the problem of metaphysics as a historical presentation of being, a presentation that involves an unconcealing/concealing: this unconcealing/concealing belongs above all to being, and yet in spite or perhaps because of this belonging to being, it fundamentally concerns our historicity, determining its "fallen" condition in the metaphysical world of *Seinsvergessenheit*. This is one of two reasons why Heidegger never manages to say, as Gadamer does in his formula mentioned above, that *being is language*. (The other reason is related to this one; it is the impossibility of saying that being *is* this or that, or indeed of using the verb "to be" as a copula at all.)' Vattimo, *The Adventure of Difference*, p 28.

16  Logocentrism is an idea Derrida uses to reveal the assumed centrality of speech over the written word to language that permeates Western thought. In its simplest terms it reveals the assumption that speech deals with what is present, whilst literature is derivative, making what is present in speech absent whilst simultaneously trying to cling to the presence of what is attached to speech. Derrida says that the interrelation between speech and literature is more complex than this, and that both involve an element of making absent and making present. Derrida uses this notion to open up a critical space between his own thought and Heidegger's, arguing that Heidegger overlooks non-metaphysical aspects in his reading of texts as well as reducing all texts from a certain period to a singular (i.e. metaphysical) totality of meaning and missing the complexity of thought that unfolds historically. For Derrida on logocentrism see

Jacques Derrida, *Of Grammatology*, trans. GC Spivak (Baltimore: Johns Hopkins University Press, 1997) and for criticism of Heidegger see Jacques Derrida, *Of Spirit: Heidegger and the Question*, trans. G Bennington and R Bowlby (Chicago: Chicago University Press, 1987).

17 Cf. *Introduction to Metaphysics*, p 144f.

18 Cf. Robert Bernasconi, *The Question of Language in Heidegger's History of Being* (New Jersey: Humanities Press, 1985), p 65f.

19 Cf. ibid., p 66.

20 Cf. ibid., p 17f.

21 Cf. Michel Haar, *The Song of the Earth*, trans. R Lilly (Indianapolis: Indiana University Press, 1993), p 73f.

22 Cf. Heidegger, *Pathmarks*, trans. Frank A Capuzzi *et al*, ed. William McNeill (Cambridge: Cambridge University Press, 1998), p 249f.

23 Cf. Bernasconi, *The Question of Language in Heidegger's History of Being*, p 76f.

24 DP Verene helpfully says of Hegel's notion of the speculative proposition that it 'has within it the dialectical motion necessary to present consciousness as alive and self-developing through its determinate shapes to the organic whole of spirit as "absolute knowing"'. Donald Phillip Verene, *Hegel's Absolute: An Introduction to Reading the Phenomenology of Spirit* (New York: State University of New York Press, 2007), p 8.

25 Cf. Robert Bernasconi, *Heidegger in Question: The Art of Existing* (New York: Humanity Books, 1996), p 190f.

26 Cf. ibid., p 195.

27 Haar, *op. cit.*, 116.

28 In his introduction to 'The Way to Language' David Farrell Krell notes the difficulty in thinking of *Ereignis* as propriation rather than the more customary 'event'. What this translation tries to convey is the sense of whatever is ownmost to a thing and reveals itself when language lets it advene under its own power, or lets it withdraw into concealment and abide on its own. Cf. Martin Heidegger, *Basic Writings*, p 395f.

29 Clark quite rightly points out that despite the widespread (if generally implicit) influence of Heidegger's readings of poets they were never intended as literary criticism as this form of thinking belongs to the kind of thinking he seeks to undermine in his readings. Cf. Timothy Clark, *Martin Heidegger* (London: Routledge, 2002), p 97.

30 History thought in terms of *Historie* is what we generally think of as the content of historiology, that is, the actual events that happen in historical time. *Geschichte*, on the other hand, is the actual *happening* of history that allows these events to take place. Cf. in particular *Being and Time*, sections 6 and 7.

31 To this end Heidegger says in 'Poetically Man Dwells' that 'man's taking measure in the dimension dealt out to him brings dwelling into its ground plan. Taking the measure

of the dimension is the element within which human dwelling has its security, by which it securely endures. The taking of measure is what is poetic in dwelling. Poetry is a measuring. But what is it to measure? If poetry is to be understood as measuring, then obviously we may not subsume it under any idea of measuring and measure' [PLT 219].

32 Interestingly, Wilhelm S Wurzer suggests that Heidegger views the word as having the power of a 'new nobility', a '*Befindlichkeit* that reveals the silent call of the earth, the sigetic region of a historical people'. Hence, for Heidegger, the word can be said to challenge nihilism insofar as it has not come up with anything that has greatness attached to it. Cf. William S Wurzer, 'Heidegger's Turn to *Germanien* – A Sigetic Venture' in *Heidegger towards the Turn: Essay on the Work of the 1930s*, p 197.

33 Ibid.

34 Zimmerman suggests, correctly, that Heidegger did not pursue a systematic ethics as this was to concern oneself with values and therefore to involve oneself with metaphysics. What is needed instead, as we shall see, is a new *ethos* or mode of dwelling, something that Heidegger thinks resides in the gift of poetry thought essentially. Cf. Michael E Zimmerman, *Heidegger's Confrontation with Modernity: Technology, Politics, Art* (Indiana: Indiana University Press, 1990), p 131f.

35 Not least amongst these is Victor Farias, in his book *Heidegger and Nazism* he accuses Heidegger of not only being a supporter of Hitler but also of supporting his racial policies, amongst much else.

36 Cf. John D Caputo, *Demythologizing Heidegger* (Indianapolis: Indiana University Press, 1993), p 132. In recent years, upon the publication of Heidegger's *Black Notebooks*, the controversy of Heidegger's involvement with the Nazis and his perceived anti-semitism has received widespread examination. For an insightful analysis of these topics and much else in the *Black Notebooks* see *Reading Heidegger's Black Notebooks 1931–1941*, eds. Ingo Farin and Jeff Malpas (Massachusetts: MIT Press, 2016).

37 In an interview Heidegger gave in 1966 to the German news magazine *Der Spiegel*, published after Heidegger's death as 'Only a God Can Save Us', Heidegger says that before his rectorship at the university, which began in 1933, he had not had any active involvement in politics. His involvement with the National Socialists only came about subsequently to his rectorship as a direct result of his attempt to prevent a party member from taking control of the university. Cf. *The Heidegger Controversy: A Critical Reader*, p 92f.

38 For example, Robin Waterfield translates this as 'A man's character is his guardian spirit'. Cf. *The First Philosophers: The Pre-Socratics and the Sophists*, trans. Robin Waterfield (Oxford: Oxford University Press, 2000), p 46.

39 Charles E Scott makes the point that what Heidegger means by authenticity in *Being and Time* is that in being confronted with its own mortality then no one, no history, no community and no subjectivity are able to authorize *Dasein*'s individual existence. Essentially, *Dasein*'s awareness of its own mortality as its ultimate possibility means,

if it is acting authentically, that its own being can no longer be thought in relation to others but that *Dasein* must resolve to be the meaning of its own life. Cf. Charles E Scott, 'Non-belonging/Authenticity' in *Reading Heidegger: Commemorations*, p 71.

40  Caputo, *op. cit.*, p 131.

41  Cf. Derrida, *Of Spirit: Heidegger and the Question*, p 37.

42  Heidegger says about his Nietzsche's lecture in 'Only a God Can Save Us' that 'anyone with ears to hear heard in these lectures a confrontation with National Socialism' [HC 101].

43  Cf. Slavoj Žižek, 'Why Heidegger Made the Right Step in 1933', in *International Journal of Žižek Studies*, Vol. 1, No. 4, 2007 (English).

# Chapter 4

1  We can see what Heidegger means by this with his example of the Greek temple in 'The Origin'.

2  Heidegger himself asks the question of the need for the poet at a time of crisis in concrete terms in 'What are Poets for?' enquiring: 'Is Rainer Maria Rilke a poet in a destitute time?' Heidegger's answer is, in short, that we can only tell by looking to his poetry. Cf. 'What are Poets for?' in *Poetry, Language, Thought*, p 89f.

3  Cf. Julian Young, *Heidegger's Philosophy of Art* (Cambridge: Cambridge University Press, 2001), p 69f.

4  Ibid.

5  Heidegger was certainly alive to the dangers of approaching the 'thinker' (*Denker*) Hölderlin as he would a philosopher, and was aware that he needed to approach Hölderlin's work in a more meditative (*denkerische*) manner, than he did that of the philosopher *per se*. Cf. (GA 39: 4f).

6  The question of metaphysics is not yet decided in Heidegger's thinking in the mid-1930s, Janicaud suggests, and Heidegger is initially seeking in Hölderlin's poetry the possibility of 'another metaphysics', rather than the overcoming (*überwinden*) of metaphysics for which his later thought calls. Cf. Dominique Janicaud, 'The "Overcoming" of Metaphysics in the Hölderlin Lectures' in *Reading Heidegger: Commemorations*, ed. John Sallis (Indianapolis: Indiana University Press, 1993), p 386f. It should also be noted that Heidegger's thinking on metaphysics undergoes a radical change from the late 1920s to the early 1940s. In *Being and Time* (1927) metaphysics is little more than a branch of philosophy, whereas in 'What is Metaphysics' (1929) it is equated with human being, before eventually becoming a mode of thought that needs to be confronted *Introduction to Metaphysics* (1935) and eventually a history that needs to be overcome.

7  This is Janicaud's translation, the original German reads: 'Man nimmt Hölderlin "historisch" und verkennt jenes einzig Wesentliche, dass sein noch Zeit-raum-loses Werk unser historisches Getue schon überwunden und den Anfang einer anderen Geschichte gegründet hat, jener Geschichte, die anhebt mit dem Kampf um die Entscheidung über Ankunft oder Flucht des Gottes.'

8  As Gosetti-Ferencei observes, Hölderlin's figure of the poet, as someone who departs from rational subjectivity, sees him directly engaging with the issues of Enlightenment thinking and its emphasis on the principle of human reason. Cf. Gosetti-Ferencei, *op. cit.*, p 107f.

9  David Constantine, *Hölderlin* (Oxford: Oxford University Press, 1990), p 26f.

10  In *On the Way to Language*, first published in 1959, Heidegger says, 'In 1910, Norbert von Hellingrath, who was killed in action before Verdun in 1916, first published Hölderlin's Pindar translations from the manuscripts. In 1914, there followed the first publication of Hölderlin's late hymns. These two books hit us students like an earthquake.'

11  Cf. Hans-Georg Gadamer, 'Thinking and Poetizing in Heidegger and in Hölderlin's "Andenken"' in *Heidegger towards the Turn: Essays on the Works of the 1930s* (New York: State University of New York Press, 1999), p 153.

12  WS Allen makes the interesting point that all of Hölderlin's writings – his poems, his novel or his letters etc., have an apostrophic nature, that is, they are always 'projected towards someone'. Thus the singularity of his writings allows Heidegger to treat him as a figure of the tradition and the most futural figure of modernity. Cf. Allen, *op. cit.*, p 124.

13  Indeed, Young sees a movement in Heidegger's thinking which means he breaks away from the tyranny of the Greek paradigm to develop a second paradigm that will do justice to Hölderlin as poet, and thinks that Heidegger is indebted to Hölderlin for this change of perspective. Cf. Julian Young, *op. cit.*, p 69f.

14  Cf. Joseph J Kockelmans, *Heidegger on Art and Art Works* (Dordrecht: MartinusNijhoff, 1995), p 196.

15  Ibid.

16  Cf. Pattison, *op. cit.*, p 165f. Amongst other differences that Pattison notes in Heidegger's thinking on Nietzsche and Hölderlin is the formers engagement with GreŽ thought involves seeing the Dionysian aspect of life as trans-historical, whilst the latter views the absence of the Greek gods as decisive, a point that speaks directly Heidegger's approach to the overcoming of metaphysics.

17  Young is speaking of the period between Heidegger's first lecture series on Hölderlin in the winter semester of 1934–5 until the essay 'Hölderlin and the Essence of Poetry' in 1936. 'The Origin of the Work of Art' was worked out over three texts, starting in 1935 and finishing in 1936, cf. Jacques Taminiaux, 'The Origin of "The Origin of the

Work of Art'" in *Reading Heidegger: Commemorations*, ed. John Sallis (Indiana: Indiana University Press, 1993), p 392.

18  Cf. ibid., p 396f.

19  My translation. The original German reads: 'Viel hat erfahren der Mensch/ Der Himmlischen viele genannt/Seit ein Gespräch wir sind/Und hören können voneinander'. For the full version of the original poem in both in German and in English translation, cf. *Friedrich Hölderlin: Poems and Fragments*, trans. Michael Hamburger (London: Anvil Press Poetry, 2004), p 512f.

20  Cf. Clark, *op. cit.*, p 102.

21  Cf. Véronique M Foti, *Heidegger and the Poets: Poiēsis/Sophia/Technē* (New York: Humanity Books, 1992) p 44f.

22  Ibid., p 46.

23  Otto Pöggeler, 'Heidegger's Political Self-Understanding' in *The Heidegger Controversy*, ed. Richard Wolin (Cambridge, MA: MIT Press, 1993), p 235. Pöggeler argues that contrary to what Heidegger thinks, Hölderlin did not see danger in the loss of meaning but in the immediate nearness of the divine such as is sought in an awakening.

24  Indeed, Paul de Man asserts: 'Hölderlin says the exact opposite of what Heidegger makes him say'. Cf. Paul de Man, 'Heidegger's Exegeses of Hölderlin' in *Blindness and Insight: Essays in the Rhetoric of Contemporary Criticism* (Oxford: Routledge, 2005), p 254.

25  For the following, cf. Allen, *op. cit.*, p 21.

26  My translation. The original German reads: 'Es reiche aber/Des Dunkeln Lichtes voll/ Mir einer den duftenden Becher'. For the complete version in both German and in English translation, cf. *Friedrich Hölderlin: Poems and Fragments*, p 577f.

27  Cf. in particular *Being and Time*, §12.

28  Pattison's use of this term hints at the essential possibility of the danger language poses to being insofar as it opens up being to conflicting interpretations, which in turn can lead to the closing off of any authentic relations to being. Cf. Pattison, *op. cit.*, p 174f.

29  Young notes a transformation in Heidegger's understanding of the fundamental mood of Hölderlin's poetry. Whereas early in Heidegger's thinking he regards it as one of loss (of the gods), as I have noted, later Young thinks that Heidegger views it as one of thankfulness (*das Danken*) in experiencing one's world as a holy place. Cf. Young, *op. cit.*, p 105.

30  Following Timothy Clark, I am using the words 'tone' and 'mood' here interchangeably to translate the German *Stimmung*. Both words hint at the notion of an attunement to being that opens up the world, with the former speaking more directly to this opening up as it occurs in the poem. Cf. Clark, *op. cit.*, p 112f.

31  Cf. Heidegger, *Basic Writings*, p 159f.

32 Heidegger makes the case for thinking of language as essentially poetic in 'Hölderlin and the Essence of Poetry' where he says that poetry is that 'whereby everything first steps into the open, which we then discuss and talk about in everyday language. Hence poetry never takes language as a material as its disposal; rather, poetry itself first makes language possible. Poetry is the primal language of a historical people. Thus the essence of language must be understood out of the essence of poetry and not the other way round' [EHP 60].

33 Gegnet is an old form of the German word Gegend (region) and is used in distinction to horizon to signify that which is open. In fact, as openness, it is that in which human horizons are sustained and delimited. Cf. Martin Heidegger 'Conversations on a Country Path' in *Discourse on Thinking*, p 66f.

34 Cf. Bret W Davis, *op. cit.*, p 176f.

35 Cf. Gosetti-Ferencei, *op. cit.*, p 57f.

36 Cf. ibid., p 134f.

37 Ibid., p 108.

38 Cf. Zimmerman, *op. cit.*, p 113.

39 To this end Heidegger says in *Introduction to Metaphysics*: 'All essential questioning in philosophy necessarily remains untimely, and this is because philosophy either projects far beyond its own time or else binds its time back to this time's earlier and *inceptive* past. Philosophizing always remains a kind of knowing that not only does not allow itself to be made timely but, on the contrary, imposes its measure on the times' [IM 9].

40 Idiosyncratic insofar as Heidegger ignores, for example, Hölderlin's engagement in his poetry with the French Revolution and instead reads into it his own concerns with Germany's confrontation with modern technology. Cf. Zimmerman, *op. cit.*, p 113.

41 George Pattison makes the point that for Heidegger, not only does what is essential to the thought of a great thinker go unsaid, but also that the truth in the poem is left in silence. Further, to understand this truth we must be genuinely about who *we are* in our own time insofar as we are concerned with what it is to be, to exist, in time. Cf. Pattison, *op. cit.*, p 170.

42 Cf. Clark, *op. cit.*, p 101.

43 Cf. Gosetti-Ferencei, *op. cit.*, p 54f.

44 Cf. Pattison, *op. cit.*, p 166.

45 Cf. Taminiaux, *op. cit.*, p 397.

46 George Pattison notes how this sense of loss unites the ancient Greeks and modern Germans insofar as Hölderlin poetically pursues a sense of harmony by envisaging a return to the luminous presence of the Greek gods on German soil. Thus Hölderlin's work can be said to be 'shot through' with a lost past that is irretrievable and yet

fating the poet to seek a destiny commensurate with his modern European reality. Cf. Pattison, *op. cit.*, p 164.

47 Cf. Davis, *op. cit.*, p 177.

48 Foti, *op. cit.*, p 54.

49 Heidegger tells us in *Identity and Difference* that 'Western Metaphysics, however, since its beginning with the Greeks has eminently been both ontology and theology, still without being tied to these rubrics. […] To those who can read, this means: metaphysics is onto-theo-logy' [IDS 54]. In other words, metaphysics determines the being of beings (ontology) in terms of a higher being (theos) which gives beings their meaning.

50 Daniela Vallega-Neu points out that Heidegger uses the concept in a lecture course delivered in 1919, in which Heidegger tries to elaborate a difference between a scientific-theoretical approach to things and a more genuine pre-theoretical approach to things. Cf. Daniela Vallega-Neu, *op. cit.*, p 141.

51 George Pattison suggests this phrase as Heidegger's notion of the fourfold should not be considered as in any sense hierarchical, as it would be misleading to single out any one element as key to understanding all the others. Cf. Pattison, *op. cit.*, p 176.

52 For an in-depth analysis of each element of the fourfold, as well as how the fourfold functions *per se*, cf. Heidegger, *Poetry, Language, Thought*, p 163f.

53 Cf. Jeff Malpas, *Heidegger's Topology: Being, Place, World* (London: MIT Press, 2008), p 311.

54 In 'The End of Philosophy and the Task of Thinking' Heidegger refers to the necessity of finding a way to think being that lies beyond that of philosophy in the following manner: 'Perhaps there is a thinking which is more sober than the irresistible race to rationalization and the sweeping character of cybernetics' [EP 72]. This is to say Heidegger thinks that we are not yet thinking being properly and that this is the very danger that lies at the heart of modernity.

# Conclusion

1 *Ponderings*, p 15.

2 Ibid., p 39.

3 Ibid., p 48.

4 Otto Pöggeler referred to *Contributions to Philosophy* as Heidegger's 'second magnum opus'. Parvis Emad calls it Heidegger's second major work after *Being and Time*, suggesting correctly that its inconclusive, nonlinear character does not diminish its

status as such. Cf. Parvis Emad, *On the Way to Heidegger's Contributions to Philosophy* (Wisconsin: University of Wisconsin Press, 2007), p xi.

5   Friedrich Nietzsche, *Human, All Too Human*, trans. RJ Hollingdale (Cambridge: Cambridge University Press, 1996), §178.

6   As with Heidegger, some commentators try to break up what is essentially a singular path of thinking in Nietzsche's work into a variety of phases that can be more easily dealt with and compartmentalized. What this misses is what is essential to understanding the thinker, the path of thought itself.

7   Cf. Chapter 1 of this text.

8   Friedrich Nietzsche, *The Gay Science*, trans. & ed.W Kauffman (New York: Vintage Books, 1974), §125.

9   Nietzsche, *Thus Spoke Zarathustra*, p 42.

10  Haase, *Starting with Nietzsche*, p 146.

11  Iain D Thomson, *Heidegger, Art and Postmodernity* (New York: Cambridge University Press, 2011), p 169f.

12  Kaufmann, *Nietzsche: Philosopher, Psychologist, Antichrist*, p 82.

# *Bibliography*

## Primary Texts (Heidegger)

*Gesamtausgabe* (Collected Works), Frankfurt: Klosterman, 1975.
*Basic Questions of Philosophy: Selected 'Problems' of 'Logic'*, trans. R Rojcewicz & A Schuwer. Indianapolis: Indiana UP, 2004.
*Basic Writings*, trans. & ed. David Farrell Krell. London: Routledge, 1993.
*Being and Time*, trans. Macquarrie and Robinson. Oxford: Blackwell Publishing Ltd, 1962.
*Contributions to Philosophy (From Enowning)*, trans. Parvis Emad and Kenneth Maly. Indianapolis: Indiana UP, 1999.
*Discourse on Thinking*, trans. John M Anderson and E Hans Freund. New York: Harper Perennial, 1966.
*The End of Philosophy*, trans. Joan Stambaugh. Chicago: Chicago UP, 2003.
*The Essence of Truth: On Plato's Cave Allegory and Theaetetus*, trans. Ted Sadler. New York: Continuum, 2002.
*Elucidations of Hölderlin's Poetry*, trans. Keith Hoeller. New York: Humanity Books, 2000.
*Four Seminars*, trans. A Mitchell & F Raffoul. Indianapolis: Indiana UP, 2003.
*The Heidegger Controversy*, ed. Richard Wolin. Cambridge: MIT Press, 1993.
*History of the Concept of Time: Prolegomena*, trans. Theodore Kisiel. Indianapolis: Indiana UP, 1985.
*Identity and Difference*, trans. Joan Stambaugh. Chicago: Chicago UP, 2002.
*Introduction to Metaphysics*, trans. Gregory Fried and Richard Polt. New Haven: Yale UP, 2000.
*Kant and the Problem of Metaphysics*, trans. Richard Taft. Indianapolis: Indiana UP, 1990.
*Mindfulness*, trans. P Emad & T Kalary. London: Continuum, 2006.
*Nietzsche*, Vol. I: *The Will to Power as Art*, trans. D. F. Krell. New York: Harper & Row, New York, 1979.
*Nietzsche*, Vol. III: *Will to Power as Knowledge and Metaphysics*, trans. D. F. Krell. New York: Harper and Row, 1987.
*Nietzsche*, Vol. IV: *Nihilism*, trans. Frank A. Capuzzi. New York: Harper & Row, 1982.
*Off the Beaten Track*, trans. Julian Young and Kenneth Haynes. Cambridge: Cambridge UP, 2002.
*On the Way to Language*, trans. Peter D Hertz. San Francisco: Harper and Row, 1971.
*Pathmarks*, trans. Frank A Capuzzi et al., ed. William McNeill. Cambridge: Cambridge UP, 1998.

*Poetry, Language, Thought*, trans. Alfred Hofstadter. New York: Harper and Row, 1971.
*Ponderings II-VI; Black Notebooks 1931-1938*, trans. Richard Rojcewicz. Indiana: Indiana UP, 2016.
*On Time and Being*, trans. Joan Stambaugh. Chicago: Chicago UP, 2002.
*On the Way to Language*, trans. Peter D Hertz. San Francisco: Harper and Row, 1971.
*What Is Called Thinking*, trans. J Glenn Gray. New York: HarperCollins, 1968.
*Zollikon Seminars*, trans. Franz Mayr and Richard Askay. New Haven: Northwestern UP, 2001.

## Studies on Heidegger

Allen (WS). *Ellipsis: Of Poetry and the Experience of Language after Heidegger, Hölderlin, and Blanchot* (New York: New York UP, 2007).
Babich (B). 'Heidegger's Will to Power', *The Journal of the British Society for Phenomenology*, Vol. 38 (1), January 2007: 37–60.
Babich (B). *Words in Blood, Like Flowers: Philosophy and Poetry, Music and Eros in Hölderlin, Nietzsche and Heidegger* (Albany: State of New York Press, 2006).
Bambach (C). *Heidegger's Roots: Nietzsche, National Socialism, and the Greeks* (Ithaca: Cornell UP, 2005).
Bambach (C). 'Who is Heidegger's Hölderlin', *Research in Phenomenology*, Vol. 47 (1), 2017: 39–59.
Bernasconi (R). *Heidegger in Question: The Art of Existing* (New York: Humanities Press, 1996).
Bernasconi (R). *The Question of Language in Heidegger's History of Being* (New Jersey: Humanities Press, 1985).
Brogan (WA). 'The Intractable Interrelation of Physis and Technē' in *Heidegger and the Greeks: Interpretive Essays*, eds. DA Hyland & JP Manoussakis (Indianapolis: Indiana UP, 2006).
Clark (T). *Martin Heidegger* (London: Routledge, 2002).
Dastur (F). 'Heidegger's Freiburg Version of the Origin of the Work of Art' in *Heidegger towards the Turn: Essays on the Work of the 1930s* (Albany: State University of New York Press, 1999).
Davis (BW). *Heidegger and the Will: On the Way to Gelassenheit* (Illinois: Northwestern UP, 2007).
De Man (P). 'Heidegger's Exegeses of Hölderlin' in *Blindness and Insight: Essays in the Rhetoric of Contemporary Criticism* (Oxford: Routledge, 2005).
Derrida (J). *Of Spirit: Heidegger and the Question*, trans. Geoffrey Bennington & Rachel Bowlby (Chicago: UCP, 1989).
Farin (I) & Malpas (J). *Reading Heidegger's Black Notebooks 1931–1941* (Massachusetts: MIT Press, 2016).
Foti (VM). *Heidegger and the Poets: Poiēsis/Sophia/Technē* (New York: Humanity Books, 1992).
Frede (D). 'The Question of Being: Heidegger's Project' in *The Cambridge Companion to Heidegger*, ed. Charles B Guignon (Cambridge: Cambridge UP, 2006).

Gadamer (H-G). 'Thinking and Poetizing in Heidegger and in Hölderlin's 'Andenken''' in *Heidegger Towards the Turn: Essays on the Works of the 1930s* (New York: State University of New York Press, 1999).

Gillespie (MA). *Hegel, Heidegger and the Ground of History* (Chicago: Chicago UP, 1984).

Gosetti-Ferencei (JA). *Heidegger, Hölderlin, and the Subject of Poetic Language: Towards a New Poetics of Dasein* (New York: Fordham UP, 2004).

Haar (M). *The Song of the Earth*, trans. Reginald Lilly (Indianapolis: Indiana UP, 1993).

Haase (U). 'Approaching Heidegger's History of Being through the Black Notebooks', *The Journal of the British Society for Phenomenology*, Vol. 51 (2), 2020: 95–109.

Haase (U). 'Δίκη and *iustitia*or: Between Heidegger and Nietzsche', *The Journal of the British Society for Phenomenology*, Vol. 38 (1), 2007: 18–36.

Janicaud (D). 'The "Overcoming" of Metaphysics in the Hölderlin Lectures' in *Reading Heidegger: Commemorations*, ed. John Sallis (Indianapolis: Indiana UP, 1993).

John D Caputo, *Demythologizing Heidegger* (Indianapolis: Indiana University Press, 1993).

Kaufmann (W). *Discovering the Mind, Volume II: Nietzsche, Heidegger and Buber* (New Jersey: Transaction Publishers, 2009).

Kockelmans (JJ). *Heidegger on Art and Art Works* (Dordrecht: Martinus Nijhoff, 1985).

Lysaker (JT). 'Language and Poetry' in *Martin Heidegger: Key Concepts* (Durham: Acumen Publishing, 2010).

Malpas (J). *Heidegger's Topology: Being, Place, World* (Massachusetts: MIT Press, 2008).

Ó Murchadha (F). *The Time of Revolution: Kairos and Chronos in Heidegger* (London: Bloomsbury, 2013).

Pattison (G). *The Later Heidegger* (London: Routledge, 2000).

Pöggeler (O). 'Heidegger's Political Self-Understanding' in *The Heidegger Controversy*, ed. Richard Wolin (Cambridge, Massachusetts: MIT Press, 1993).

Polt (R). 'Being and Time' in *Martin Heidegger: Key Concepts*, ed. Bret W Davis (Durham: Acumen, 2010).

Richardson (WJ). 'Toward the Future of Truth' in *Heidegger and the Greeks: Interpretive Essays*, eds. (DA) Hyland & (JP) Manoussakis (Indiana: Indiana UP, 2006).

Ruin (H). '*Gestell*: Enframing as the Essence of Technology' in *Martin Heidegger: Key Concepts*, ed. Bret W Davis (Durham: Acumen, 2010).

Scott (CE). 'Non-belonging/Authenticity' in *Reading Heidegger: Commemorations*, ed. John Sallis (Indiana: Indiana UP, 1993).

Sheehan (T), *Making Sense of Heidegger: A Paradigm Shift* (New York: Rowman & Littlefield, 2015).

Sinclair (M). *Heidegger, Aristotle and the Work of Art: Poiesis in Being* (New York: Palgrave Macmillan, 2006).

Taminiaux (J). 'The Origin of "The Origin of the Work of Art"' in *Reading Heidegger: Commemorations*, ed. John Sallis (Indiana: Indiana UP, 1993).

Thomson (ID). *Heidegger, Art, And Postmodernity* (Cambridge: CUP, 2011).

Vattimo (G). *The Adventure of Difference: Philosophy after Nietzsche and Heidegger*, trans. C Blamires & T Harrison (Cambridge: Polity Press, 1993).

Wurzer (WS). 'Heidegger's Turn to Germanien – A Sigetic Venture' in *Heidegger towards the Turn: Essay on the Work of the 1930s*, ed. J Risser (New York: State University of New York Press, 1999).

Young (J). *Heidegger's Philosophy of Art* (Cambridge: Cambridge UP, 2001).

Zimmerman (M). *Heidegger's Confrontation with Modernity: Technology, Politics, Art* (Indiana: Indiana UP, 1990).
Žižek (S). 'Why Heidegger Made the Right Step in 1933', in: *International Journal of Žižek Studies*, Vol. 1, (4), 2007, (English): 1–43.

# Other Texts

Aristotle. *Metaphysics*, trans. WD Ross (Oxford: Clarendon Press, 1924).
Aristotle. *Physis*, trans. RP Hardie & RK Gaye (New Jersey: Princetown UP, 1984).
Barnes (J). *Early Greek Philosophy* (London: Penguin, 1987).
Behler (E). 'Nietzsche in the Twentieth Century' in *The Cambridge Companion to Nietzsche*, eds. B Magnus & KM Higgins (Cambridge: Cambridge UP, 1996).
Blond (LP). *Heidegger and Nietzsche: Overcoming Metaphysics* (London: Continuum, 2010).
Constantine (D). *Hölderlin* (Oxford: Oxford UP, 1990).
Critchley (S). *Very Little... Almost Nothing* (London: Routledge, 1997).
Cunningham (C). *Genealogy of Nihilism: Philosophies of Nothing and the Difference of Theology* (London: Routledge, 2002).
Derrida (J). *Of Grammatology*, trans. GC Spivak (Baltimore: Johns Hopkins UP, 1997).
Descartes (R). *Mediations on First Philosophy*, trans. John Cottingham (Cambridge: Cambridge UP, 1996).
Fink (E). *Nietzsche's Philosophy*, trans. G Richter (London: Continuum, 2003).
*Friedrich Hölderlin: Poems and Fragments*, trans. Michael Hamburger (London: Anvil Press Poetry, 2004).
Gillespie (MA). *Hegel, Heidegger and the Ground of History* (Chicago: Chicago UP, 1984).
Gillespie (MA). *Nihilism before Nietzsche* (Chicago: CUP, 1995).
Haase (U). *Starting with Nietzsche* (London: Continuum, 2008).
*The Holy Bible* (London: Catholic Truth Society, 1966).
Jaspers (K). *Nietzsche: An Introduction to the Understanding of His Philosophical Activity*, trans. C Wallraff & F Schmitz (Baltimore: Johns Hopkins UP, 1997).
Kaufmann (W). *Nietzsche: Philosopher, Psychologist, Antichrist* (New Jersey: Princetown UP, 1974).
Lindley (D). *Uncertainty: Einstein, Heisenberg, Bohr and the Struggle for the Soul of Science* (New York: Anchor Books, 2008).
Magnus (B) & Higgins (K). 'Nietzsche's Works and Their Themes' in *The Cambridge Companion to Nietzsche*, eds. B Magnus & K Higgins (Cambridge: Cambridge UP, 1996).
McNeill (W). 'Traces of Discordance' *Nietzsche: A Critical Reader*, ed. PR Sedgwick (Oxford: Blackwell, 1995).
Nehamas (A). 'Nietzsche, Modernity, Aestheticsim' in *The Cambridge Companion to Nietzsche* (Cambridge: Cambridge UP, 1996).

Nietzsche (F). *The Anti-Christ, Ecce Homo, The Twilight of the Idols and Other Writings*, trans. J Norman (Cambridge: Cambridge UP, 2005).
Nietzsche (F). *Beyond Good and Evil*, trans. M Faber (Oxford: Oxford UP, 1998).
Nietzsche (F). *The Birth of Tragedy and Other Writings*, trans. R Speirs (Cambridge, Cambridge UP, 1999).
Nietzsche (F). *The Gay Science*, trans. W Kauffman (New York: Vintage Books, 1974).
Nietzsche (F). *Human, All Too Human*, trans. RJ Hollingdale (Cambridge: CUP, 1996).
Nietzsche (F). *Thus Spoke Zarathustra*, trans. RJ Hollingdale (London: Penguin, 2003).
Nietzsche (F). *Twilight of the Idols*, trans. Duncan Large (Oxford: Oxford UP, 1998).
Nietzsche (F). *The Will to Power*, trans. W Kauffman & RJ Hollingdale (New York: Vintage Books, 1968).
Pearson (KA) & Morgan (D). 'Introduction: The Return of Monstrous Nihilism' in *Nihilism Now! Monsters of Energy*, eds. KA Pearson & D Morgan (London: Macmillan, 2000).
Plato. *Phaedo*, trans. Hugh Tredennick (Harmondsworth: Penguin, 1954).
Plato. *Republic*, trans. Paul Shorey (Massachusetts: Harvard UP, 1930).
Picht (G). 'Nietzsche – Thought and the Truth of History', trans. U Haase in *The Journal of the British Society for Phenomenology*, Vol. 38, (1), January 2007.
Pinker (S). *The Language Instinct* (New York: Harper Collins, 2007).
Salaquarda (J). 'Nietzsche and the Judeo-Christian Tradition' in *The Cambridge Companion to Nietzsche*, eds. B Magnus & KM Higgins (Cambridge: Cambridge UP, 1996).
Spinks (L). *Nietzsche* (London: Routledge, 2003).
Vattimo (G). *Dialogue with Nietzsche*, trans. William McCuaig (New York: Columbia UP, 2000).
Vattimo (G). *The End of Modernity: Nihilism and Hermeneutics in Post-modern Culture*, trans. JR Snyder (Cambridge: Polity Press, 1988).
Verene (DP). *Hegel's Absolute: An Introduction to Reading the Phenomenology of Spirit* (New York: State University of New York Press, 2007).
Waterfield (R). *The First Philosophers: The Pre-Socratics and the Sophists* (Oxford: Oxford UP, 2000).

# Index

**A**

abandonment 9, 13, 24, 43, 48, 49, 51, 65, 141, 159
absence of the gods 112, 134, 135, 137, 141, 152
absencing 51, 63, 81, 167
abyss 29, 53, 152
abyssal 4, 98, 142
aesthetics 96, 105, 106, 113
*a-letheia* 59, 64, 82
*aletheia* 59, 66–8, 87, 127, 164
Allen W.S. 78, 82, 83, 118, 168, 169, 173, 174, 179
*Anwesenheit* 68
appropriated 84, 85, 92, 95, 124, 141, 165
*arche* 61
Aristotle 5, 48, 56, 57, 61, 62, 64, 67, 166, 167, 180, 181
art 5, 7, 8, 25, 26, 43, 66, 70–3, 78, 79, 85, 96, 97, 102, 103, 105–7, 137, 138, 166, 169–74, 177–81
artwork 5, 72, 78, 79, 85, 97, 113, 126, 137, 169
attunement 48, 49, 54, 124–6, 128, 134, 156, 165, 174
*Auseinandersetzung* 7, 102, 159
authentic 47, 54, 60, 94, 101, 110, 112, 120, 128, 130, 156, 163, 164, 168, 169, 174
authenticity 101, 171, 172, 180

**B**

Babich, B. 54, 163, 166, 179
beginning 1, 4, 7, 38, 43–7, 50, 51, 53, 55, 60, 73, 86, 88, 93, 101, 103, 105, 107, 109, 111, 124, 132, 135, 136, 141, 142, 146, 147, 156, 158, 161, 164, 165, 176
Behler, E. 40, 164, 181
being-historical 25, 146, 151, 152
being and time 5, 6, 32, 45, 47, 49, 50, 53, 75, 76, 79, 84, 97, 100, 101, 112, 122, 124, 126, 130, 145, 146, 158, 165, 166, 169, 170, 172, 174, 176, 178, 180
being-in-the-world 75, 79, 122
Bernasconi, R. 86, 87, 89, 91, 92, 170, 179
*Bestand* 69
birth of tragedy 24, 134, 162, 163, 182
black notebooks 145, 159, 171, 179, 180
Brentano, F. 5
Brogan, W.A. 65, 167, 179

**C**

calculative thinking 139
Caputo, J.D. 100, 102, 103, 171, 172
christian god 16, 18, 138
Christianity 16–18, 22, 148
Clark, T. 96, 97, 115, 131, 170, 174, 175, 179
Constantine, D. 108, 173, 181
*Contributions to Philosophy* 1, 43, 50, 135, 141, 146, 152, 155, 156, 159, 164, 165, 176–8
Copernican Revolution 16
crossing 46, 47, 50, 53, 55, 60, 165
cybernetics 143, 176

**D**

*Da-sein* 85, 145, 146, 151, 155, 156
Davis, B.W. 128, 137, 164, 166, 175, 176, 179, 180

decision 4, 5, 7, 31, 45, 51, 53, 61, 105, 110, 132, 134, 136, 137, 140, 142, 151, 152
Derrida, J. 84, 91, 92, 102, 169, 170, 172, 179, 181
Descartes, R. 18, 41, 74, 121, 161, 181
destiny 3, 10, 31, 37, 46, 51–3, 55, 69, 82, 133, 134, 136, 145, 147, 176
destitute time 106, 172
*Destruktion* 57, 166
*Dichtung* 3, 97, 98, 114, 125
dwell poetically 98, 107, 123

### E

earth 73, 96, 98, 99, 132, 141–3, 171, 180
*Ecce Homo* 27, 162, 182
*eidos* 62, 63, 67
elegiac mood 134, 140
emergence 3, 61, 67, 82, 83
Enlightenment 16, 17, 108, 173
*Entschlossenheit* 128
*Ereignis* 45–7, 52, 53, 81, 85, 87, 92, 94, 95, 97, 111, 115, 122, 124, 127, 130, 132, 141, 147, 152–4, 156, 157, 164, 165, 170
*Erschrecken* 49, 152, 165
essence 3, 7, 10, 12, 25, 33, 39, 44, 52, 53, 56–9, 61, 63–5, 68, 69, 71, 74, 76–8, 80–3, 86–95, 97, 98, 100, 102, 103, 109–11, 113–15, 119, 120, 123, 127, 133–5, 155, 164, 165, 167–9, 173, 175, 178, 180
On the Essence and Concept of Φύσις in Aristotle's Physics B, I 56, 57, 61, 65, 167
On the Essence of Truth 89
essencing 88
essential 1, 3, 10, 12, 21, 23, 43, 47, 50, 51, 57, 59, 71, 73, 75, 84, 85, 89, 93, 102, 106, 107, 109, 110, 112–17, 119, 120, 126, 127, 129, 131–5, 137–40, 142, 143, 151–6, 165, 174, 175, 177
essential naming 126, 137
essential sway 47, 51, 59, 153, 156, 165
ethical 99–104, 132, 165
*ethos* 100, 104, 171

### F

fate 20, 33, 34, 40, 45, 48, 51, 52, 54, 98, 119, 121, 132, 133
*Fehl* 124
Fink 39, 40, 160, 161, 164, 181
flight of the gods 4, 138
forgetting of being 1, 2, 49
Foti, V.M. 116, 117, 174, 176, 179
*Four Seminars* 76, 178
Frege, G. 74
French Revolution 108, 117, 175

### G

Gadamer, H.-G. 109, 163, 169, 173, 180
*Gelassenheit* 53, 54, 128, 137, 163, 166, 179
*genesis* 63
George, S. 114
Germanien 107, 171, 180
*Geschichte* 87, 97, 98, 130, 133, 170, 173
*Geschick* 51, 55, 133
*Gespräch* 114, 174
*Gestell* 69, 70, 141, 168, 180
*Geviert* 125, 140–2
Gillespie, M.A. 44, 45
Gosetti-Ferencei, J. 2, 69, 128, 129, 132, 158, 168, 173, 175, 180
*Of Grammatology* 91, 170, 181
*Grundbegriffe* 56
*Grundfrage* 50, 53, 55, 165
*Grundstimmung* 48, 112, 124, 125, 156

### H

Haar, M. 87, 88, 93, 170, 180
Haase, U. 21, 26, 150, 159–62, 164, 177, 180–2
Hegel G.W.F. 5, 75, 89–91, 105, 108, 121, 164, 180, 181
*Heidegger's Confrontation with Modernity* 130, 171, 181
*Heilige* 139
Heraclitus 58, 59, 61, 64, 84, 100, 166
hermeneutic ontology 83
hermeneutical circle 78, 79
hermeneutics 102, 159, 182

hiddenness 2, 3, 7, 53, 55, 88, 132, 147, 152, 164
historical thinking 7, 8, 146
historicity 169
historico-political 117
*Historie* 97, 133, 170
historiographical 107
historiology 170
*History of Being* 1, 146, 159, 170, 179, 180
the history of beyng 152, 154, 155, 157
history of metaphysics 2, 5, 7, 12, 21, 27, 29, 32, 33, 44–6, 48, 50, 51, 54, 56–8, 71, 78, 86, 88, 101, 104, 105, 135, 151, 152, 154, 163
Hobbes, T. 74
Hölderlin and the Essence of Poetry 109, 110, 113, 120, 127, 173, 175
*Hölderlin's Hymn 'der Ister'* 137
holy 119–23, 131, 139–41, 160, 174, 182
holy mourning 140
Homecoming/To Kindred Ones 125
*Human, All Too Human* 148, 177, 181
Hume, D. 74
Husserl, E. 74, 121

**I**
inauthenticity 101
*Introduction to Metaphysics* 84, 158, 165, 167, 170, 172, 175, 178

**J**
Jacobi, F. 13
Janicaud, D. 107, 172, 180
Jaspers, K. 40, 160, 181

**K**
Kant, I. 18, 60, 178
Kaufmann, W. 17, 27, 30, 157, 160–3, 177, 180, 181
*Kehre* 86, 147
*kinesis* 61
Kockelmans, J.J. 111, 173, 180

**L**
leap 116, 152, 156
Leibniz, G.W. 121
*Leitfrage* 50, 55, 165
*Leitwort* 86, 89–91, 93, 94
Letter on Humanism 52, 55, 76, 81, 82, 89, 95, 99, 100, 139, 145, 168
logocentrism 84, 169
*logos* 81–5, 127, 168
Lysaker, J.T. 76, 81, 168, 169, 180

**M**
Malpas, J. 143, 171, 176, 179, 180
McNeill, W. 41, 164, 170, 178, 181
meaning of being 2, 5, 6, 50, 52, 53, 57, 85, 133, 140, 143, 165
meaninglessness 9, 15
measure 24, 25, 82, 98, 122, 123, 127, 130, 135, 141, 170, 171, 175
metaphysical tradition 1, 2, 32–4, 37, 41, 87, 166, 167
metaphysician 30, 37, 39, 40, 145
*Mindfulness* 1, 146, 152, 154, 155, 157, 178
Murchadha, Ó. F. 5, 51, 60, 158, 167, 180
mystery 77, 78, 93, 98, 114, 152

**N**
new beginning 1, 4, 7, 55, 86, 105, 111, 132, 135, 136, 141, 142
*Nietzsche in the Twentieth Century* 40, 164, 181
nietzsche's word: god is dead 10, 33, 36
nihilism 1, 2, 7–16, 18–21, 23, 26–35, 37, 38, 41, 43–5, 48, 51, 54, 58, 64, 65, 69, 70, 73, 85, 92, 101, 103, 111, 143, 145, 148, 149, 159–61, 171, 178, 181, 182

**O**
oblivion of being 55, 89, 116, 127, 141
Only a God can save us 101, 171, 172
ontic 6, 97, 103
ontological 6, 32, 72, 75, 97–100, 103, 129, 137, 159, 165
ontotheology 138

onto-theo-logy 176
open region of being 122, 128, 139
Origin of the Work of Art 72, 102, 169, 173, 179, 180
other beginning 43, 45, 46, 50, 51, 53, 55, 60, 147, 156
*ousia* 46, 92, 167
overcoming 7, 28, 29, 33, 36, 44–6, 51, 54, 106, 158, 172, 173, 180, 181
overcoming nihilism 7, 54
overhuman 28–32, 35–40, 52, 54, 150, 151, 162

**P**

Parmenides 84, 166
Pattison, G. 55, 69, 111, 123, 134, 166, 168, 173–6, 180
*Phaedo* 22, 161, 182
phenomenology 82, 83, 121, 159, 160, 163–5, 170, 179, 180, 182
*physis* 55–70, 72, 84, 166, 167, 179, 181
Picht, G. 160, 182
Pinker, S. 74, 168, 182
Plato 16, 21–3, 27, 29, 33, 48, 62, 92, 134, 161, 182
poem 4, 5, 7, 70, 71, 73, 107, 110, 113–16, 118–20, 122–6, 129–34, 138, 140, 174, 175
poesy 71
poet 1, 7, 8, 70, 106, 108–10, 112–16, 118, 120–6, 128–39, 145, 152, 153, 172, 173, 176
Poetically Man Dwells 98, 170
poetics 97, 158, 180
poetry 3, 4, 7, 8, 71, 73, 85, 95–8, 104–14, 116–20, 122–5, 127, 129–41, 145, 152, 166, 168, 171–6, 178–81
*poiesis* 67–70, 72, 73, 104, 109, 110, 119, 166, 180
poietic 8, 70, 153, 155
Polt, R. 48, 165, 178, 180
positivism 13, 18, 30, 32, 135
presencing 3, 41, 47, 51, 55, 61, 64, 67, 68, 80, 81, 93, 95, 100, 114, 122, 123, 142, 166
privation 63, 87, 167

**Q**

On the Question of Being 92
Question Concerning Technology 66, 69–71, 168

**R**

Remembrance 120
revaluation of all values 26, 27, 35
rift-design 80–2, 93
Ruin, H. 69, 167, 168, 180

**S**

sacred mourning 112
*Sage* 80, 93
Schelling, F.W.J. 108
*sein* 2, 46, 82, 85, 135, 138, 159, 164, 173
*Seiende* 46, 138
*Seiendheit* 2, 62
*Seinsgeschichte* 48, 128, 165
*Seinsvergessenheit* 1, 49, 155, 169
Several 5
*The Several Senses of Being in Aristotle* 5
*Seyn* 46, 154, 164
Socrates 22, 134
speech 76, 78–81, 83, 93, 168, 169
startled dismay 49, 152, 155, 165
*steresis* 63, 167
Stimmung 125, 174
substance 28, 46, 130

**T**

Taminiaux, J. 112, 134, 173, 175, 180
*techne* 65–70, 167
technology 65, 66, 68–71, 99, 102–4, 106, 111, 167, 168, 171, 175, 180, 181
*thaumazein* 48
Thomson, I.D. 156, 177, 180
*Thus Spoke Zarathustra* 28, 162, 163, 177, 182
truth 2–9, 15–26, 28–31, 36, 37, 39, 44–53, 55–7, 59, 60, 62–73, 75, 81, 82, 84–94, 97, 100, 102–6, 109, 110, 112–14, 119–24, 126, 127, 131–5, 137, 138, 140–3, 145–7, 151, 153–6, 159–61, 163–7, 175, 178, 180, 182

Turgeniev, I. 13
turning 1, 12, 57, 105, 106, 109, 147, 163

**U**
*Übergang* 50
unconcealment 47, 64, 65, 67, 80, 82, 88, 96, 119, 133, 143, 166
*Unheimlich* 98
unpoetic 99
untimely 118, 130, 175
untruth 17, 45, 51, 108
Utilitarianism 13, 14

**V**
Van Gogh, V. 126
Vattimo, G. 10, 32, 38, 83, 159, 160, 163, 169, 180, 182

**W**
*On the Way to Language* 76, 86, 91, 93, 94, 114, 173, 178
The Way to Language 78, 79, 170
*Weltanschauung* 74

*Wesen* 47, 86, 102, 135, 164
western thought 2, 12, 15, 16, 31, 33, 44, 48, 56, 60, 99, 100, 131, 134, 143, 160, 163, 169
*What is Called Thinking* 5, 32, 116, 117, 163, 179
*Wiederholung* 60
will to power 1, 2, 13, 23–30, 33, 35–41, 48, 54, 109, 151, 160–3, 178, 179, 182
*Wink* 138
withdrawal 2–4, 59, 60, 63, 83, 116, 120, 132
Wurzer, W.S. 99, 171, 180

**Y**
Young, J. 106, 107, 110, 111, 172–4, 178, 180

**Z**
Zimmerman, M.E. 99, 130, 131, 171, 175, 181
Žižek, S. 103, 172, 181
*Zollikon Seminars* 74, 168, 179

www.ingramcontent.com/pod-product-compliance
Lightning Source LLC
Chambersburg PA
CBHW061833300426
44115CB00013B/2364